NAVIGATING COVID-19 IN ASIA AND THE PACIFIC

EDITED BY

BAMBANG SUSANTONO, YASUYUKI SAWADA, AND CYN-YOUNG PARK

SEPTEMBER 2020

ASIAN DEVELOPMENT BANK

ADB

© 2020 Asian Development Bank
6 ADB Avenue, Mandaluyong City, 1550 Metro Manila, Philippines
Tel +63 2 8632 4444; Fax +63 2 8636 2444
www.adb.org

Some rights reserved. Published in 2020.

ISBN 978-92-9262-355-5 (print); 978-92-9262-356-2 (electronic); 978-92-9262-357-9 (ebook)
Publication Stock No. TCS200247-2
DOI: http://dx.doi.org/10.22617/TCS200 247-2

Notes:
In this publication, "$" refers to United States dollars.
ADB recognizes "China" as the People's Republic of China, and "Korea" as the Republic of Korea.
All photos by ADB unless otherwise indicated.

Cover design by Achilleus Coronel.

Contents

Tables and Figures

Tables

Figures

About the Editors

Bambang Susantono is the Vice-President for Knowledge Management and Sustainable Development of the Asian Development Bank (ADB). He is the first Indonesian in this position.

He holds a PhD in Infrastructure Planning, and has two master's degrees in Transportation Engineering, and City and Regional Planning from the University of California, Berkeley. He graduated with a Bachelor of Engineering from the Civil Engineering Department, the Bandung Institute of Technology.

Dr. Susantono is responsible for managing knowledge in ADB, and coordinating research and studies on various topics such as energy, transport, education, health, finance, and urban development; and also cross-cutting nexus themes such as climate change, governance, gender, social development, environment, rural development and food security, and regional cooperation. He also coordinates ADB annual flagship publications such as the *Asian Development Outlook, Key Indicators for Asia and the Pacific,* and *Asian Economic Integration Report.*

Prior to this, Dr. Susantono was the Acting Minister and Vice-Minister of Transportation of Indonesia, and Deputy Minister for Infrastructure and Regional Development at the Coordinating Ministry for Economic Affairs. He was also Member of the Board for airline, port, telecommunications, and media companies.

He has chaired several research institutes and taught in universities. He is actively doing research, has published several books, and has written articles on the subject of infrastructure, transportation, urban and regional planning, sustainable development, and climate change.

Dr. Susantono has received several accolades, including *Bintang Mahaputra Utama, Satya Lencana Pembangunan, Satya Lencana Wira Karya, Rekor MURI 2015, Sustainable Leadership Award 2018, Ganesha Widya Jasa Adiutama (ITB) 2019,* and *Top 100 Fintech for SDG Influencer 2019.*

Yasuyuki Sawada is the Chief Economist of ADB and Director General of its Economic Research and Regional Cooperation Department. He is the chief spokesperson for ADB on economic and development trends, and leads the production and dissemination of ADB's flagship knowledge products, as well as ADB's support for various regional cooperation fora such as Association of Southeast Asian Nations (ASEAN)+3 and Asia-Pacific Economic Cooperation (APEC).

Before joining ADB, Mr. Sawada was Professor of Economics at the University of Tokyo. A leading figure in development economics, he has served as a visiting professor at Stanford University, adjunct professor of economics at Korea University, and AJRC Research Associate, Australian National University. He has led a number of development policy research projects in a variety of institutions, such as the ADB Institute in Tokyo, the World Bank, the International Rice Research Institute (IRRI), the Economic Research Institute for ASEAN and East Asia (ERIA), the Japan International Cooperation Agency (JICA) Research Institute, the Research Institute of Economy, Trade and Industry (RIETI), Bangladesh Institute of Development Studies (BIDS), BRAC, and Pakistan Institute of Development Economics (PIDE).

He is a recipient of various awards such as the Ishikawa Prize of the Japanese Economic Association, Nikkei Book Prize, and Masayoshi Ohira Memorial Prize. His key research areas are macro- and micro-development economics, economics of disasters, and field surveys and experiments. Mr. Sawada obtained his PhD in Economics and his master's degree in International Development Policy from Stanford University.

Cyn-Young Park is Director of the Regional Cooperation and Integration Division in the Economics Research and Regional Cooperation Department of the ADB. In her current capacity, she manages a team of economists to examine economic and policy issues related to regional cooperation and integration (RCI) and develop strategies and approaches to support RCI. During her progressive career within ADB, she has been a main author and contributor to ADB's major publications including *Asian Development Outlook* (ADB's flagship publication), *Asian Economic Integration Report, Asia Capital Markets Monitor, Asia Economic Monitor, Asia Bond Monitor,* and ADB *Country Diagnostic Study Series.* She has also participated in various global and regional fora including the G20 Development Working Group, ASEAN, ASEAN+3, APEC, and Asia-Europe Meeting (ASEM). She has written and lectured extensively about the Asian economy and financial markets. Her work has been published in peer reviewed academic journals including the *Journal of Banking and Finance,* the *Journal of Financial Stability,* the *Journal of Futures Markets,* the *Review of Income and Wealth*, and the *World Economy*.

Prior to joining ADB, she served as Economist (1999-2002) at the Organisation for Economic Co-operation and Development (OECD), where she contributed to the OECD Economic Outlook. She received her PhD in Economics from Columbia University. She holds a bachelor's degree in International Economics from Seoul National University.

Authors

Abdul Abiad is director of the Macroeconomics Research Division, Economic Research and Regional Cooperation Department (ERCD), Asian Development Bank (ADB).

Mia Arao is a consultant, ERCD, ADB.

Preety Bhandari is chief of the Climate Change and Disaster Risk Management Thematic Group, concurrently director, Climate Change and Disaster Risk Management Division, Sustainable Development and Climate Change Department (SDCC), ADB.

Steven Beck is advisor (trade and supply chain finance), Private Sector Operations Department (PSOD), ADB.

Bruno Carrasco is chief of the Governance Thematic Group, Thematic Advisory Service Cluster, SDCC, ADB.

Arup Chaterjee is principal financial sector specialist, Finance Sector Group, Sector Advisory Service Cluster, SDCC, ADB.

Joris van Etten is senior urban development specialist, Urban Development and Water Division, Southeast Asia Department (SERD), ADB.

Jesus Felipe is advisor, Office of the Chief Economist and Director General, ERCD, ADB.

Benno Ferrarini is principal economist, Office of the Chief Economist and Director General, ERCD, ADB.

Raymond Gaspar is a consultant, ERCD, ADB.

Colin Gin is assistant general counsel, Office of the General Counsel, ADB.

Arjun Goswami is chief of Regional Cooperation and Integration Thematic Group, Thematic Advisory Service Cluster, SDCC, ADB.

Sanjay Grover is public–private partnership specialist, Office of Public-Private Partnership, ADB.

Matthias Helble is an economist, Regional Cooperation and Integration Division, ERCD, ADB.

Jan Hinrichs is a senior natural resources economist in the Environment, Natural Resources and Agriculture Division, East Asia Department, ADB.

Jingmin Huang is director, Urban Development, Water Supply and Sanitation Division, Pacific Department, ADB.

Jules Hugot is a young professional, Office of the Director General, PSOD, ADB.

Ancilla Marie Inocencio is a consultant, ERCD, ADB.

Christian Jabagat is a consultant, ERCD, ADB.

Amir Jilani is a young professional, Social Development Thematic Group, Thematic Advisory Service Cluster, SDCC, ADB.

Sameer Khatiwada is a social sector specialist (information and communications technology), Human and Social Development Division, SERD, ADB.

Kijin Kim is an economist, Regional Cooperation and Integration Division, ERCD, ADB.

Sunae Kim is a natural resources and agriculture specialist, Environment, Natural Resources and Agriculture Division, South Asia Department, ADB.

Editha Lavina is a senior economics officer, Macroeconomics Research Division, ERCD, ADB.

Junkyu Lee is chief of the Finance Sector Group, Sector Advisory Service Cluster, SDCC, ADB.

Anouj Mehta is principal infrastructure specialist and unit head of Green and Innovative Finance and the ASEAN Catalytic Green Finance Facility, SERD, ADB.

Naeeda Crishna Morgado is a senior climate finance specialist (consultant), ASEAN Catalytic Green Finance Facility, SERD, ADB.

Badri Narayanan is a consultant, ERCD, ADB.

Ilan Noy is chair of economics of disasters and climate change, Victoria University of Wellington.

Susan Olsen is a senior investment specialist, Infrastructure Finance Division 1, PSOD, ADB.

Patrick Osewe is chief of the Health Sector Group, Sector Advisory Service Cluster, SDCC, ADB.

Jesson Pagaduan is a consultant, ERCD, ADB.

Brajesh Panth is chief of the Education Sector Group, Sector Advisory Service Cluster, SDCC, ADB.

Cyn-Young Park is director, Regional Cooperation and Integration Division, ERCD, ADB.

Donghyun Park is principal economist, Macroeconomics Research Division, ERCD, ADB.

Jesper Pedersen is principal procurement specialist, Office of the Director General, Procurement, Portfolio and Financial Management Department, ADB.

Nigel Phair is director, UNSW Canberra Cyber.

Reizle Platitas is a consultant, ERCD, ADB.

Hanif Rahemtulla is principal public management specialist, Governance Thematic Group, Thematic Advisory Service Cluster, SDCC, ADB.

David Robinett is a senior public management specialist (state-owned enterprise reforms), Governance Thematic Group, Thematic Advisory Service Cluster, SDCC, ADB.

Peter Rosenkranz is an economist, Regional Cooperation and Integration Division, ERCD, ADB.

Susann Roth is principal knowledge sharing and services specialist, Knowledge Advisory Services Center, SDCC, ADB.

Arghya Sinha Roy is a senior climate change specialist (climate change adaptation), Climate Change and Disaster Risk Management Division, SDCC, ADB.

Malika Shagazatova is a social development specialist (gender and development), Gender Equity Thematic Group, Thematic Advisory Service Cluster, SDCC, ADB.

Shigehiro Shinozaki is a senior economist, Office of the Chief Economist and Director General, ERCD, ADB.

Akmal Siddiq is chief of the Rural Development and Food Security (Agriculture) Thematic Group, Thematic Advisory Service Cluster, SDCC, ADB.

Bambang Susantono is vice-president, knowledge management and sustainable development, ADB.

Aiko Kikkawa Takenaka is an economist, Economic Analysis and Operational Support Division, ERCD, ADB.

Mara Claire Tayag is a senior economics officer, Regional Cooperation and Integration Division, ERCD, ADB.

Tiffany Tran is a human settlements expert (consultant), SERD, ADB.

Paul Vandenberg is principal economist, Economic Analysis and Operational Support Division, ERCD, ADB.

James Villafuerte is a senior economist, Regional Cooperation and Integration Division, ERCD, ADB.

Marianne Vital is a consultant, ERCD, ADB.

Ingrid van Wees is vice-president, finance and risk management, ADB.

Meredith Wyse is a senior social development specialist (elderly care), Social Development Thematic Group, Thematic Advisory Service Cluster, SDCC, ADB.

Jeffrey Jian Xu is a senior education specialist (education technology), Education Sector Group, Sector Advisory Service Cluster, SDCC, ADB.

Al-Habbyel Yusoph is assistant professor and chair, Department of Accounting and Finance, University of the Philippines.

Qingfeng Zhang is director, Environment, Natural Resources and Agriculture Division, East Asia Department, ADB.

Juzhong Zhuang is a former senior economic advisor, Office of the Chief Economist and Director General, ERCD, ADB.

Lotte Schou-Zibell is regional director, Pacific Liaison and Coordination Office, ADB.

Acknowledgments

This publication was made possible by a team led by Cyn-Young Park, director, Regional Cooperation and Integration Division (ERCI), Economic Research and Regional Cooperation Department, Asian Development Bank (ADB). Paulo Rodelio Halili, senior economics officer, ERCI, efficiently managed the production process with assistance from Aleli Rosario and Carol Ongchangco.

Contributions from the blog authors who permitted the use of their material and also updated information are gratefully appreciated. They are Abdul Abiad, Mia Arao, Steven Beck, Preety Bhandari, Bruno Carrasco, Arup Chaterjee, Joris van Etten, Jesus Felipe, Benno Ferrarini, Raymond Gaspar, Colin Gin, Arjun Goswami, Sanjay Grover, Matthias Helble, Jan Hinrichs, Jingmin Huang, Jules Hugot, Ancilla Marie Inocencio, Christian Jabagat, Amir Jilani, Sameer Khatiwada, Kijin Kim, Sunae Kim, Editha Lavina, Junkyu Lee, Anouj Mehta, Naeeda Crishna Morgado, Badri Narayanan, Ilan Noy, Susan Olsen, Patrick Osewe, Jesson Pagaduan, Brajesh Panth, Cyn-Young Park, Donghyun Park, Jesper Pedersen, Nigel Phair, Reizle Platitas, Hanif Rahemtulla, David Robinett, Peter Rosenkranz, Susann Roth, Arghya Sinha Roy, Malika Shagazatova, Shigehiro Shinozaki, Akmal Siddiq, Bambang Susantono, Aiko Kikkawa Takenaka, Mara Claire Tayag, Tiffany Tran, Paul Vandenberg, James Villafuerte, Marianne Vital, Ingrid van Wees, Meredith Wyse, Jeffrey Jian Xu, Al-Habbyel Yusoph, Qingfeng Zhang, Juzhong Zhuang, and Lotte Schou-Zibell.

ERCI staff who provided chapter summaries and coordinated the updates include Rolando Avendaño, Matthias Helble, Jong Woo Kang, Kijin Kim, Rogelio Mercado Jr., Peter Rosenkranz, and James Villafuerte.

Valuable advice and assistance was provided by Vicky Tan, principal director, Department of Communications (DOC), ADB. John Larkin assisted in connecting with the blog authors and shared suggestions on style.

James Unwin edited this publication. The cover design was created by Achilleus Coronel while Michael Cortes did the typesetting. Lawrence Casiraya proofread the publication with assistance from Paulo Rodelio Halili, Aleli Rosario, and Carol Ongchangco. Support was provided by the DOC Publishing Team.

Abbreviations

ADB	Asian Development Bank
ASEAN	Association of Southeast Asian Nations
COVID-19	coronavirus disease
GDP	gross domestic product
ICT	information and communication technology
ILO	International Labour Organization
IMF	International Monetary Fund
Lao PDR	Lao People's Democratic Republic
MERS	Middle East respiratory syndrome
MSMEs	micro, small, and medium-sized enterprises
PRC	People's Republic of China
SARS	severe acute respiratory syndrome
UNICEF	United Nations Children's Fund
US	United States
WHO	World Health Organization

Introduction

Bambang Susantono, Yasuyuki Sawada, and Cyn-Young Park

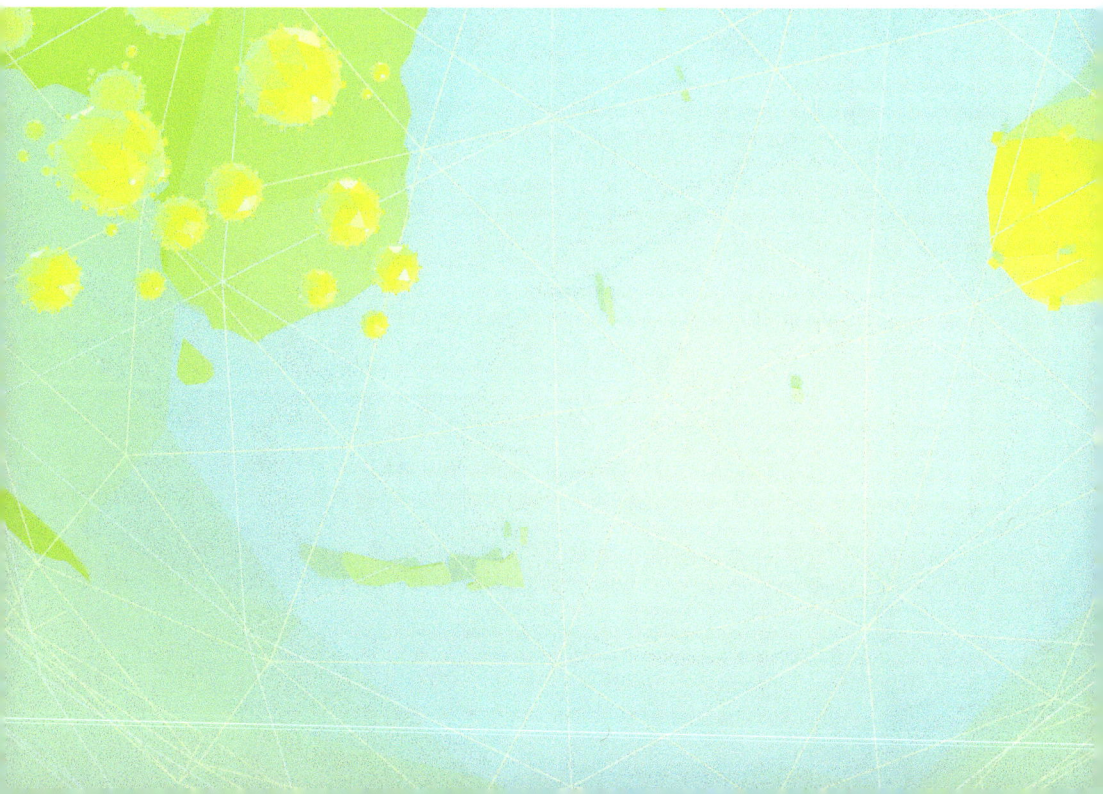

The coronavirus disease (COVID-19) pandemic is presenting unprecedented health, economic, and social challenges throughout the world. Infections have claimed nearly three-quarters of a million lives and containment strategies have disrupted nearly every aspect of people's routines.[1] As the pandemic continues to evolve through the second half of 2020, efforts to protect livelihoods imperiled by the coronavirus resurgence, safely return social activities to normal functioning, and support struggling economies across the globe must contend with uncertainties that, for many, point to an unparalleled pace of change.

The crisis calls for collective ideas. This publication gathers blogs and short policy pieces contributed by Asian Development Bank (ADB) staff and experts in an attempt to tackle immediate challenges and prepare for what may lie beyond the horizon. It brings together snapshots of intellectual efforts that aim to help make sense of unprecedented times.

Through the first half of 2020, international travel bans and domestic lockdowns brought much of global economic activity to a stop with a jolt never before experienced.[2] The pandemic's impact proved much worse than anticipated when COVID-19 jumped borders in January, and estimates for global economic growth since have repeatedly been revised downward. The June 2020 projection of the International Monetary Fund (IMF) for the world economy this year is −4.9%, while significantly flattening its expectations for a quick recovery. Similarly, ADB forecasts that economic growth in developing Asia will be only 0.1% in 2020, its lowest since 1961, with this projection dashing earlier confidence in a V-shaped recovery.[3]

The pandemic has exposed the depth of many unresolved development issues facing the region, including inequality, socioeconomic vulnerability, and environmental challenges. Collective efforts are needed to find immediate solutions to pressing problems such as ensuring supply of personal protective equipment and developing vaccines. But amid the urgency, we should contemplate the pandemic's long-term consequences—how our world, development strategies, and priorities will be reshaped—and prepare for them.

---

[1]   As of 10 August 2020, the World Health Organization (WHO) Coronavirus Disease (COVID-19) Dashboard reported 728,013 deaths.

[2]   As of 8 May 2020, 219 countries, territories, and areas implemented a total count of 60,711 travel restrictions, according to the International Organization for Migration.

[3]   In April 2020, ADB forecast that economic growth in developing Asia was expected to fall to 2.2% in 2020 due to the COVID-19 outbreak before rebounding sharply to 6.2% in 2021.

As this publication illustrates, the biggest economic casualty has been micro and small businesses. The pandemic has been particularly tough on the poor and most vulnerable groups, threatening to reverse hard-won gains in global poverty reduction since the 1990s. In some economies, the spotlight falls on crowded and unsanitary living conditions of the urban poor. In others, it shines light on hourly workers forced to continue working despite their illness. Glaring gaps in public health services, unemployment insurance, and social protection have also compounded containment efforts.

As a development organization on the frontline of the fight against poverty, ADB stands side by side with its developing member economies in mitigating the devastating social and economic impacts of COVID-19, and in crafting a vision for a more inclusive and resilient future when the pandemic ends.

Timely policy responses in health, education, labor, and social protection, combined with well-considered monetary and fiscal policies, will be critical to rebooting the global economy and to ensuring inclusive and resilient recovery in the post-COVID-19 era. Stronger regional cooperation is also needed to keep trade flowing, minimize the interruption to transportation and essential travel, and safeguard financial stability. In contrast to previous pandemics—and as this publication highlights—a much broader set of policy tools is now available.

While the COVID-19 crisis has created unparalleled challenges, it also offers a window to rethink Asia's most fundamental development policies. Addressing the long-term challenges highlighted in this publication— including the rapid adoption of digital technologies, adequate supply of quality infrastructure, climate change and disaster management, and strengthening regional cooperation—will play a crucial part in shaping post-pandemic conditions.

Broadly we face evolving issues of staggering complexity posed by the pandemic impact and its long-term consequences. Yet, this is also a time of great opportunity, as the pandemic is inevitably forcing a rethink of priorities and, through necessity, will propel invention and innovation across the development agenda, bringing themes of resilience, sustainability, and inclusion to the fore. The unprecedented nature of the pandemic means that countries will need to do things differently, and in unison. Knowledge and thoughtful policy advice geared toward change for the better are now welcomed and needed more than ever.

Although the trajectory of a post-pandemic recovery remains uncertain, ADB staff and experts featured in this publication have shared insights and experiences on the ground to help mitigate its effects. Their diverse expertise includes assessment of the economic and social impact of the pandemic, policy analysis for better crisis responses, and policy options and suggestions for arresting market panic, supporting small businesses and jobs, and protecting the poor and most vulnerable. Contributions also highlight the medium-term challenges of food security, trade and digital transformation, and insights for post-pandemic recovery. Together, they represent an earnest attempt to help develop policy strategies and action plans to limit the short-term impact, prepare for medium-term challenges, and build back better for a resilient future.

It is our hope that this collective effort will help make progress through the uncharted territory that policy makers will encounter as they navigate many cross-cutting themes, both during the pandemic and beyond. We also hope this is the first of many more collections to come, motivating policy makers, academics, development practitioners, and other stakeholders to engage in open dialogue, and join in translating knowledge and wisdom into policy actions for a more effective fight against COVID-19.

Chapter Summaries

Chapter 1: Economic Impact and Policy Responses

The pandemic and related strict containment measures—restrictions to transport, labor mobility, and workplace closures—are supply and demand shocks that could cost the global economy as much as $8.8 trillion (9.7% of global gross domestic product [GDP]), according to estimates from ADB in a scenario where the pandemic could be contained within 6 months.[4] Losses to Asia and the Pacific in that now optimistic-looking scenario were as much as $2.5 trillion (or 9.3% of the region's GDP) and accounted for more than a third of projected global losses. The region's job losses were a disproportionate 70% of the global losses projected in the analysis.

---

[4] Asian Development Bank (ADB). 2020. An Updated Assessment of the Economic Impact of COVID-19. ADB Briefs No. 133. Manila.

Significant expansion of government macroeconomic stimulus packages to protect lives, support businesses, and keep jobs—including increased health spending and direct income and revenue support—could soften the COVID-19 impact by as much as 40%–50%, to $3.5 trillion–$4.4 trillion (3.9%–4.8% of global GDP). The longer the containment period, the more difficult and prolonged the recovery will be, according to ADB's analysis.

As COVID-19 drives economies into recession, many jobs are at risk. But some industries and jobs, such as in tourism, are hit harder than others. As the pandemic drives further digital transformation, job polarization, and the displacement of middle-skilled workers, concerns arise in terms of income polarization, inequality, and inadequate social protection. *Cyn-Young Park and Ancilla Marie Inocencio* argue that, given significant reallocation of jobs in coming years, there is an urgent to increase job training programs and support workers' transition and adaptation to digital transformation and technology disruption with well-considered education and labor policies.

The pandemic is putting the spotlight on 91 million international migrants from Asia and the Pacific who face unemployment or reduced income, or being stranded in their host economies. Official data show that the pandemic is taking its toll on remittance flows to some developing Asian economies, while *Aiko Takenaka, James Villafuerte, Raymond Gaspar,* and *Badri Narayanan* note that for full-year 2020, remittances to Asia are expected to drop between $31.4 billion (in a baseline scenario) and $54.3 billion (in the worst case), equivalent to 11.5% and 19.8% of the baseline remittances. More than half is explained by lower remittances from the Middle East. Special policy attention would be needed for a sudden drop which may put households at risk of falling into poverty.

The severe acute respiratory syndrome (SARS) outbreak in 2003 provides insights on how the health and economic impact of COVID-19 can be mitigated, according to *Ilan Noy, Benno Ferrarini,* and *Donghyun Park,* whose reflections on events nearly 2 decades ago support the case for society and governments to work closely together to fight COVID-19. They recommend forceful fiscal and monetary policy responses by governments to reduce the negative impact and prepare the ground for a quicker and more complete recovery.

Jesus Felipe and *Al-Habbyel Yusoph* look at how economies have been providing income support, liquidity injections, and credit to combat the impact of the pandemic. Globally, total policy packages to combat COVID-19 reached $21 trillion in June 2020. Of this, ADB's developing members' total package is $3.1 trillion while its other members' total package is $13.7 trillion. Central banks continue to play a significant role in promoting liquidity and credit creation and financing government fiscal measures. International assistance in Asia from ADB and other institutions has increased significantly since April 2020 and may continue to rise in the near future. International loans and grants to ADB's developing members also increased twelvefold since April.

Chapter 2: Tackling the Financial Fallout

The pandemic has sent a shockwave through global financial markets and strained the banking sector, threatening financial stability in the process. Consequently, concerted action is needed to cushion the impact of the ongoing crisis and confront a possible financial fallout ahead. This chapter examines current risks to Asia's financial systems and proposes policy options to strengthen the region's financial resilience.

Cyn-Young Park, Peter Rosenkranz, and *Mara Claire Tayag* call attention to Asian banks' reliance on United States dollars funding markets which exposes the structural vulnerability of the region's financial system in times of crisis. Asia's cross-border assets and liabilities have risen considerably since the global financial crisis, and most are denominated in the United States dollars. With high financial interconnectedness of Asian banking systems, both regionally and globally, a sudden strain on United States dollars liquidity can rapidly spill over to emerging Asian economies. This, in turn, can prompt a sudden reversal in capital flows and an increase in financial volatility.

The economic slowdown from continuing measures to stem COVID-19's spread also increases risks of corporate defaults and, according to *Cyn-Young Park,* raises the specter of a debt crisis. A decade of low interest rates has raised global debt levels and widened financial imbalances across many economies. Amid increased financial interconnectedness of Asian and global financial markets, developing Asian economies remain particularly vulnerable to a financial fallout should loan defaults trigger banking crises in advanced economies. *Bambang Susantono* notes that falling corporate earnings and incomes add to the vulnerabilities of Asian banks, as these may push loan defaults higher. The significance of this potential risk to financial stability is underscored by the region's financial systems still being heavily bank-based.

The pandemic is damaging many state-owned enterprises across the region, with implications for a buildup of nonperforming loans in state-owned banks and other financial institutions. *David Robinett* argues that circular debts involving big loss-making state-owned enterprises spread the pain more widely. Many state-owned enterprises require deeper restructuring to improve fiscal and financial performance while still delivering crucial public services.

As governments continue to grapple with the many COVID-19-related risks to Asian financial markets, a coordinated response is needed to ensure timely, collective, and effective action. The pandemic provides an opportunity for regional financial cooperation to regain reform momentum. Suggested policy considerations in this chapter include deepening and strengthening the regional financial safety net to weather future financial volatilities, and improving mechanisms to allow for the swift resolution of nonperforming loans as they emerge.

Chapter 3: Supporting Micro, Small, and Medium-Sized Enterprises

Micro, small, and medium-sized enterprises (MSMEs) form the backbone of nearly every economy in Asia and Pacific, employing of more than 70% of all workers and accounting for more than 95% of all business establishments.[5] *Cyn-Young Park* and *Shigehiro Shinozaki* review the policy measures to provide MSMEs with financial support to survive the current economic slowdown, including emergency loans and low-cost credit provided by some governments and guarantees offered to help access credit indirectly. Moratoriums or forbearance on repayments and debts along with debt restructuring have featured in fiscal packages across the region. The authors argue that eligibility criteria of MSMEs for various funding facilities should be carefully attuned to help only enterprises at risk of collapse, and support should be temporary, with clear time-bound measures.

---

[5] Asian Development Bank. 2020. *Asia Small and Medium-sized Enterprise Monitor 2020*. Manila.

The impact of COVID-19 on MSMEs was further illustrated by a recent ADB survey of MSMEs in Indonesia, the Lao People's Democratic Republic, the Philippines, and Thailand, covering March to May 2020. *Shigehiro Shinozaki* presents key survey findings which show a sharp fall in MSME sales and revenues following strict public health measures in all four countries. Most MSMEs in the survey also reported they would run out of working capital within 1 month and had already started to reduce their workforce. The author recommends that governments should continue to support MSMEs, employing a more targeted approach to make better use of limited budgets.

Paul Vandenberg and *Matthias Helble* argue that supporting MSMEs is critical for the post-crisis recovery. The measures can include deferring payments by businesses to the government, such as on taxes, duties, and social security contributions, which allows MSMEs to conserve needed operating capital in the short term. Governments can also pay a portion of the payroll for workers who would otherwise be laid off during the pandemic to maintain employment. Providing business support during a temporary crisis can be a valuable investment for governments as it allows firms to quickly reboot once the crisis is over. Reconstituting businesses is often a costly and lengthy process.

How can banks best serve MSMEs during the pandemic? This is an issue explored by *Susan Olsen*. The author recommends that banks deploy business continuity plans, boost cash in hand, and avoid the debt trap of borrowing short to lend long. Further, banks should accelerate the transition toward digital solutions, particularly for mobile money payments and micro and small loan applications, and partner with non-traditional actors with strong distribution to help low-income consumers purchase goods. They could also help customers by opening channels for transfers of government subsidies or insurance.

Lotte Schou-Zibell studies how governments could improve the business environment to help MSMEs. One possibility is to overhaul business laws and regulations to remove bureaucratic red tape and to allow businesses to open and operate as quickly as possible when COVID-19 restrictions are eased. Governments should rethink the role of state-owned enterprises and allow MSMEs to enter their markets, and improve competition and consumer protection frameworks to help reduce prices. Finally, women should be offered targeted training to realize their potential to run businesses.

Chapter 4: Mitigating the Impact on the Poor and Vulnerable

The COVID-19 pandemic is worsening the conditions of vulnerable groups, including the urban and rural poor, people in informal and low-skilled work, the elderly, and women. The higher poverty and income inequality that this causes could hurt the chances of stable, inclusive, economic recovery. Studies in this chapter offer policy considerations on how to address the effects of the pandemic on vulnerable groups by highlighting the importance of financial support, social safety nets, and the provision of basic services.

As the ongoing pandemic continues to take a heavy toll on the health, livelihood, and well-being of billions of people across the region, *Juzhong Zhuang* explains that the poor and vulnerable groups are hardest hit. Informal sector workers suffer the most from layoffs, wage cuts, and health care costs, while the absence of written contracts, paid leave, or access to employment insurance benefits can push their households into poverty, increasing income inequality. *Joris van Etten* and *Tiffany Tran* argue that addressing infrastructure and basic services gaps can help the urban poor in Indonesia, who are vulnerable to COVID-19 because they lack adequate basic amenities, including access to clean water, and often live in overcrowded places with limited space for social distancing. COVID-19 presents a pressing opportunity to rethink public health, infrastructure provision, and social protection systems, according to the authors. *Amir Jilani* takes up the social protection theme, digging deep into how assistance can be given to the poor workers and families disproportionately affected by disease outbreaks.

Meredith Wyse highlights that COVID-19 points to the need to strengthen programs and policies affecting older people, who are among the most vulnerable during the pandemic because they often have chronic underlying diseases, and if in informal employment, face an increased risk of being infected at work. The large share of the retired elderly in Asia and the Pacific who lack adequate pensions struggle to respond to the pandemic. Similarly, *Malika Shagazatova* explains the importance of a gender-sensitive response to the crisis. Women are more vulnerable to the pandemic and worsening economic conditions than men as they tend to earn less, work in informal sectors and labor-intensive industries like services and health care, and spend more time caring for sick family members.

Junkyu Lee and *Arup Kumar Chatterjee* show that informal sector microenterprises in the region are at particular disadvantage from pandemic-related restrictions on mobility, delays in payments, and limited access to credit as they have no or poor-quality collateral. The authors emphasize the importance of financial support packages to cushion the severity of the pandemic on livelihoods and incomes. Emergency cash transfers to the vulnerable should be an essential element of the financial relief packages, which can benefit from innovative approaches such as the digital national identity *Aadhaar* card in India. *Arup Kumar Chatterjee* also argues that given a dizzying array of financial support to households and businesses, financial literacy programs for vulnerable groups will be crucial to help sustain long-term economic and financial resiliency in the region.

Chapter 5: Ensuring Food Security and Sustainable Agriculture

Hunger and malnutrition were urgent global concerns even before the pandemic. Despite impressive economic growth, 326 million people in Asia and the Pacific still live below the poverty line and 86 million or about one in four children below the age of five suffer stunted growth.[6] Meanwhile, farmers face shrinking natural resources, degrading environments, declining labor availability, and stresses from climate change and financial problems.

The COVID-19 pandemic has deepened these impacts, *Akmal Siddiq* finds, while lockdowns imposed to deal with the pandemic are hitting the entire food value chain from "farm to fork." These have led to labor shortages at planting and harvesting, while stoppage of transport services has hampered distribution of food to consumers. International supply chains are also impeded by limited port operations and logistics, while some countries have imposed export bans to protect domestic food stocks.

The pandemic should be used as an opportunity to accelerate reforms to increase food safety and security and swiftly improve rural development, according to *Kijin Kim, Sunae Kim,* and *Cyn-Young Park*, whose research highlights how rural development is strongly linked to poverty reduction, food security, and a reduction in rural-urban disparities. Smallholder farmers, who provide 80% of the region's food and yet are most vulnerable, could be given access to quality seeds, fertilizers, and pesticides. The region also

---

[6]   The UNICEF/WHO/WB Joint Child Malnutrition Estimates (JME) group released new data.

needs highly functioning markets for nutritious but perishable foods with a particular attention to potential wastage.

Qingfeng Zhang and *Jan Hinrichs* outline how digital technology can play a key role in improving food access and preventing waste through two-way flow of information between buyer and seller and feedback loops on price, origin, and safety of food production. COVID-19 has catalyzed an increasing role for digitization in the world's food supply, including in locked-down urban communities, where the trend toward online platforms for food purchases has accelerated.

Infrastructure investments, alongside policies to ensure digitization benefits are shared, should be increased to improve productivity, sustainability, and climate resilience. According to an ADB study, investments in agricultural research and development, market infrastructure, irrigation, and water use efficiency should increase from the current $42 billion to as much as $79 billion per year if international goals to end hunger are to be achieved.[7] The evolving impacts of the pandemic suggests this should now be higher.

Chapter 6: Building Resilient Trade and Supply Chains

A sharp fall in domestic and external demand due to mobility restrictions has been propagated through global value chains. *Abiad et al.* assess the impact of the COVID-19 pandemic using ADB's Multi-Region Input-Output Tables (MRIOT) to capture spillovers through trade and production linkages. They use country-specific information on outbreak severity, stringency of containment measures, and declines in mobility outside the home to calibrate the size of domestic demand declines resulting from the outbreak. The estimated domestic demand and external demand shocks are fed into the ADB MRIOT which traces all domestic and international sectoral linkages across 62 economies, with each economy disaggregated into 35 sectors.

Even with borders closing on movement of people, it is important to keep trade flowing for goods and services. Of immediate importance is to maintain supplies of medical masks, protective suits, googles, and gloves, and cooperation between countries to bring an end to shortages that have put frontline

---

[7] ADB. 2019. *Ending Hunger in Asia and the Pacific by 2030: An Assessment of Investment Requirements in Agriculture.* Manila.

health care workers at risk. *Susann Roth* and *Jesper Pedersen* highlight how the pandemic exposes the vulnerabilities of supply chains, not just in the market for personal protective equipment, but across many industries. This calls for policy makers' renewed attention to build and sustain resilient trade and supply chains in the wake of crisis and its aftermath.

The crisis underlines that countries need safe access to medicines, medical equipment, and other goods vital to the health of their populations through seamless trade flows. In this vein, *Steven Beck* describes ADB's efforts through trade and supply chain finance to support companies manufacturing and distributing medicines and other items needed to combat the virus. A recently devised supply chain mapping tool from ADB adds to the global armory of knowledge, bridging the information gap among the suppliers of personal protective equipment and reducing supply chain blockages to better respond to disease outbreaks. For example, if a shortage of rubber gaskets were holding up production of ventilators, someone using the ADB tool could quickly look up companies that make those gaskets and see if they were a match for their needs. The mapping tool represents innovative support offered by ADB's trade and supply chain finance programs.

Arup Kumar Chatterjee, Arjun Goswami, Jules Hugot, and *Marianne Vital* expand the trade and investment finance discussion to make the case for greater regional cooperation to strengthen the role of export credit agencies for greater cross-border trade and investment. Regional cooperation could lead to the creation of a multilateral agency with a good credit standing to facilitate access to trade and investment finance across Asia, particularly in the countries where credit availability is limited. Lessons learned from existing multilateral and national export credit agencies in Asia should be carefully considered in the new regional agency's design to keep trade and investment finance flowing.

Chapter 7: Accelerating Digital Transformation

Digital technologies have proven useful and necessary to manage the COVID-19 crisis. Digital platforms could be critical to reshaping the way we work, socialize, and create economic value in the post-pandemic world, *James Villafuerte* claims. Online platform companies open opportunities for efficiency gains, rapid economic growth, greater inclusion, and job creation. Yet, success is not preordained: how policies create an ecosystem and incentives while addressing regulatory challenges will be key to unlocking the economic potential of the digital economy—and to finding smarter solutions for growth and economic recovery in the time of COVID-19.

Steven Beck argues that the crisis should drive aggressive digitalization of global trade and supply chains to make the recovery stronger and economies more robust. As the pandemic continues to spread, this will also help economies become more secure. Although successful digitalization in the banking sector has made the trade finance market quite resilient, more can be done to standardize entity identifiers, make digitalization laws internationally compatible, and promote harmonized standards and protocols that improve interoperability across different systems.

COVID-19 might be speeding up the digitalization and automation process, according to *Sameer Khatiwada*. With restrictions on mobility and social distancing causing shops to close and shift to selling online, some jobs could be displaced and better ones emerge. Although technological progress has always driven growth and improvement in living standards, it is important that government prepares the workforce of the future by aligning education and training with the changing demand for labor.

On the education front, the pandemic has also forced a full shift to online learning which could further exacerbate the existing learning crisis in low-income and middle-income economies in Asia and the Pacific. *Brajesh Panth* and *Jeffrey Jian Xu* note that before the pandemic access was not much of an issue in education, but now the digital divide could lead to a decline in literacy and numeracy skills of the next generation. Better organization of government policies, IT infrastructure, schools and teachers, parents and students, and private providers of education technology is crucial. The delivery systems and management of online learning, so-called education technology or EdTech, are expected to continue to blend and evolve through and after the pandemic.

In a Pacific region case study, *Lotte Schou-Zibell* and *Nigel Phair* find COVID-19 is changing consumer behavior and expectations, particularly in using digital tools for financial transactions. Yet, the region needs a more efficient system to support contactless payment and government distribution of cash transfers during the pandemic. Deficiencies in infrastructure, database registries, identification systems, and bank information for most of the population are challenging. Investing in data connectivity, mobile technology, digital banking, and financial technologies is critical. The introduction of a digital access tool in Papua New Guinea and the launch of a mobile wallet in Fiji have improved financial inclusion. But more needs to be done to develop universal access, build trust and confidence, expand education and financial literacy, comply with international rules, and build regulations that make digital payments safe.

Chapter 8: Rebooting Asia in the Time of COVID-19

This chapter presents the questions about how economies in lockdown can best be restarted during and after the COVID-19 pandemic. The best approach is gradual, allowing flexibility for different regions or sectors to open up, according to *Patrick Osewe*, who highlights the uncertainty governments must grapple with when devising strategies to reboot their economies. Early evidence from the People's Republic of China suggests that a gradual approach can keep a second wave of infections at bay while an economy restarts. In developing a plan to reopen the economies, governments can follow a set of questions to assess the readiness of each sector, different areas, subregions, communities, and cities.

With travel restrictions and fear of traveling set to decimate international tourist arrivals in Asia and the Pacific, *Matthias Helble* examines two strategies to restart the tourism industry: first, promoting domestic tourism, and second, forging agreements on travel bubbles that allow business and leisure travelers to move between partner economies. Domestic tourism has the potential to close the gap left by the absence of international travelers in many economies, with the exception of those that rely heavily on international tourism, according to the analysis. Travel bubbles may be an attractive option for those heavily dependent on international tourism, although a sudden resurgence in infections could make them challenging to maintain.

Sanjay Grover, Hanif Rahemtulla, and *Colin Gin* discuss how to manage public–private partnerships for infrastructure investment during the post-pandemic recovery. They highlight that the current crisis has led to a high demand in certain infrastructure sectors, like health and information and communication technology (ICT), while airports and others have seen demand dry up. Governments need to quickly assess the potential short-term impact of reduced demand and increased costs across their public–

private partnership portfolios, differentiating between types of project, and assessing government exposure. Amid shrinking economies and with fiscal headroom reducing new sources of revenue such as bonds, land value capture and asset recycling need to be mobilized. Multilateral financial institutions will also have a big role to play in supporting governments with capacity building, technical, and financial assistance in this transitionary period. As *Arjun Goswami* points out, COVID-19 is a reminder that we are highly interconnected and disease does not respect national boundaries. It is therefore crucial to redouble regional cooperation efforts to coordinate effective responses to mitigate pandemic crises and engineer sustainable and resilient recovery.

Matthias Helble and *Susann Roth* highlight that strong regional cooperation is needed to facilitate development and distribution of safe and effective COVID-19 vaccines in sufficient quantities, and to make them accessible to the region's poorest countries. Asia and the Pacific accounts for over one-third of all confirmed active vaccine candidates,[8] and most efforts are coming from smaller private sector manufacturers. With six Asia and the Pacific countries among the top 20 vaccine exporters worldwide, the region can build on its substantial experience to take a lead in developing and distributing new vaccines.

Chapter 9: Building Back Better Together

ADB's strategy for long-term recovery from the pandemic is focused on the principles of building back better, differently, and together, according to *Bambang Susantono*. Better, by improving disaster preparedness, strengthening response systems, and facilitating early recovery. Differently, by adopting innovative tools. Together, by strengthening regional cooperation and building resilience across all sectors. Recovery will need to be based on key principles of resilience, sustainability, and inclusiveness, which cut across important areas of infrastructure investment, environmental protection, and climate change.

On post-pandemic infrastructure investments, *Bruno Carrasco* and *Hanif Rahemtulla* stress that quality considerations must prevail, and as Asia and the Pacific comes out of the crisis with significantly larger public debts,

---

[8] T.T. Le et al. 2020. The COVID-19 Vaccine Development Landscape. *Nature.* 9 April.

projects will need to be efficient, affordable, and sustainable. The crisis offers an opportunity to adopt higher standards that take a broader approach to project design and environmental and social sustainability safeguards, and to use technologies to create resilience against natural disasters. *Benno Ferrari* explains that building resilience in recovery and reconstruction would be crucial for developing Asia, which is highly prone to disasters triggered by natural hazards. The region accounted for more than half of 60,000 disaster fatalities and more than a quarter of total economic damage worldwide from 2000 to 2018. *Jingmin Huang* further stresses that the nature of COVID-19 infections makes policies toward improving water and sanitation critical.

The COVID-19 crisis also offers opportunities to take action to reverse decades of environmental neglect and damage. Indeed, *Preety Bhandari* and *Arghya Sinha Roy* argue that now is the time to ramp up actions on climate resilience so that society can beat the COVID-19 crisis while reducing the impact of climate threats. *Anouj Mehta* and *Naeeda Crishna Morgado* state the case for making investments in climate-resilient infrastructure a central part of economic stimulus to rebuild Asia's economies. To do this, putting in place adequate principles for guiding green infrastructure choices is a first step that governments in the region can take. The introduction of green bonds guidelines, such as the Climate Bonds Standard, will help distinguish bonds that support green objectives and guide investors to determine their impact. In Southeast Asia, the governments can also tap the Association of Southeast Asian Nations (ASEAN) Catalytic Green Finance Facility to prepare and finance infrastructure projects that promote environmental sustainability.

A sustainable response in a post-COVID-19 world cannot underestimate the importance of oceans and the "blue economy" according to *Ingrid van Wees*. Besides their pivotal economic role and importance for biodiversity, oceans absorb about a third of the carbon dioxide emissions generated by human activities—and yet they are threatened. Attracting finance to this sector has been challenging because of a lack of bankability and low revenue streams. Yet, renewed efforts that draw private capital through blended finance instruments, including "blue credits," are promising.

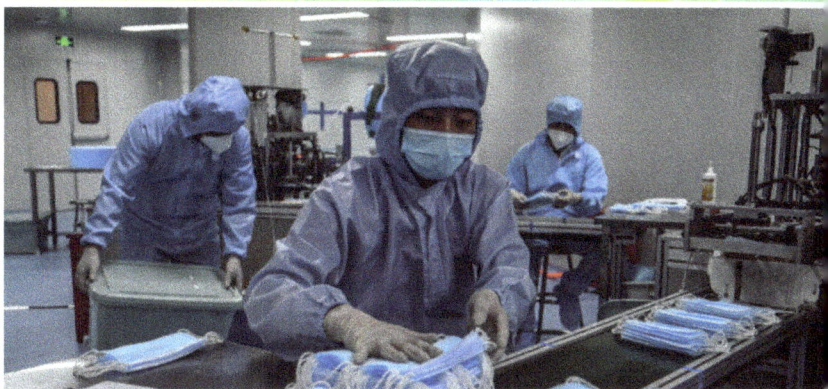

1. Economic Impact and Policy Response

Photos on previous page: [Top] Workers at an assembly line for medical masks. [Bottom] Closed metro station during lockdown announced by government to help decrease number of people infected by COVID-19, 4 August 2020 (photo by Elmar Estefayev).

The COVID-19 Economic Impact

James Villafuerte

The coronavirus disease (COVID-19) pandemic continues to weigh heavily on health and economic systems around the world. Millions have been infected and hundreds of thousands have lost their lives. Border controls continue to be strictly implemented in many countries, impairing global production capacity, and creating one of the most serious crises in history.

The ongoing pandemic is a "crisis like no other," according to the June *World Economic Outlook Update* of the International Monetary Fund (IMF), which has cut its global growth forecast to -4.9% for 2020. The World Bank, in its *Global Economic Prospects,* in June cut its forecast to -5.2% and called the crisis one of the deepest recessions in over 150 years, next to recessions after World War I, in the 1930s, and after World War II. Meanwhile, the Asian Development Bank (ADB) also cut its growth projection for developing Asia by over 2%—since April— to 0.1% in 2020, the lowest regional growth outcome in 6 decades.

ADB estimates the COVID-19 economic impact will range from $5.8 trillion if the outbreak is contained and economic conditions normalize in 3 months, to $8.8 trillion if it takes longer or 6 months to rein in the virus and normalize economic conditions. As a share of global gross domestic product (GDP), the damage could range from 6.4% to 9.7%, excluding the impact of government measures taken to mitigate its impact. About 30% of this global impact will be accounted for by Asia, where in the two scenarios output will fall by $1.7 trillion and $2.5 trillion, which is 6.2% to 9.3% of regional GDP.

The ADB study also notes severe employment effects from the pandemic. Globally, 158 million to 242 million jobs will be lost in the two scenarios

(6.0% and 9.2% of total employment). For Asia, the drop in employment will reach 109 million to 167 million jobs—or as much as 69% of total employment losses globally. This estimated impact is more than seven times the employment decline in Asia during the 2008–2009 global financial crisis—which reduced employment by about 22 million people, measured on a full-time job equivalent basis.

Moreover, the pandemic will also likely reverse some of the hard-won development gains that Asia has achieved since the global financial crisis. For example, relative to a scenario without COVID-19, the long containment scenario—where it takes 6 months to contain the virus and normalize economic conditions—will see 56 million people moved into extreme poverty, earning $1.90 or less a day, and 140 million surviving on $3.20 a day.

For these reasons, strong government support of households and businesses is warranted. This could take the form of payroll support, subsidies, unemployment assistance, and help for jobseekers. Cash transfers to those in the informal employment sector, and the distribution of essential services and commodities, including through community feeding programs, are also vital. Incorporating this type of government policy response, could soften the COVID-19 economic impact by as much as 30%–40%, reducing global economic losses to $4.1 trillion–$5.4 trillion (4.5%–5.9% of global GDP), according to the ADB study.

Policy makers should continue to focus on three key actions at this time. First, governments must do all they can to contain the pandemic as soon as possible to reduce the economic costs. Sufficient testing, tracing and isolation, effective social distancing, and securing protective and medical equipment are critical elements.

Second, it is important for governments to help struggling families and businesses mitigate adverse impacts of the pandemic and to head off the long-term consequences for growth and development that could otherwise occur.

Third, governments also need to manage supply chain disruptions, support e-commerce and technology solutions for delivering goods and services, and prepare for a gradual opening of economies when things get better— and they will get better.

COVID-19, Technology, and Polarizing Jobs

Cyn-Young Park and Ancilla Marie Inocencio

As COVID-19 drives economies into recession, many jobs are at risk. However, not all jobs are equally affected—some industries and jobs are more severely hit than others. Several factors seem to be at play, such as labor intensity (traditional services such as restaurants and retail shops and labor-intensive manufacturing sectors), low-skill (manual and routine) jobs, and informality (inadequate employment protection).

Indeed, COVID-19 effects are fueling trends of job polarization and widening wage inequality among employees that had already been exposing middle-skilled workers to displacement and lower working hours and incomes.

Without conscious effort and effective policies, the unequal impact of COVID-19 on jobs will hit the most vulnerable individuals and communities. They will continue to face greater risks of unemployment, financial losses, and health hazards, exacerbating socioeconomic inequalities and undermining inclusive growth efforts. To break and reverse the vicious cycle, it is essential to understand the relationship between technologies and job polarization, how COVID-19 exposes middle-skilled workers to job displacement and aggravates job polarization, and what the policy priorities should be after the pandemic.

Technology and Polarization of Jobs

Earlier economic literature investigated the possible causes of job polarization and suggested a hypothesis of skill-biased technical change. Such change implies that technological advances have boosted the productivity of skilled labor relatively more than that of unskilled labor, benefiting skilled workers more than unskilled workers. The evolution of new technologies—such as information and communication technology (ICT)—have increased returns from skill. Autor and Katz (1999) presents a survey of the skill-biased technical change hypothesis.[1]

Autor, Levy, and Murnane (2003) note that skills and tasks are distinct.[2] They argue that while some tasks can be easily displaced, codified, and automated, it is more difficult for other tasks. Tasks can be categorized as "cognitive" (analytical or interactive) versus "manual" and "routine" versus "nonroutine." Jobs that are at risk tend to be a combination of manual and routine tasks, while jobs that remain are (i) manual and nonroutine, typical of the service sector; and (ii) cognitive and nonroutine, which are often found in managerial, professional, and creative occupations. This so-called routine-biased technological change hypothesis suggests that technological change leads to polarization of low- and high-skilled jobs and hollowing out of middle-skilled ones, typically of a routine nature, such as clerical and administrative occupations.

Job polarization displaces middle-skilled workers into lower-paying work, which drives wages of low-skilled workers even lower, while widening wage gaps between high-skilled and low-skilled workers. The phenomenon of job polarization is not limited to developed countries. Maloney and Molina (2016) show that middle-skilled occupations (intensive in routine cognitive and manual tasks) have decreased across developing countries.[3] Fleisher et al. (2018) find evidence of job polarization in the People's Republic of China (PRC) from 1995 to 2013.[4] Dao et al. (2017) argue that developing countries with higher routinization of tasks and greater participation in global value chains experience more declines in the labor income share of medium-skilled workers.[5]

[1]   D. Autor and L. Katz. 1999. Changes in the Wage Structure and Earnings Inequality. In O. Ashenfelter and D. Card, eds. *Handbook of Labor Economics*. 3A: pp. 1463–1555.

[2]   D. Autor, F. Levy, and R. Murnane. 2003. Computer-Based Technological Change and Skill Demands: Reconciling the Perspectives of Economists and Sociologists. In E. Appelbaum, A. Bernhardt and R. J. Murnane, eds. *Low-Wage America: How Employers Are Reshaping Opportunity in the Workplace*. New York: Russell Sage Foundation.

[3]   W. Maloney and C. Molina. 2016. Are Automation and Trade Polarizing Developing Country Labor Markets, Too? *Policy Research Working Paper* No. 7922. Washington, DC: World Bank Group.

[4]   B. Fleisher et al. 2018. Innovation, Wages, and Polarization in China. *IZA Discussion Paper* No. 11569. IZA Institute of Labor Economics.

[5]   M. Dao et al. 2017. Why Is Labor Receiving a Smaller Share of Global Income? Theory and Empirical Evidence. *IMF Working Paper* No.17/169. IMF.

COVID-19 and Unequal Impacts on Jobs

The International Labour Organization (ILO) confirms that the hardest-hit industries by the COVID-19 crisis are accommodation and food services, manufacturing, wholesale and retail trade, and real estate and business activities.[6] In Asia and the Pacific, prolonged and extended lockdown measures have hit wholesale and retail trade, accommodation and food services, and transportation sectors severely—these sectors account for 14% (1.9 billion workers) of total employment (Figure 1.1). Manufacturing (16% of total employment in the region)—such as automobiles and textiles, clothing, leather, and footwear—has also suffered severe domestic and global value chain disruptions.

Estimates based on the different measures implemented by the Republic of Korea and the United Kingdom also show that low-skilled work, where face-to-face interaction is unavoidable (i.e., service sector and retail), were hardest hit by blanket lockdowns.[7] As seen in Figure 1.2, developing countries, where 50%–90% of total employment is in the informal economy, will also be hit hard because of lower health care capacity, poor governance, and less fiscal space.[8]

On the other hand, employment in some sectors, particularly in the tech and pharma industries, has held up relatively well. Since the outbreak early this year, many employees in Facebook, Google, and other tech giants have been working from home. A recent study in the United States, in the context of COVID-19, show that 37% of jobs can be done at home. However, these vary significantly across location and industry. The top five includes (i) educational services; (ii) professional, scientific, and technical services; (iii) management; (iv) finance and insurance; and (v) information. The bottom five include (i) transportation and warehousing; (ii) construction; (iii) retail trade; (iv) agriculture, forestry, fishing, and hunting; and (v) accommodation and food services.[9]

---

[6]   International Labour Organization (ILO). 2020. ILO Monitor: COVID-19 and the World of Work. 29 April. Third edition.

[7]   S. Aum, S. Lee, and Y. Shin. 2020. Inequality of Fear and Self-Quarantine: Is There a Trade-off between GDP and Public Health? *NBER Working Paper* No. 27100. National Bureau of Economic Research.

[8]   N. Loayza and S. Pennings. 2020. Macroeconomic Policy in the Time of COVID-19: A Primer for Developing Countries. *Research & Policy Briefs* No. 28. Washington, DC: World Bank Group.

[9]   J. Dingel and B. Neiman. 2020. How Many Jobs Can Be Done at Home? *NBER Working Paper* No. 26948. National Bureau of Economic Research.

Figure 1.1: Employment Sectoral Distribution by Subregion, 2019

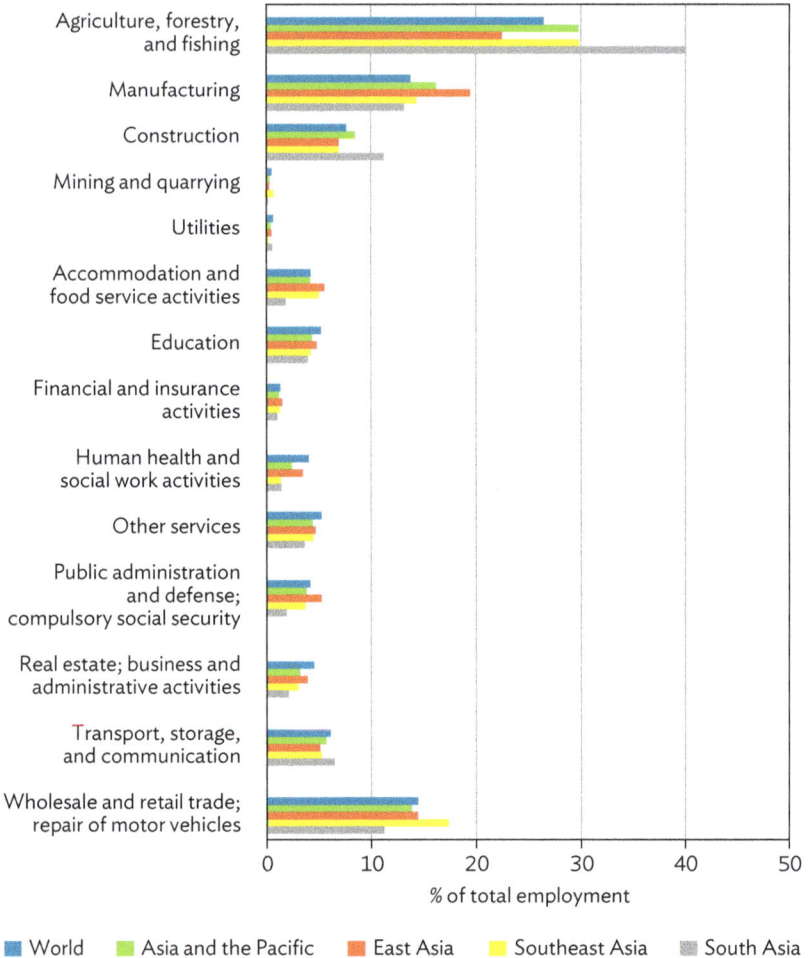

Source: International Labour Organization. Employment by Sex and Age — ILO Modelled Estimates. ILOSTAT database, https://ilostat.ilo.org/data (accessed 25 June 2020).

Automation also gains prominence in addressing supply chain disruptions arising from pandemic-induced mobility restrictions. In the PRC, Cadillac had already begun fully automating its car welding and painting production lines.[10] As the coronavirus spreads, companies' reliance on non-human labor

---

[10] Baker McKenzie and Oxford Economics. 2020. Beyond COVID-19: Supply Chain Resilience Holds Key to Recovery. https://www.bakermckenzie.com/-/media/files/insight/publications/2020/04/covid19-global-economy.pdf.

Figure 1.2: Share of Informal Employment in Non-Agriculture Sector (%)

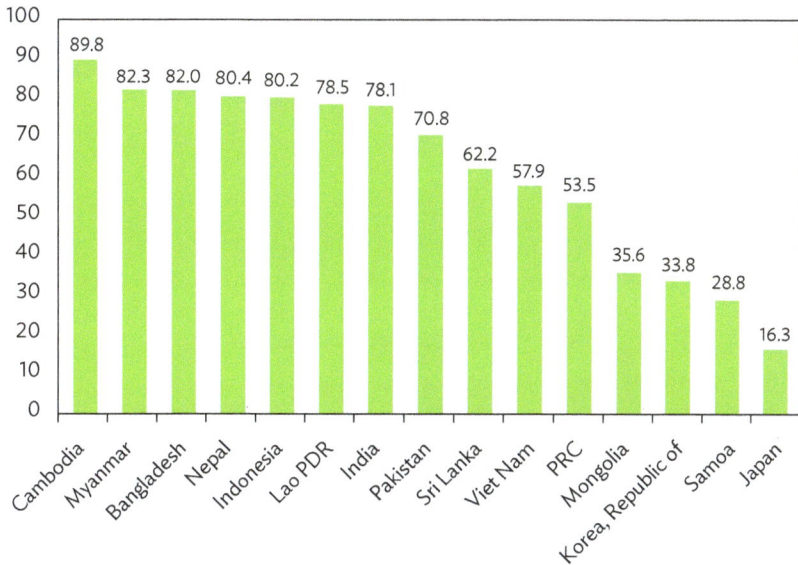

Lao PDR = Lao People's Democratic Republic, PRC = People's Republic of China.
Source: International Labour Organization (2018).

will also likely grow, while e-commerce and e-business models based on digital platforms continue expanding rapidly. Robotics are also likely to be used more for public health in a wide range of tasks such as disinfection or measuring vital signs, while protecting frontline health care workers.[11]

As automation happens for routine and manual jobs, workers who do not have the skills for the nonroutine and nonmanual jobs will be at greater risk. Khatiwada and Maceda Veloso (2019) use models to determine who is more likely to be successful in emerging new jobs associated with new technologies.[12] They find that males, those with education, the urbanized, and those working in the service sector have an advantage, consistent with finding by Egana del Sol (2020) that people with higher levels of education

[11] G. Yang et al. 2020. Combating COVID-19—The Role of Robotics in Managing Public Health and Infectious Diseases. *Science Robotics.* 5 (40). DOI: 10.1126/scirobotics.abb5589.

[12] S. Khatiwada and M. Maceda Veloso. 2019. New Technology and Emerging Occupations: Evidence from Asia, *ADB Economics Working Paper Series*, No. 576. Manila: Asian Development Bank.

face lower risks from automation.[13] On the other hand, most workers in developing Asia are low-skilled (50%–80%) and have at most primary education (30%–65%).[14]

Informal workers are at particular risk. A large share of informal employment is in sectors that are relatively more vulnerable, such as manufacturing, wholesale and retail trade, transportation and storage, and accommodation and food services (Figure 1.3).

Informal sector employment features low skills, low productivity, and low capital investment, and is subject to a higher risk of job losses. Workers in the informal sector typically earn low wages and have little access to social protection coverage. The ILO reports that 1.3 billion people work informally in Asia and the Pacific—65% of the world informal employment (footnote 14). Around 7 in 10 workers in developing Asia are in the informal economy. Informal employment accounts for the highest share of total employment in South Asia (89%), followed by Southeast Asia (76%) and Central Asia (70%). For example, almost 9 in 10 workers are in informal sectors in Bangladesh, India, and Nepal.

The situation is often worse among women, youth, and rural workers. Women make up a larger share of the informal economy with 92.1% in low-income and 84.5% in lower middle-income countries—versus men at 87.5% and 83.4% (footnote 14). Women also have less education and lower incomes than men. In developing countries, only 32% of female workers are in the formal economy, compared to 36% of male workers (Figure 1.4). The difference is highest for South Asia and Africa, with 26% and 31% more men in the formal sector, respectively. Women are also often overrepresented in low-skill services such as housekeeping, wholesale and retail trading, agricultural activities, and labor-intensive manufacturing sectors. Women typically earn much less than men. In addition, a considerable share of women is engaged in family employment, working for no pay at all, either caring for family members or as unpaid employees.

---

[13] P. Egana del Sol. 2020. The Future of Work in Developing Economies: What Can We Learn from the South? GLO Discussion Paper, No. 483, Global Labor Organization.

[14] ILO. 2018. Women and Men in the Informal Economy: A Statistical Picture (third edition). Geneva: International Labour Office.

Figure 1.3: Informal Employment by Sector in Select Asian Countries

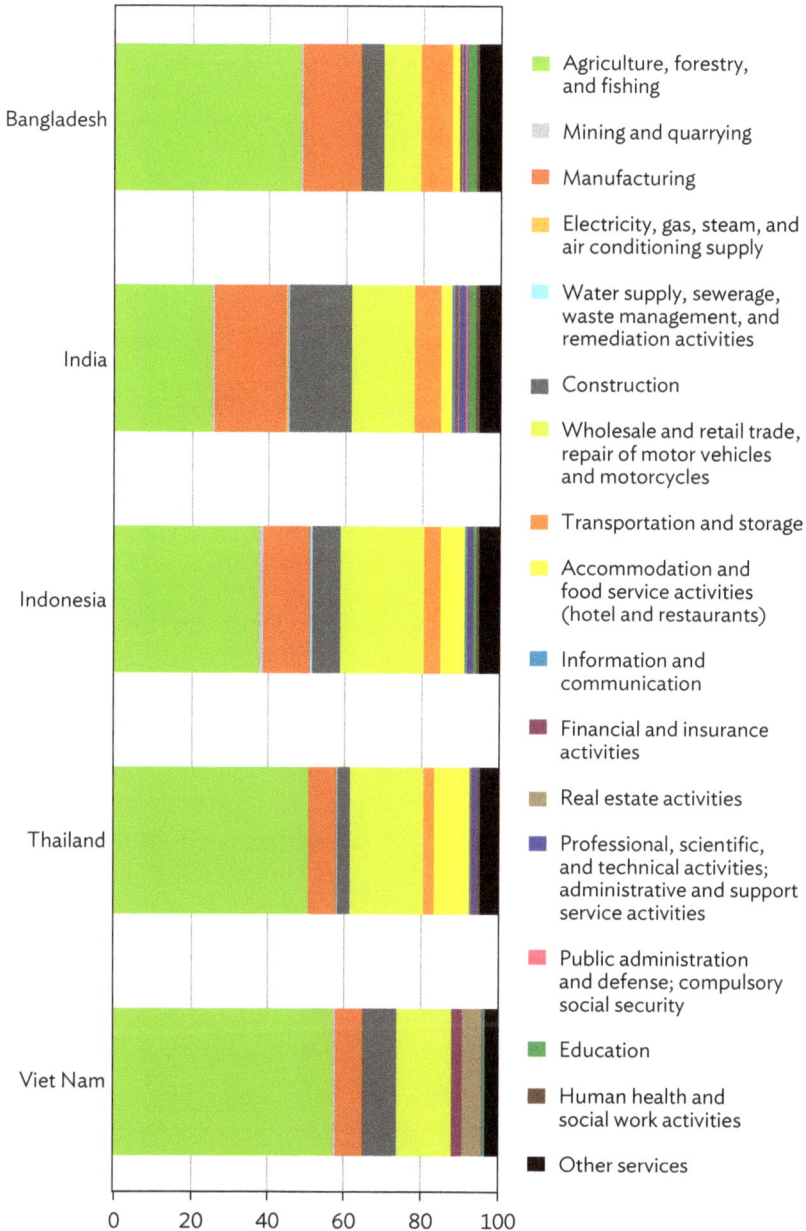

Source: Asian Development Bank calculations based on country microdata: Labor Force Surveys for Bangladesh (2016), India (2011–2012), Indonesia (2017), Thailand (2018), and Viet Nam (2016).

Figure 1.4: Regional Average Share of Formal Employment to Total Employment by Gender

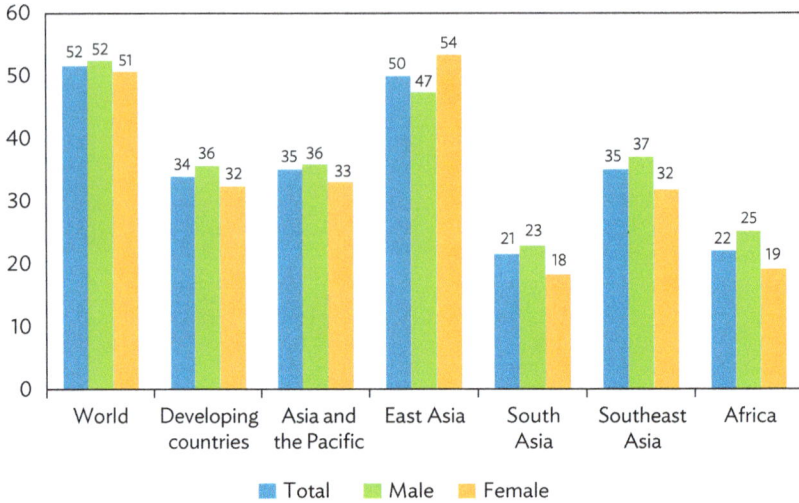

Source: International Labour Organization (2018).

Policy Implications for the Post-COVID-19 Work and Workplace

COVID-19 will likely spur digital transformation in work and workplace. Country experiences underscore the importance of technology in mitigating the effects of COVID-19 not only on health, but also on economic outcomes.[15] In the post-COVID-19 era, digital tools and technologies will be further prioritized in schools, workplaces, and across different sectors.

However, as digital transformation accelerates, job polarization and displacement of middle-skilled workers are raising concerns about income polarization, inequality, and inadequate social protection.

The trend of job polarization indicates significant reallocation of jobs could occur in coming years, increasing the urgency for job training programs and appropriate labor policy. Indeed, the trend could worsen inequality and skill-bias, with still worse impacts on old workers, who are typically low skilled

---

[15] The Republic of Korea is often cited as a successful case of using digital technology to contain the pandemic by contact tracing: see *What We Can Learn from the Korean Response to COVID-19* in ADB's Development Asia platform.

and do routine jobs.[16] Past experiences in developed nations also suggest developing countries need to prepare for labor market disruptions coming from increasing automation and a reduction in offshored jobs.[17]

Policy makers should agonize over policy strategies and options that help mitigate the impact of these post-crisis structural changes on the workforce and the most vulnerable, who deserve timely and human-centered attention.

Invest in digital readiness

Digital readiness has proved a crucial factor in allowing some economies to successfully contain the spread of the virus and others to continue normal activities (or as close as possible to normal) during the pandemic. Developing the enabling infrastructure, nurturing cooperative ecosystems, and building digital skills and education are all critical for digital transformation.

A recent study by United Nations Conference on Trade and Development (UNCTAD) noted significant gaps in digital readiness across borders, with the least-developed countries lagging considerably behind.[18] Gaps range from ICT infrastructure to online platforms, mobile payment solutions, skills, and legal and regulatory frameworks. The digital divide also remains significant between rich and poor, urban and rural, young and old, and men and women in many developing countries, posing a meaningful social challenge. The gap in digital readiness and various forms of the digital divide can also have longer-term and lasting impact on inequality among individuals and in social groupings and countries.

Investment in ICT and digital infrastructure, digital skills development, and in the regulatory framework will be critical to bridge the gap in digital readiness and facilitate digital transformation.[19]

---

[16] P. Lewandowski et al. 2017. Routine and Ageing? The Intergenerational Divide in the Deroutinisation of Jobs in Europe. *IZA Discussion Paper* No. 10732. Bonn: IZA Institute of Labor Economics.

[17] M. Das. 2018. Automation and Job Displacement in Emerging Markets: New Evidence. *VoxEU*. 13 November. https://voxeu.org/article/automation-and-job-displacement-emerging-markets.

[18] United Nations Conference on Trade and Development (UNCTAD). 2020. *The COVID-19 Crisis: Accentuating the Need to Bridge Digital Divides*. New York: United Nations.

[19] M. Chinn and R. Fairlie. 2007. The Determinants of the Global Digital Divide: A Cross-Country Analysis of Computer and Internet Penetration. *Oxford Economic Papers*, Oxford University Press. 59 (1). pp. 16–44.

Develop skills for the digital economy

Skills development programs can help the low-skilled unemployed find work once countries open up. Prolonged unemployment is a serious challenge, especially for low-skilled workers, although it will affect workers of all skill levels. Some countries have increased their investment in skills development of people unemployed and furloughed due to the pandemic. In Indonesia, as millions filed for jobless allowances, the government allotted $227 million for upskilling programs through vocational training on digital platforms and some allowance.[20]

The COVID-19 impact on education also has implications for the future workforce. With school closures, e-learning has increased substantially. While this offers opportunities to develop or deepen digital skills, not every student is capable of going online. Moreover, despite the noticeable improvement in digital skills education, the pandemic has thrown a spotlight on the key constraints in current education systems, including lack of digital curricula, teaching tools, and materials.

Reforms and policies related to digital technology in the education system are needed to integrate ICT into teaching methods. They are also needed to give teachers ICT skills and reshape their roles, helping them to become facilitators of knowledge, to nurture digital capability and competency among students, and to promote creative and innovative ideas in classes. At the same time, policy makers should not lose sight of the groups often falling behind and excluded, such as the elderly, poor, and rural communities. It is important to provide targeted support to enhance digital literacy and reduce digital exclusion.

Strengthen social protection for the unemployed and vulnerable

The COVID-19 pandemic has exposed serious gaps in social protection systems in many developing economies. Effective social protection systems are essential to support the unemployed and vulnerable, especially during crises. However, national systems often remain limited in coverage and

---

[20] E. Listiyorini and H. Suhartono. 2020. Four Million Indonesians Seek Jobless Funds While Virus Spreads. *Bloomberg.* 14 April. https://www.bloomberg.com/news/articles/2020-04-14/four-million-indonesians-seek-jobless-funds-while-virus-spreads.

efficiency of delivery. They need significant upgrading to respond effectively to a crisis like COVID-19.

Developing economies can explore targeted or semi-targeted policies, according to risk, as economies reopen. In the pandemic context, Acemoglu et al. (2020) suggest that optimally targeted policies—such as limiting strict lockdowns to older populations, allowing the less vulnerable to rejoin the economy gradually—can reduce both mortality and economic damage more than policies that apply to everyone can.[21]

Public policy responses should also limit the impact of unemployment on workers and their families by providing temporary income support (i.e., unemployment insurance systems, redundancy payments, and social assistance programs) and employing active labor market policies (i.e., labor exchanges or mobility assistance, education and training, and business support or subsidized employment).[22] According to IMF, at least 20 countries have provided targeted support to the informal sector or the self-employed.[23]

---

[21] D. Acemoglu et al. 2020. A Multi-Risk SIR Model with Optimally Targeted Lockdown. *NBER Working Paper* No. 27102. National Bureau of Economic Research.

[22] A. Schmillen. 2020. Causes and Impacts of Job Displacements and Public Policy Responses. *Research & Policy Briefs* No. 33. Washington, DC: World Bank Group.

[23] IMF. 2020. Policy Responses to COVID-19. 8 May. https://www.imf.org/en/Topics/imf-and-covid19/Policy-Responses-to-COVID-19#S.

COVID-19 Impact on International Migration, Remittances, and Recipient Households in Developing Asia

Aiko Kikkawa Takenaka, James Villafuerte, Raymond Gaspar, and Badri Narayanan

The COVID-19 pandemic has devastated economies worldwide, slashing jobs and incomes. ADB estimates that employment in Asia and the Pacific will fall as much as 167 million person months in 2020 should containment measures last 6 months from when the outbreak first intensified.[24] In turn, wage incomes in the region are projected to fall by $359 billion to $550 billion.

Migrant workers are among the hardest-hit groups, as border control restrictions have limited job security and protection. Crucial remittances they send home to their families are expected to decline dramatically.

Asian Migrants' Jobs at Risk

Asia and the Pacific accounted for 33% (91 million) of the 272 million migrant workers worldwide in 2019. Major destination regions for Asian migrants included Asia (35%), the Middle East (27%), Europe inclusive of the Russian Federation (19%), and North America (18%). COVID-19 has hit all of these regions hard, with economic output in these economies projected to contract by 6.7%–10.2% in 2020.

The overall economic conditions of host countries and the sector affiliation determine impact, with severe losses of migrant jobs reported in retail trade, manufacturing, hospitality and recreation, and accommodation and food service sectors. Workers have been laid off and, in many cases, stranded in host economies as strict quarantines were imposed, borders closed, and air

---

[24] ADB. 2020. An Updated Assessment of the Economic Impact of COVID-19. *ADB Briefs* No. 133. Manila.

travel halted. Worse still, departures of new migrant workers from Asia have been put off until further notice.

Remittance Flows to Developing Asia to Plunge amid the Pandemic

The pandemic is taking a heavy toll on remittance flows to developing Asian economies. Official central bank data on remittance inflows show significant declines, although magnitude and consistency vary across countries. Some altruistic migrant workers may still be able to send money home to families in extremely difficult situations, but prevailing weak economic forecasts suggest remittances will plunge.

Using the Bilateral Labor Migration or GMig2 Model and Database of the Global Trade Analysis Project, we analyzed COVID-19's effect on remittance inflows. The analysis assumes that the pandemic has reduced GDP growth through anticipated country-specific declines in tourist arrivals, domestic consumption, investment and production, and increase in trade costs, as reported in an ADB assessment published in May 2020 (footnote 24). The outbreak has also undermined demand for and price of oil, which hits employment and wage differentials between home and host countries. These shocks hurt migrant employment and their ability to send remittances.

In the analysis, if outbreak control and normalization takes about a year—with the pandemic effects on the economy halving in the last quarter of the year as containment efforts and reopening takes effect—global remittances are expected to decline $108.6 billion in 2020, equivalent to 18.3% of the baseline remittances globally (Table 1.1). Remittance receipts in Asia will fall $54.3 billion, equivalent to 19.8% of the baseline remittances in 2018. By subregion, remittances in South Asia will fall most—by $28.6 billion (24.7% of 2018 baseline). Remittances to Central Asia follow (declining $3.4 billion, 23.8%), then Southeast Asia ($11.7 billion, 18.6%) and East Asia excluding the PRC and Japan (1.7 billion, 16.2%). Remittances to the Pacific will also fall ($267 million, 13.2%).

Table 1.1: Impact on Global Remittance Inflows

Remittance Recipients	Amount ($ million)	% of Baseline
Global	-108,617	-18.3
Asia	-54,255	-19.8
Australia and New Zealand	-299	-10.8
Central Asia	-3,366	-23.8
East Asia	-1,660	-16.2
Japan	-497	-13.3
PRC	-7,886	-12.6
Southeast Asia	-11,660	-18.6
South Asia	-28,621	-24.7
Pacific	-267	-13.2
United States	-482	-7.4
European Union + United Kingdom	-17,889	-14.4

PRC = People's Republic of China.
Note: Data presented for East Asia do not include those for the PRC and Japan.
Source: Asian Development Bank estimates.

Remittance-Dependent Households at Risk of Falling into Poverty

International remittance inflows are critical in Asia's efforts to uplift the lives and welfare of poor people in the region. In a cross-country study involving the 10 migrant-sending countries in Asia, Yoshino, Taghizadeh-Hesary, and Otsuka (2017) estimate that a 1-percentage-point increase in the share to GDP of remittance inflows from overseas is associated with a 22.6% reduction in the poverty gap ratio and 16% decline in the poverty severity ratio.[25]

Families in migrant-sending households use remittances to buy essential items such as food, clothing, shelter, health, and education. Indeed, hundreds of thousands of households in countries of origin depend on remittance incomes. Nearly 90% of households in Tonga, 80% in Samoa, and more than 40% in Fiji are reported to receive some amount of remittances from overseas (Figure 1.5).

---

[25] N. Yoshino, F. Taghizadeh-Hesary, and M. Otsuka. 2017. International Remittances and Poverty Reduction: Evidence from Asian Developing Countries. *Asian Development Bank Institute (ADBI) Working Paper 759.* Tokyo: ADBI.

Figure 1.5: Share of the Recipient Households with International Remittances

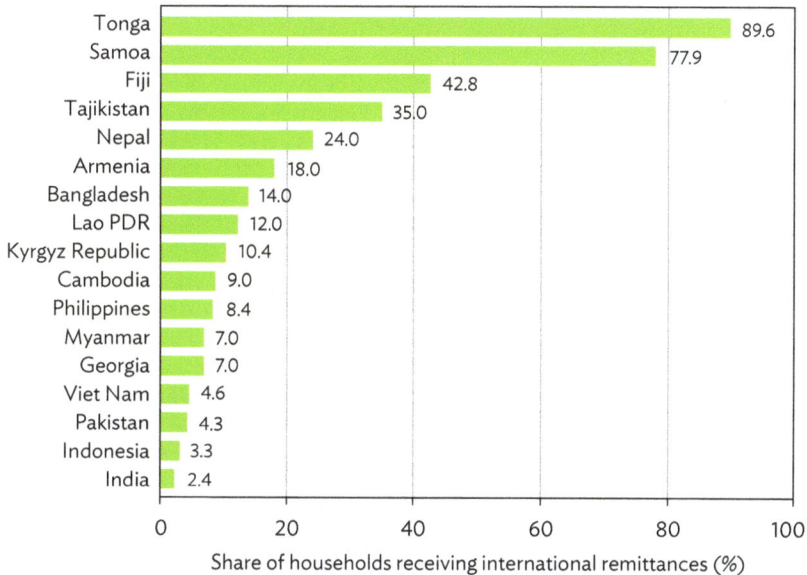

Country	Share (%)
Tonga	89.6
Samoa	77.9
Fiji	42.8
Tajikistan	35.0
Nepal	24.0
Armenia	18.0
Bangladesh	14.0
Lao PDR	12.0
Kyrgyz Republic	10.4
Cambodia	9.0
Philippines	8.4
Myanmar	7.0
Georgia	7.0
Viet Nam	4.6
Pakistan	4.3
Indonesia	3.3
India	2.4

Share of households receiving international remittances (%)

Lao PDR = Lao People's Democratic Republic.
Sources: ADB compilation using data from household surveys/various years.

Unexpected reduction or suspension of these remittances can leave recipients particularly vulnerable. In the Kyrgyz Republic, for example, remittances constitute 75% of recipient households' average income.[26] Concerns are even greater for households comprising older people or with no additional income earner. In the Philippines, senior citizens are the most likely to receive remittances, at over 21%.[27] Many existing government emergency social protection measures are linked to employment (e.g., unemployment benefits, minimum wage guarantee program) and these by design will not reach hard-hit remittance recipient households.

---

[26] X. Gao, A. Kikkawa, and J. W. Kang. 2020. Evaluating the Impact of Remittances on Human Capital Investment in the Kyrgyz Republic. Draft.

[27] Philippine Statistics Authority. 2020. Domestic Remittances are Just as Important as International Remittances (Results from the 2018 National Migration Survey). Press release.

Recommended Policy Actions

International migration, cross-border mobility of workforces, and flows of worker remittances are essential features of today's globalized economy. As such, the COVID-19 pandemic has undermined the social and employment status of migrant workers and their families and host and source countries are encouraged to provide them effective support.

Authorities in these countries can take several measures to help. They are encouraged to:

- Extend temporary health and social services to assist stranded and returned migrants.

- Expand social protection coverage to low-income remittance recipient households who may fall back into the poverty trap.

- Design comprehensive national migration policy frameworks that encompass immigration, health, and labor policies to support migrant workers and improve their rights and welfare.

- Ensure the continuity of remittance services and enabling business environments for service providers, including through use of digital and online platforms to better serve migrants and their families.

COVID-19 and SARS: An Epidemiological and Economic Comparison

Ilan Noy, Benno Ferrarini, and Donghyun Park

Much is still unknown about SARS-CoV-2, the virus that causes COVID-19, and its destructive potential, but from the information known at this point, several facts are pertinent. First, it belongs to the same family of coronaviruses that cause severe acute respiratory syndrome (SARS), which spread in a global pandemic in 2003, and Middle East respiratory syndrome (MERS) that appeared in 2012 and continues to persist, mostly in the Middle East with other occasional hotspots elsewhere. Like these diseases, the main symptoms of COVID-19 appear in the upper respiratory system and it has most often more potent symptoms in older patients.

Second, and most importantly, the global mortality rate of 6.6%, based on more than 1.99 million reported cases and 130,885 deaths as of 16 April, is significantly lower than 10% for SARS and 35% for MERS, according to the United States (US) Centers for Disease Control and Prevention. Further, 6.6% may be a substantial overestimate. For example, a scientific analysis of cases aboard the Diamond Princess cruise ship yielded an estimate of 1.2%.[28] However, much uncertainty remains about reporting of caseloads. Also, as the disease is spreading to low-income and lower middle-income countries with limited public health systems, the mortality rate may rise significantly.

While we probably have an accurate count of the number of people who died from the disease in some of the countries affected, we do not know the number of people who were infected, since many display only mild symptoms. The current death rate among reported Chinese patients is about 4%, but it is likely that some milder cases have not yet been diagnosed as diagnostic resources are being prioritized for those who are symptomatic

---

[28] T. Russell et al. 2020. Estimating the Infection and Case Fatality Ratio for COVID-19 Using Age-Adjusted Data from the Outbreak on the Diamond Princess Cruise Ship. *Eurosurveillance*. 25 (12). 26 March.

(and in many countries only for those who are severely ill). Outside of the PRC, the mortality rate among reported cases is currently about 6.7%.

Third, even though it is of zoonotic origins (emerging from animal hosts), it is by now being spread through human-to-human contact. Its infection rate appears higher than SARS (and much higher than MERS), but not as high as the seasonal flu. Its infection rate may be as high as the flu only if there are a lot of undiagnosed cases (some epidemiological modeling suggests that).

Fourth, comparisons of this event with the deadly 1918–1919 flu pandemic are unwarranted. This is because that earlier flu virus was both infectious and very deadly, it affected most severely prime-age patients, and the state of the global health system at the time was drastically inferior than at present.

Is COVID-19 the Same as SARS?

SARS emerged in November 2002 and infected individuals across 26 countries during the course of several months. Like COVID-19, it appears to have originated from animal markets. The SARS virus was contained relatively rapidly, ultimately infecting around 8,500 people with a mortality rate of around 10%. As mentioned above, the preliminary evidence seems to suggest that the COVID-19 mortality rate is much lower than SARS though it has managed to spread further and infect more people (Figure 1.6). This is partly because there are a lot of mild or asymptomatic infections of COVID-19, so that the sick cannot be identified as rapidly and isolated. In these cases, carriers continue to spread the virus, not aware they are infected. Some estimates suggest there might be tens of thousands of asymptomatic carriers.

The SARS outbreak did not lead to any long-lasting damage to public health, except of course to the families of those who died. Affected national health systems actually learned from the experience and improved their response capacity. This is in contrast to MERS, which appears to be entrenched and re-emerges in new clusters of infections (fortunately, it is less infectious). It is not yet clear whether COVID-19 will end up like SARS (with no long-term impact on health expenditures) or MERS (some need for long-term spending on prevention and treatments), or become a recurring epidemic, and what will be the interactions between the public health prevention efforts targeting the seasonal flu and COVID-19.

Figure 1.6: The SARS and COVID-19 Infection and Death Numbers Compared

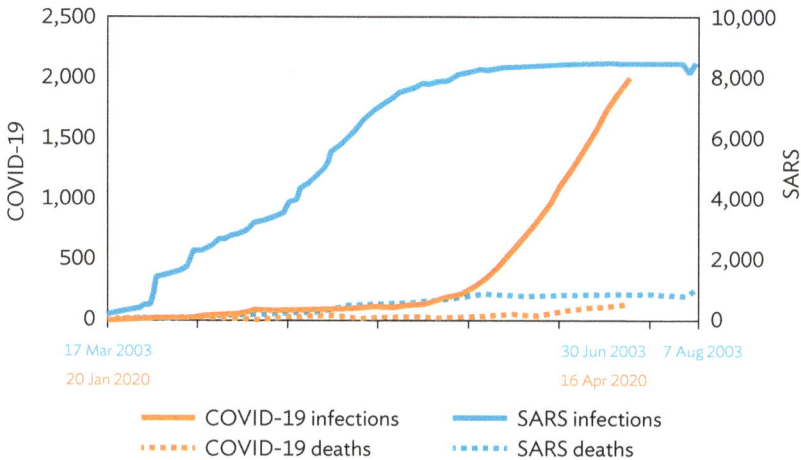

SARS = severe acute respiratory syndrome.
Source: ADB calculations using data from CEIC and World Health Organization (accessed 17 April 2020).

Lastly, one big epidemiological difference between COVID-19 and SARS is that while SARS spread primarily in the PRC, COVID-19 has reached all corners of the world. By late March 2020, the US had the largest number of cases, while the disease showed signs of receding in the PRC. Other countries that suffered large outbreaks included France, Germany, Iran, Italy, the Republic of Korea, Spain, Switzerland, and the United Kingdom, and caseloads have been on the rise in Japan and in most developing countries worldwide, where testing is substantially less widespread. The difference is partly due to the highly infectious nature of COVID-19 and partly due to closer links between countries. COVID-19 has not yet run its full course and its future epidemiological trajectory is highly uncertain. What is certain is that it is exacting a far heavier toll on global public health than its earlier coronavirus cousin SARS.

SARS was contained relatively rapidly, but the epidemic caused significant economic losses. These economic costs did not stem from the 8,500 people who were directly infected. The economic effect of SARS occurred by changing the behavior of hundreds of millions of individuals who sought to avoid becoming infected by the virus, and by corporations and governments who implemented various changes to their operations by instituting travel bans, for example. People changed their daily routine, such as staying home rather than going out to restaurants and shopping malls. These changes ended up causing much of the economic dislocation.

COVID-19 poses an incomparably larger risk to global public health and world economy. Though less deadly than SARS, COVID-19 has infected almost the entire world whereas SARS was largely confined to the PRC and a few other hotspots. The number of COVID-19 confirmed cases and fatalities are of an altogether different magnitude than the figures for SARS.

What Can We Learn from the SARS Outbreak?

Nevertheless, some lessons from SARS remain valid for COVID-19. While news headlines are dominated by the number of new cases and fatalities, as was the case with SARS, the economic impact of COVID-19 does not directly stem from those who are infected. Instead, they stem from the containment policies that governments put in place to contain the disease, in particular community quarantines and travel bans, as well as precautionary behavior of individuals. All of these will be amplified many times over since COVID-19 is a much bigger epidemic than SARS, implying much larger overall economic damage.

There are four main channels through which COVID-19 will affect economies in Asia and beyond. First and foremost, the service sector, in particular the leisure, hospitality, and retail industries, is hit very hard as people stay home. Domestic tourism also suffers. Second, worldwide travel bans exact a heavy toll on international tourism. Countries that attract a lot of foreign tourists, such as Maldives, Palau, and Thailand take a bigger blow, but the effect on tourism will reverberate globally. Third, COVID-19 disrupts global supply chains and thus manufacturing sectors. This is especially important for Asia, where countries form a regional production network—i.e., so-called Factory Asia—anchored around the PRC. Fourth, the draconian containment policies may induce credit defaults by businesses and households, causing financial sector distress and even a financial crisis.

Further, if the disease persists for an extended period, as is currently widely expected, other long-term effects will kick in. The heavy burden of taking care of COVID-19 patients may compromise the capacity of hospitals to provide adequate care for other patients, thereby harming the overall health of the population. The COVID-19 crisis may have other long-term effects on the world economy. For example, the crisis may accelerate trends toward self-sufficiency and away from free trade. Heavy dependence on imports of medical supplies and other personal protective equipment—especially those needed for COVID-19, such as masks and ventilators—may be used by some to advocate economic nationalism and protectionism.

Is Social Networking Good or Bad for this Crisis?

Fear, propagated and amplified by social media, exacerbates the economic damage from COVID-19. Panic today travels much more widely and deeply because of social media, which was much less developed during SARS. Social media has allowed for the propagation of many myths about COVID-19—e.g., drinking water can flush coronavirus from your system or young people cannot get infected—that can potentially undermine efficient public response to crises.

At the same time, social media and more broadly ICT can also mitigate the negative effects of COVID-19. Social media is being used to alert millions of residents to community quarantines, curfews, and other relevant information. And work-from-home arrangements adopted by companies would simply not have been possible without ICT. Online shopping substitutes for trips to the mall and distance learning substitutes for classroom lectures.

How Can We Recover?

Forceful fiscal and monetary policy response of governments are reducing the negative impact and preparing the ground for a quicker and more complete recovery.[29]

Finally, while COVID-19 is a once-in-a-lifetime global crisis, if society and government work closely together to fight COVID-19, there is every chance of defeating the disease and reviving the economy. One prominent example is government-mandated community quarantines and social distancing restrictions. They are proving to be effective in containing the coronavirus in many countries, especially if the public adheres to them and stay home.

---

[29] I. Noy, B. Ferrani, and D.Park. 2019. Build Back Better: What is it, and What should it be? *ADB Economics Working Paper Series No. 600*. Manila.

Key Responses to COVID-19 by Economies in Asia and the Pacific: An Update from the ADB COVID-19 Policy Database

Jesus Felipe and Al-Habbyel Yusoph

ADB's Economic Research and Regional Cooperation Department launched the *ADB COVID-19 Policy Database* on 20 April 2020. It provides information on the key economic measures that authorities are taking to combat the COVID-19 pandemic. Measures are classified according to how they work their way through the financial system, and how they affect the financial positions of different sectors of society. Some of the key findings from the database in the past two months are discussed here.

Total global package to combat COVID-19 is at $21 trillion as of June 2020. The world's total package to combat COVID-19 in June sums to $21 trillion, up from $15 trillion in April. The total package of ADB's developing members is $3.1 trillion while the total package of ADB's other members is $13.7 trillion. The total package of the European Central Bank and the European Union is $4.9 trillion.

The increase in ADB's developing members' packages is mainly driven by the PRC and India. From $2 trillion in April, the total package of ADB's developing members has increased to $3.1 trillion. This is mainly driven by the increases of the PRC accounting for 58% of the total, and India accounting for 28% of the total. The PRC package increased from $1.3 trillion to $1.9 trillion in the last 2 months, while India's package increased from $64 billion to $351 billion.

By measure, 64% of the increase in ADB's developing members' total package is accounted for by direct income support (measure 5). This is followed by support to the normal functioning of money markets (measure 1), which accounts for 16% of the total increase. The PRC almost doubled its efforts in terms of direct income support. India's direct income support increased fivefold and its support to the normal functioning of money markets increased more than sevenfold.

48.5% of ADB's developing members' $3.1 trillion package is intended for direct income support. The priorities of ADB's developing members have not changed since April. Direct income support still accounts for the highest share, followed by support to the normal functioning of money markets (Table 1.2). Direct income support remains the largest measure in all five ADB regions with Central and West Asia having the largest share (Figure 1.7).

Table 1.2: Share of Each Economic Measure as of 20 April and 1 June 2020

Measure	As of April 20 (%)	As of June 1 (%)
Measure 1: Functioning money markets	20.65	19.12
Measure 2: Credit creation	4.12	5.68
Measure 3: Lending to non-financial sector	9.22	7.14
Measure 4: Equity claims on the private sector	0.43	0.29
Measure 5: Direct support to income	40.73	48.54
Measure 9: International assistance (lender/donor)	1.02	0.75
No breakdown*	23.83	18.48

* This measure captures those actions that governments have not been explicit about regarding their allocation into one or more of the other measures.
Source:ADB COVID-19 Policy Database. https://covid19policy.adb.org.

Central bank financing in ADB's developing members increased by 75%. ADB's developing members' central banks have funded a significant portion of governments' operations in response to the pandemic. This includes direct lending, reserve drawdowns, and purchases of government bonds. These, in turn, fund governments' fiscal, liquidity, and lending measures. Since April, significant increases in central bank financing have been seen in India, Indonesia, the Republic of Korea, Singapore, and the Philippines. Direct lending by central banks are important policy actions to monitor. For instance, the Philippine central bank purchased PHP300 billion of government securities from the Bureau of Treasury under a repurchase agreement. As of 28 May 2020, the Indonesian central bank had directly purchased IDR23.98 trillion of *sharia* sovereign bonds through a government auction in the primary market. Central bank financing in ADB's other members increased by 35% mainly due to increased government

Figure 1.7: Share of Each Measure in Region's Total Package (%)

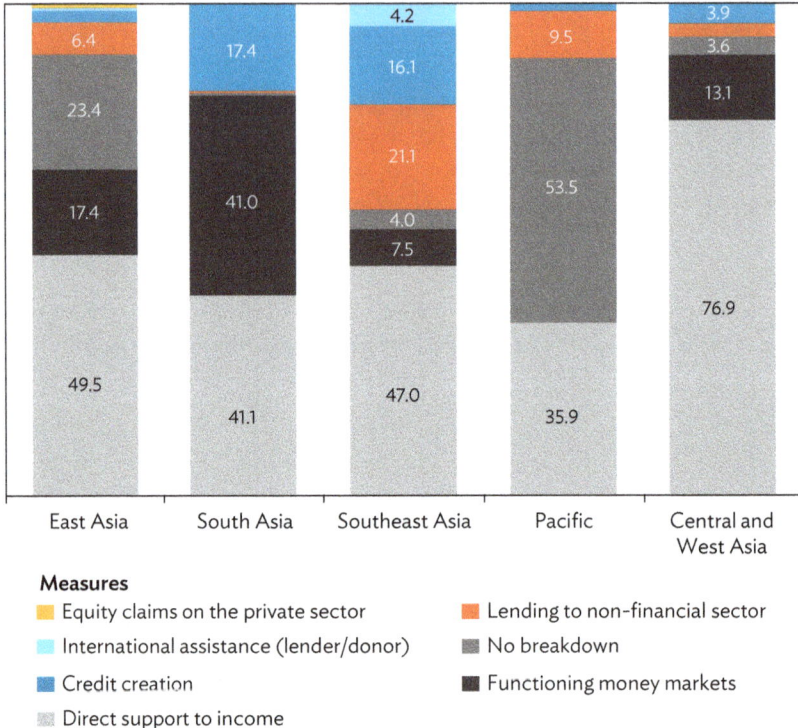

East Asia: Equity claims (top), 6.4, 23.4, 17.4, 49.5

South Asia: 17.4, 41.0, 41.1

Southeast Asia: 4.2, 16.1, 21.1, 4.0, 7.5, 47.0

Pacific: 9.5, 53.5, 35.9

Central and West Asia: 3.9, 3.6, 13.1, 76.9

Measures
- Equity claims on the private sector
- International assistance (lender/donor)
- Credit creation
- Direct support to income
- Lending to non-financial sector
- No breakdown
- Functioning money markets

Source: ADB COVID-19 Policy Database, https://covid19policy.adb.org/ (accessed June 2020).

security purchases by the US, the United Kingdom, and Australia. Central banks also continued to promote liquidity and credit creation by conducting open market operations, secondary market purchase of long-term assets, and implementing interest and other regulatory changes.

International loans and grants received by ADB's developing members increased twelvefold. International assistance to ADB's developing members in the form of grants and loans increased twelvefold since April. Out of the recorded $16 billion international assistance, 41% came from ADB, while 59% came from other institutions like the IMF, World Bank, United Nations (UN), Asian Infrastructure Investment Bank, and the US Agency for International Development.

Measures, Packages, and Caveats

The database classifies the measures into five types: (i) actions to support the normal functioning of money markets; (ii) encouraging private credit creation; (iii) direct long-term lending to households, businesses, and local governments and forbearance; (iv) increasing equity claims on the private sector; and (v) direct support to income or revenue of households, businesses, and local governments. The database also tracks four additional funding measures that effectively "double count" measures 1 to 5 from an accounting perspective. Measure 6 is reallocation of previously budgeted spending. Measure 7 is central bank purchases of national government bonds or direct lending to government. Measure 8 is international assistance received by borrower/recipient countries. Measure 9 is international assistance given by lender/donor countries.

Figure 1.7 provides a summary of the nine measures and how they are financed. There is a use and funding relationship between Measures 1 to 5 and Measures 6 to 8, which is the accounting corollary of the "double counting" for these measures.

From the point of view of the uses, Measures 1 to 4 are mostly self-funded by the central bank and also partly by the government. Measure 5 is funded by the government's bond sales to the non-government sector, which may be purchased in the secondary market by the central bank (Measure 7B), central bank loans or primary market purchases of government bonds (Measure 7A), drawdown of existing reserves (Measure 7A), and also partly by international assistance (Measure 8B).

From the point of view of the funding sources, Measure 6 is also a source of government spending, lending, or investment, but is mutually exclusive from Measures 1 to 5 in this taxonomy since "where" the spending has been reallocated to is already in Measure 6. As noted, in Measure 7, the central bank directly or indirectly funds the government, which then appears in the latter's actions across Measures 1 to 5. Central bank swaps directly go to the central bank, providing funding for activities in Measure 1. Finally, as noted, international assistance is a source of funds for the government and likely ends up in Measure 5.

The total package, as used in the database, is the sum of Measures 1 to 5. International assistance given and measures with no definite breakdown are also included in the total package for individual economies and regions. The world's total package, however, excludes Measure 9 to prevent "double counting" (Figure 1.8).

Figure 1.8: The COVID-19 Measures and Funding

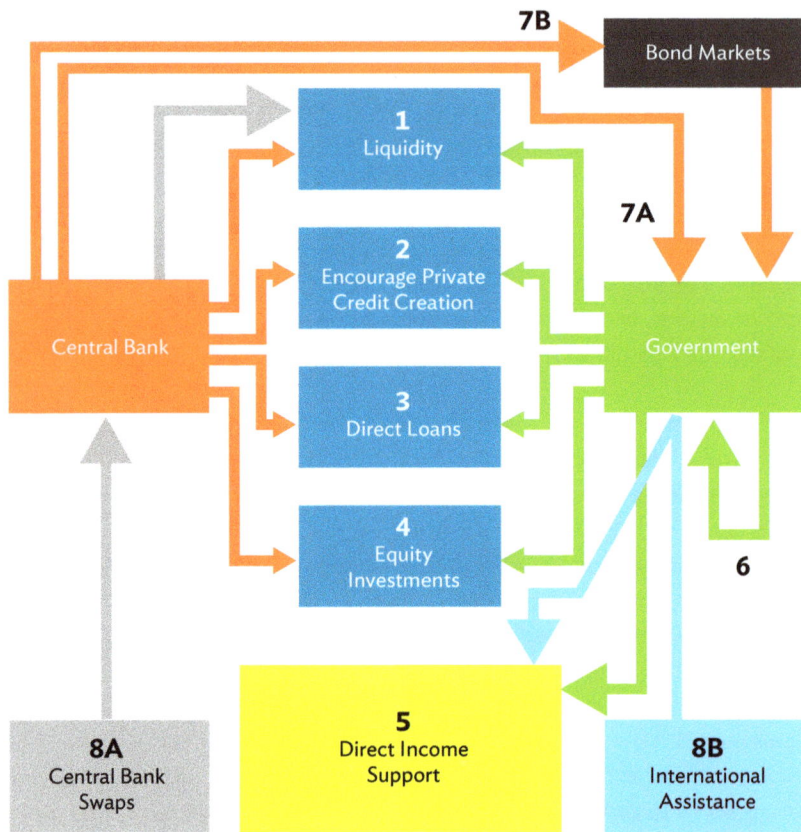

7B

Bond Markets

1
Liquidity

7A

Central Bank

2
Encourage Private Credit Creation

Government

3
Direct Loans

4
Equity Investments

6

8A
Central Bank Swaps

5
Direct Income Support

8B
International Assistance

Source: J. Felipe and S. Fullwiler. 2020. The ADB COVID-19 Policy Database: A Guide. Forthcoming (September 2020 issue), Asian Development Review.

Caution should be exercised in using and interpreting the data. Measures and packages included in the database are mostly intentions and announcements of authorities. Information on actual amounts spent or transacted are not always available. Some measures only have estimated amounts such as liquidity injected to the economy due to lower reserve requirements. Moreover, measures are not always announced with a defined period of implementation or effectivity and intended amounts have changed in some cases. Lastly, the database does not make any judgment on the appropriateness of the type and amount of measures.

Conclusion: Key Policy Responses to COVID-19

The updates on the ADB COVID-19 Policy Database have shown that economies have remained active in pursuing income support, liquidity support, and credit creation measures. Central banks continue to play a significant role, not just in promoting liquidity and credit creation, but also in financing government fiscal measures. International assistance, both from ADB and other institutions, has increased significantly since April, and may continue to rise in the near future.

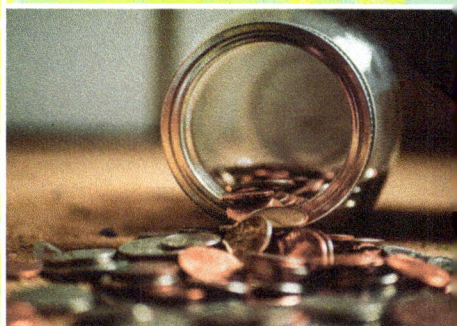

2. Tackling the Financial Fallout

Photos on previous page: [Top] The COVID-19 pandemic struck
as Asian banks struggled with large amounts of debt (photo by Josh
Appel). [Bottom] Critical utilities, such as water and power, are
provided to millions of people in Asia by state-owned enterprises that
are in jeopardy due to the pandemic (photo by Mi Pham).

COVID-19 Exposes Asian Banks' Vulnerability to United States Dollars Funding

Cyn-Young Park, Peter Rosenkranz, and Mara Claire Tayag

The unfolding COVID-19 pandemic has precipitated a sharp projected slowdown in the region's growth, raising the specter of financial instability. Past episodes of financial crisis highlighted the region's financial vulnerability given greater interconnectedness in global financial markets and institutions. The rapid globalization of financial markets, substantial short-term capital flows, uneven development of local capital markets, and deficient currency hedging mechanisms—combined with the region's continued reliance on foreign borrowing and investment and insufficient crisis control mechanisms—underpinned the unfavorable dynamics of financial volatility during times of economic uncertainty and stress.

The COVID-19 pandemic has yet again unraveled global financial markets, putting Asia's financial resilience to the test. As the economic losses associated with the pandemic are set to rise, Asian stocks have plunged and short-term portfolio flows reversed sharply in March 2020, putting local currencies under severe pressure. Amid flight to safety, global demand for the United States dollars soared, risking the tightening of local financial conditions in emerging Asian economies which remain heavily exposed to United States dollars funding risks. While multiple factors are behind the surge in demand, it is a global rush to unwind carry trades that have driven a rise in global United States dollars funding costs.

The London Interbank Offered Rate (LIBOR)–Overnight Index Swap (OIS) spread, exhibiting a pattern similar to that of the global financial crisis, indicates that interbank money markets came under severe strain due to a spike in United States dollars demand during the COVID-19 pandemic (Figure 2.1). The cross-currency basis swap widened for a number of

Figure 2.1: LIBOR–OIS Spread—Global Financial Crisis versus COVID-19
(basis points)

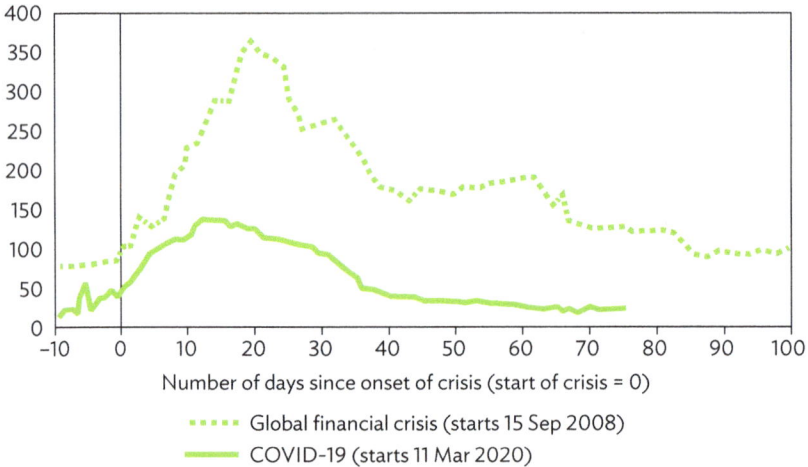

LIBOR = London interbank offered rate, OIS = overnight index swap.
Source: Bloomberg (accessed 25 June 2020).

emerging Asian currencies and to a much greater degree than it did for the euro, the British pound, or the Japanese yen (Figure 2.2). As in past financial crises, emerging Asian financial markets and currencies have borne the heaviest brunt, reflecting their underlying structural vulnerabilities to United States dollars funding risks. Measures taken by the US Federal Reserve to establish swap lines and introduce a temporary repo facility helped arrest panic on the United States dollars funding market.[1]

The global reliance on short-term dollar funding was the Achilles' heel of the international monetary and financial system more than a decade ago—and it still is. Non-US global banks have become major intermediaries of United States dollars-denominated cross-border lending and international debt issuance. Prior to the global financial crisis of 2008, European banks had sharply increased their United States dollars-denominated lending to

---

[1]   In addition to the US Federal Reserve's standing swap lines with major central banks, the establishment of nine temporary dollar liquidity swap lines (19 March 2020), including with regional central banks in Australia, New Zealand, the Republic of Korea, and Singapore, as well as the introduction of the temporary foreign and international monetary authorities repo facility (31 March 2020) to a broader group of foreign central banks and other international monetary authorities, were effective in arresting panic on the United States dollars funding market.

Figure 2.2: Cross-Currency Basis Swap
(basis points)

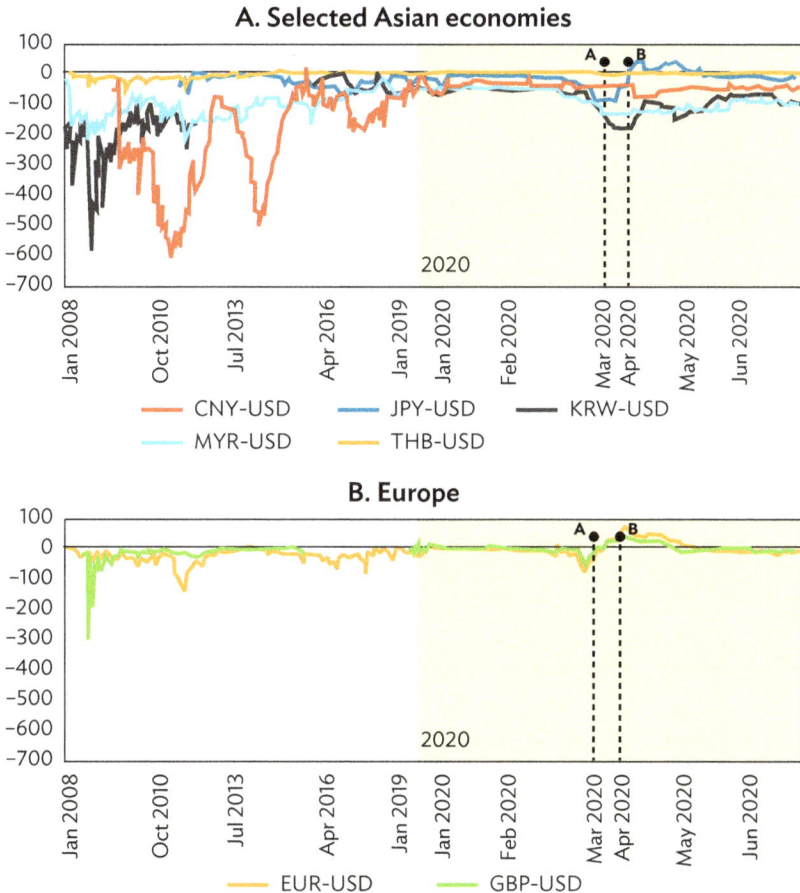

A. Selected Asian economies

Legend (Panel A): CNY-USD, JPY-USD, KRW-USD, MYR-USD, THB-USD

B. Europe

Legend (Panel B): EUR-USD, GBP-USD

- - -● A (1 Mar 2020): US Federal Reserve established nine temporary dollar liquidity swap lines[a]

- - -● B (30 Mar 2020): US Federal Reserve introduced temporary foreign and international monetary authorities repo facility

[a]   In addition to the US Federal Reserve's standing swap lines with major central banks, the establishment of nine temporary dollar liquidity swap lines (19 March 2020), including with regional central banks in Australia, New Zealand, the Republic of Korea, and Singapore, as well as the introduction of the temporary foreign and international monetary authorities repo facility (31 March 2020) to a broader group of foreign central banks and other international monetary authorities were effective in arresting panic on the United States dollars funding market.

CNY = yuan (People's Republic of China), EUR = euro, GBP = pound sterling (United Kingdom), JPY = yen (Japan), KRW = won (Republic of Korea), MYR = ringgit (Malaysia), THB = baht (Thailand), USD = United States dollar.

Notes: Three-month cross-currency basis swap for CNY-USD, EUR-USD, GBP-USD, JPY–USD, and MYR-USD; 6 months for THB-USD; and 3 months versus 6 months for KRW-USD.

Source: Bloomberg (accessed 25 June 2020).

emerging market economies, with subsequent massive deleveraging of European banks causing financial stress to emerging market borrowers.

Despite the improved health of Asian banks relative to past crisis periods, fundamental weaknesses remain. Post-crisis reforms have improved banking and financial soundness across many economies in Asia, with stronger regulation and supervision. However, international activity at Asian banks has increased substantially over the past 2 decades, the majority of which is denominated in foreign currency (primarily in United States dollars)— approximately 80% as of the third quarter of 2019. United States dollars-denominated lending has increased across banks in high-income Asian economies while dollar-denominated borrowing ticked up across emerging Asian economies. The rapid growth in cross-border banking activities underscores United States dollars funding needs of Asian banks through foreign exchange swap markets. However, while Asian banks' exposure to United States dollars funding risks rises, currency hedging mechanisms and instruments remain underdeveloped in the region.

Consequently, a sudden tightening of global United States dollars liquidity conditions during times of financial stress can pose a threat to financial stability in emerging Asian economies. First, a sudden squeeze in dollar funding liquidity associated with unwinding of carry trades by non-US global banks can quickly spill over to emerging market borrowers, as evidenced during the global financial crisis and the COVID-19 crisis. Second, some high-income Asian economies have now replaced European banks in credit expansion to emerging Asian economies. When high-income Asian economies face financial distress arising from high dollar funding costs, they will be forced to curtail their lending to emerging Asian economies, amplifying and propagating financial shocks to regional economies. Lastly, during times of financial stress, emerging market borrowers are also typically vulnerable to capital flow and exchange rate volatility. Our research shows empirically that economies with higher exposure to United States dollars funding tend to be more vulnerable to stress in the United States dollars funding market. This can, in turn, trigger nonresident investors to pull out their investments.

To address this vulnerability to United States dollars liquidity during times of crisis, regional policy makers in Asia need to take bold actions now to strengthen crisis preparedness and mitigate the impacts through better management of global and regional financial safety net arrangements. At this stage, one cannot discount the possibility of another financial turmoil, and of some countries experiencing financial crises, starting from defaults and bankruptcies in the private sector, leading to a credit crunch or even a financial crisis. This would exacerbate Asia's vulnerability to United States dollars funding, amplifying negative spillovers to financial markets. However, given Asia's strong underlying economic fundamentals, timely and appropriate policies can help avoid a prolonged recession and steer toward a swift recovery. In fact, This COVID-19 pandemic also offers an opportunity to strengthen regional financial cooperation to address the issue over the long term.

First, the current policy priority is to sustain market confidence and ensure adequate liquidity. Containment efforts and stimulus packages by central banks and governments of large scale can help significantly decrease the probability of recession.[2] Maintaining macrofinancial policies that are supportive of the economy and markets is key. To mitigate the stress on the banking sector and credit markets, central banks must be ready to provide ample liquidity and take necessary actions to avoid massive defaults, especially by small businesses and household sectors. Some Asian central bankers have already intervened in the repo market or purchased domestic bonds to provide liquidity, including bond purchase programs in Indonesia, the Philippines, and Thailand.

Second, while the region's macrofinancial positions remain sound, policy makers should remain vigilant against the risk of financial turmoil. Across the region, reforms after the Asian financial crisis and global financial crisis have contributed significantly to the adoption of sound macroeconomic policies and adequate foreign exchange reserves, which has helped maintain economic and financial stability during the COVID-19 crisis. However, multiple risks remain that can lead to a financial crisis, including rising debt and debt-servicing burdens on household and corporate sectors, a buildup of financial fragility in the banking system, disruptions in global United States dollars funding markets, sudden stops in capital flows, and a sharp rise in public spending and collapse in revenues. Authorities should continue monitoring the development of macrofinancial conditions in their respective economies with sound macroprudential policies in place and keep inflation expectations well anchored. Maintaining adequate foreign

---

[2]   ADB estimates the global impact of COVID-19 would range from $5.8 trillion to $8.8 trillion (6.4%–9.7% of global GDP), with Asia accounting for about 30% of the overall decline in global output, depending on the length of containment measures. It also shows that policy interventions can significantly soften the GDP impact of COVID-19—reducing the impact by 30%–40%.

exchange reserves also helps support market confidence and financial stability, while bilateral swap lines with the US Federal Reserve also help arrest market panic at a time of extreme financial volatility.

Third, an orderly exit from fiscal and monetary stimulus is as important as the stimulus itself to maintain financial stability. Governments and international organizations need to design and implement an exit strategy to carefully navigate the transition from extra stimulus to normal economies in an orderly way to ensure economic and financial stability. As the pandemic is contained and financial conditions of distressed firms and households normalize, an orderly exit from the emergency financial relief should be carefully managed to avoid large corporate debt overhang and excessive burdens on the banking sector. Large fiscal stimuli and increased borrowing in developing countries can be a source of financial instability in the post-COVID-19 period. There should be a careful review of debt sustainability and a gradual unwinding of extraordinary policy support and budget expansion over the medium to long term.

Fourth, Asian economies need to deepen regional cooperation to strengthen regional financial safety nets and improve financial resilience. Reforms after the Asian financial crisis and regional cooperation efforts under the ASEAN+3 initiatives contributed to stronger regional financial safety nets through (i) the Chiang Mai Initiative Multilateralization to provide emergency dollar liquidity, (ii) the ASEAN+3 Macroeconomic Research Office for macrofinancial surveillance, and (iii) deepening of local currency capital markets. Expanding and strengthening the Chiang Mai Initiative Multilateralization and its capacity can shore up defense against United States dollars liquidity shortages. The surveillance capacity of the ASEAN+3 Macroeconomic Research Office can also be strengthened to help detect and prevent any buildup of financial vulnerabilities.[3]

Fifth, the region should continue developing and nurturing vibrant local currency bond markets to help tackle the currency and maturity mismatches of Asian financial systems. The ASEAN+3 Asian Bond Markets Initiative has helped promote the development of regional capital markets. Greater availability of local currency long-term securities can reduce short-term United States dollars funding needs. Under the initiative, authorities have significantly improved national regulatory frameworks, developing market

---

[3]   ASEAN+3 comprises the 10 members of the ASEAN plus Japan, the People's Republic of China, and the Republic of Korea.

infrastructure, and promoting the issuance of—and demand for—bonds denominated in local currencies. Further efforts should be made to increase the size of and liquidity in secondary markets; refine and upgrade supporting market infrastructure; broaden the institutional investor base; and facilitate cross-border issuance, trading, and settlements for more integrated regional capital markets.

Finally, persistent and big demand for United States dollars funding by non-US banks reveals fundamental issues in the current international monetary system. The heavy reliance on a single national currency (the United States dollars) as an international reserve currency is inherently unstable. The global rush for the United States dollars at any sign of market turbulence will easily swamp global United States dollars funding markets, no matter how big daily foreign exchange swap transactions can be. Efforts to redesign the global financial architecture should embrace renewed discussion of the reform of the international reserve system to include multiple currency units down the road.

How Can Asia Avoid Fallout if COVID-19 Triggers a Debt Crunch?

Cyn-Young Park

The COVID-19 pandemic raises the specter of another global debt crisis. The global economy is deep in debt—to the tune of an estimated $250 trillion in 2019—after a decade of historically low interest rates. Global debt-to-GDP hit a record high of over 320%, according to the Institute of International Finance.[4]

A pandemic-induced economic slowdown implies lower corporate earnings and greater debt-servicing burdens on companies. This would lead to increasing defaults, plunging investor confidence, and potentially a widespread credit crunch.

How policy makers respond now will be crucial in avoiding this worst-case scenario, and deciding whether the recovery path will be V, U, or L-shaped.

Economists have warned for years of the risks posed by massive debt accumulation. While the corporate sector ratcheted up its borrowing, financial engineering also played a role in expanding and leveraging loans. Leveraged loans are a type of loan extended to companies with below investment grade credit ratings (i.e., subprime corporate borrowers). Investors were enticed by 10 years of very low interest rates to buy them, as they typically pay higher interest rates.

The Bank for International Settlements has estimated that outstanding leveraged loans worldwide reached $1.4 trillion at the end of 2018, more than

---

4   E. Tiftik and K. Mahmood. 2020. *High and Rising Debt Levels: Should We Worry?* Institute of International Finance.

double the amount a decade ago (Figure 2.3).[5] Yet, the Bank of England has estimated this figure at around $2.2 trillion.[6] For comparison, the stock of US mortgages at the time of the US subprime mortgage crisis was estimated at about $2.3 trillion, of which subprime mortgages were $1.3 trillion.

About half of US leveraged loans are repackaged into collateralized loan obligations, which were estimated by the US Federal Reserve at $617 billion at the end of 2018.[7] Collateralized loan obligations are similar to collateralized debt obligations and mortgage-backed securities—touted as the root causes of the global financial crisis.

Figure 2.3: Leveraged Loans
($ trillion)

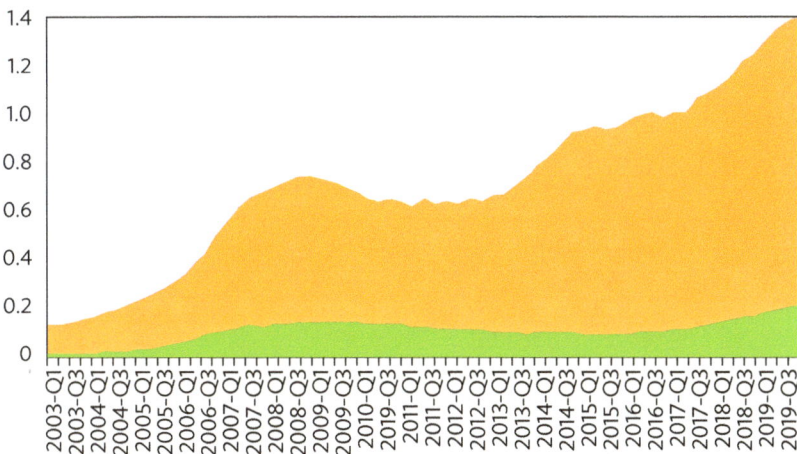

Notes: For institutional leveraged loans, outstanding amounts are based on the S&P-LSTA leveraged loan index for the United States and the S&P European leveraged loan index for Europe (LSTA = Loan Syndications and Trading Association).
Source: Bank for International Settlements. 2019. BIS Quarterly Review. International banking and financial market developments. September.

Collateralized loan obligations are collateralized debt obligations made up of bank loans (or corporate debt) instead of household mortgages. Another important similarity is the complexity and opacity of collateralized

---

[5]   S. Aramonte and F. Avalos. 2019. Structured finance then and now: a comparison of CDOs and CLOs. Basel: Bank for International Settlements.

[6]   Bank of England. 2019. *How Large is the Leveraged Loan Market? Bank Overground.*

[7]   E. Liu and T. Schmidt-Eisenlohr. 2019. Who Owns U.S. CLO Securities? *FED Notes.*

loan obligations, although there has been significant improvement in transparency of these products compared to collateralized debt obligations and banks hold only a limited share of them thanks to tighter financial regulations since the global financial crisis.

Still, it is unclear exactly how big and widely held they are among nonbank investors. The Financial Stability Board has already sounded alarms, as leveraged loans and collateralized loan obligations have risen fast in recent years.[8]

The US Federal Reserve estimates that banks hold about 15% of US-collateralized loan obligations. Nonbank institutional investors, including insurance companies, mutual funds, and pension funds, hold more than 50%. The rest is held by hedge funds, private debt investors, and other investment vehicles, which remain obscure to regulators. If collateralized loan obligations incur substantial losses among nonbank investors, banks might still be indirectly exposed. Asian investors are also exposed to collateralized loan obligations, particularly institutional investors from high-income economies.

With COVID-19 roiling economies and markets, concerns are rising many subprime corporate borrowers could default on their loans. This could set off chain reactions in the global financial system just as the US subprime mortgage market did a decade ago through holdings of collateralized debt obligations and mortgage-backed securities among banks and nonbank financial institutions.

Some corporate sectors are particularly vulnerable to COVID-19. Airlines, travel, and leisure services companies are at greater risk among US-collateralized loan obligation issuers. Additionally, large swings in oil prices threaten earnings for oil and other commodities. Significant global supply chain disruptions can deepen the economic malaise.

Ratings agencies have reported an increase in the share of lower rating (or speculative grade) issuers in collateralized loan obligations in recent years. S&P Global Ratings reported that about 20% of the US-collateralized

---

[8] Financial Stability Board. 2019. Vulnerabilities associated with leveraged loans and collateralised loan obligations. Basel.

loan obligation issuers are rated B- and below.[9] Lower rating issuers tend to be subject to more downgrades and defaults when the economy turns sour. Fitch Ratings has estimated about 12% of US-collateralized loan obligation issuers under its surveillance are highly vulnerable to an economic slowdown due to COVID-19.[10]

Developing countries are often vulnerable to a global credit crunch. The external debt-to-GDP ratio for developing Asia was 33% in 2018, only slightly lower than 34% during the global financial crisis. Though macroeconomic conditions in Asia are generally sound, the previous crisis made it clear that developing Asia is far from immune to a financial crisis originating in advanced economies.

At the time of the US subprime mortgage crisis, US banks directly hit by deterioration in asset quality curtailed credits particularly, drying up liquidity in interbank markets. The troubled banks in advanced economies also rushed to withdraw funds from emerging economies. International spillovers tend to be large when troubled banks are big lenders and systemically important to the global financial system.

Given the greater financial interconnectedness compared to a decade ago, Asian banks could expect significant shocks if loan defaults reverberate throughout broader banking systems in advanced economies.

But this challenge can be overcome if stakeholders work together. Here are three avenues of approach that policy makers can take to avoid a debt crisis.

First, G20 policy makers should immediately coordinate actions to provide timely and effective policy support to avoid market panic while taking aggressive, preemptive measures to contain the spread of the virus.

The G7 statement in March announcing a commitment to "use all appropriate policy tools" was welcome. But it was the US government's announcement of economic stimulus and $50 billion financial assistance to state and local governments that helped arrest a market panic. This shows that actions speak louder than words. The interdependence of global value

---

[9]   S&P Global Ratings. 2019. Credit Trends: The Expansion of The 'B-' Segment Is Feeding Growing Vulnerabilities. New York.

[10] Fitch Ratings. 2020. Coronavirus Risk to US Leveraged Finance Issuers, CLOs. New York.

chains and financial systems also calls for much broader participation of the G20 to take actions to be effective and credible.

Second, coordinated efforts within and across borders are needed to manage business continuity, shore up confidence, prevent massive defaults through tax relief and emergency loans, and provide adequate liquidity in the financial systems.

COVID-19 is causing substantial disruptions in business and productivity due to restrictions on the movement of goods and people, as well as increased costs of capital and doing business. Depending on fiscal space and other circumstances, national governments can consider unconventional measures like payroll tax cuts and unconditional cash transfers. Health care subsidies could include waivers and cost sharing on fees related to coronavirus testing and treatments.

Third, regulators should carefully monitor and guide orderly reduction of undue exposures to leveraged loans and collateralized loan obligations among banks and nonbank investors, particularly those that are systemically important.

Some high-income Asian economies with direct exposures to leveraged loans and collateralized loan obligations should review and reduce their exposures. Policy makers must remain vigilant, maintain prudential macroeconomic policies, keep debt levels (especially external debt) in check, and prepare to provide timely liquidity support through financial safety net arrangements. Emerging economies often experience strains in dollar funding and capital flow reversals at times of global financial stress. Regional and global cooperation is crucial to provide emergency liquidity within and across borders as needed.

Luckily, Asia's economies generally maintain sound macroeconomic policies with healthy fiscal and external buffers after the two most recent financial crises. If this resilience is reinforced by good policies, the region can withstand this latest challenge and emerge even stronger.

Pandemic Highlights the Need to Manage Asia's Debt Problem

Bambang Susantono

The COVID-19 pandemic is hitting economies already reeling from global trade tensions and geopolitical uncertainties. It threatens to trigger a sustained downturn in the global and regional economy that will ripple across industries and sectors. We are already seeing stunted trade and investment, disrupted supply chains, fragile consumer and investor confidence, and volatile financial markets.

This could spell trouble for Asian banks and corporations. While some industries might be hit harder than others, reduced corporate earnings and tighter credit conditions could lead to more nonperforming loans—debilitating debts that are at or near default. With corporate clients—particularly airline, travel, and retail industries—facing difficulties paying back their debts, local banks could be saddled with more troublesome defaults. Micro, small, and medium-sized enterprises (MSMEs) are also particularly at risk. Given the dominant role of banks in Asia's financial systems, this could breed widespread financial instability.

Bank-held nonperforming loans across Asia and the Pacific rose 23% from end-2018 to August 2019, reaching $640 billion. Nonperforming loans are often sensitive to an economic downturn.

These bad debts were a salient feature of past financial crises, including the 1997–1998 Asian financial crisis, the 2008 US subprime mortgage crisis, and the 2009 European debt crisis. Even after these crises were addressed, nonperforming loans had long-lasting, detrimental effects on economic recovery and financial stability in Asia and around the world.

Monetary policies that stimulated economic activity by lowering interest rates drove recovery after the 2008–2009 global financial crisis. But they also created new financial imbalances and distortions in many economies. For example, the private debt-to-GDP ratio rose sharply in many Asian economies. Housing prices in many economies have also soared.

Against this backdrop, a significant decline in economic activity may invite corporate debt downgrades and defaults, while a collapse in asset prices could lead to a serious deterioration in the quality of banks' assets, leading to tighter credit conditions. These conditions pose a considerable risk to banking system stability in the region.

The good news is that, across the region, policy makers are trying to preempt a pandemic-induced loan crisis. Many central banks have already cut interest rates. But more action is needed. Central banks should provide backstop measures against potentially massive defaults and a credit crunch. Some have already introduced programs to purchase commercial paper and provide a range of credit to households and businesses. Temporary financial relief for indebted households and small businesses can be also considered. With the support from the governments, banks are already granting deferments or temporary forbearance of loans and repayments. These measures should be properly targeted and clearly time bound.

However, a widespread economic slowdown suggests some increases in nonperforming loans might be inevitable after the temporary relief. Therefore, authorities should also prepare to act swiftly to avoid a massive buildup of nonperforming loans in national banking systems. This requires the authorities, together with banks, to develop clear action plans to effectively resolve nonperforming loans.

There are many obstacles to effective resolution of nonperforming loans. These include information asymmetry, coordination failures, and institutional impediments. The region's policy makers must address demand-side, supply-side, and structural challenges while developing a nonperforming loan resolution framework as part of financial safety nets.

On the demand side, the price investors will pay for nonperforming loans can be far less than what banks like to accept. Transaction costs, the underlying collateral values, and the cost of recovery, all exacerbate the divide between buyer and seller. As a result, nonperforming loan markets tend to be dominated by a few large investors with concentrated market power.

On the supply side, banks may not want to sell at a discounted price. Banks usually prefer holding on to nonperforming loans until asset prices recover. Selling nonperforming loans below current book values would be counted as losses on a bank's books and negatively affect its capital. Additionally, banks' reluctance to sell nonperforming loans may stem from their desire to avoid the first-mover disadvantage.

Structural challenges include poor legal frameworks, legislation, or sufficiently transparent collateral enforcement and insolvency proceedings. These can delay recovery in asset values and add to recovery costs. All of these will limit investment into nonperforming loan markets and keep them from functioning efficiently.

To address these impediments, it is important to enhance data availability, transparency, and integrity. Further, strong public support, institutional quality, oversight, contract enforcement powers, and governance are essential.

What can countries do to help prevent these nonperforming loans from exacerbating economic problems created by the current crisis? Here are three policy lessons we have learned from our work in the region.

First, an early and preemptive response is key to addressing nonperforming loans and preventing them from contributing to banking instability and market panic. Preventive restructuring frameworks can ensure proper action is taken to preempt corporate defaults. This gives companies a second chance at debt rehabilitation. The efficiency of insolvency frameworks is another important element in reducing a buildup of nonperforming loans and for a well-functioning nonperforming loan market. Also, facilitating out-of-court enforcement for financial collateral will allow banks to recover the value of collateral without going to court, and help speed up the resolution process.

Second, developing private nonperforming loan markets allows financial institutions to dispose of distressed portfolios at fair and efficient market prices. A functioning secondary market allows banks to remove nonperforming loans from their balance sheets and sell them to interested buyers. Without this, banks have to keep nonperforming loans on their balance sheets, pressuring their profitability and limiting capacity to lend to new clients. Secondary markets for nonperforming loans can be promoted by addressing barriers to loan servicing and to the transfer of bank loans to third parties.

And third, crises have taught us that we need stronger regional financial cooperation, with policy makers working collectively on risk identification, mitigation, and response. Safeguarding financial stability requires Asian policy makers to work together through a combined focus on adequate national regulatory policies, effective monitoring and surveillance frameworks, and regional cooperation for emergency liquidity support.

COVID-19 is a significant risk to the region's financial systems. But one that can be managed through coordinated policy responses to address its impact on economies and finances.

Reform State-Owned Enterprises to Avoid a COVID-19 Debt and Investment Crisis

David Robinett

State-owned enterprises supply energy, transport, and water to millions of citizens in Asia and the rest of the world. Globally, state-owned enterprises account for 55% of infrastructure investment and hold trillions of dollars in assets, according to the IMF.

COVID-19 has had a direct and highly damaging impact on many state-owned enterprises, including airlines, airports, and other tourism-linked enterprises that have seen revenues plummet. As have national oil companies and other state-owned commodity producers, state-owned enterprises are also helping to bail out the wider economy.

This is especially true for state-owned banks, which also face losses and loan impairment from the economic slowdown. State-owned utilities and service providers will also see lower revenue, including from providing forbearance to both other state-owned enterprises and private sector clients that may have certain fees and charges waived.

Bailouts also mean that new state-owned enterprises are being created, as governments inject equity into airlines, banks, and other private companies, and salvaged company assets. Government ownership will also grow from recapitalizing listed state-owned enterprises, which make up a large part of Asia's capital markets.

Growth of state-owned enterprise liabilities would be matched by growing fiscal pressure on governments as tax revenues fall and government spending ballooned. Governments would need to reduce state-owned enterprise losses, increase profitability, and better manage state-owned enterprise liabilities.

In a V-shaped recovery scenario, most state-owned enterprises would begin to bounce back early 2021. The fiscal impact would be limited—though in some tourism and oil dependent economies, new debt would still hit around 10%–20% of GDP. Only a handful of companies would get equity injections.

If the decline in tourism, oil prices, and overall economic activity were to persist well into 2021, the impact would be all the greater. State-owned enterprises would need bigger bailouts even as they were doing more for the overall economy. More private companies, perhaps many more, would be nationalized with equity injections needed across a range of those highly indebted.

Circular debts involving big loss-making state-owned enterprises would spread the pain more widely, and nonperforming loans will pile up in state-owned banks. Fiscal pressure would be worse, with governments looking for any way to boost revenues and reduce spending and liabilities.

Under these conditions, short-sighted and haphazard policies should be avoided. Rushed privatizations and poorly designed public-private partnerships may offer relief in the short run, but will actually weaken governments' fiscal position and fuel further political opposition to effective private sector engagement.

This mix of state-owned enterprise debt, fiscal deterioration, and a growing role for state ownership frames the challenges for the years to come. Reform will be needed for state-owned enterprises to remain financially viable while maintaining delivery of crucial services. State-owned enterprises will have to quickly transition from being a drain on the state budget to net contributors.

Broad-based and ambitious state-owned enterprise reform is needed to achieve the same or better service delivery with improved fiscal and financial performance. This includes corporate governance reform, introduction of performance management systems, and greatly enhanced transparency. It must include the proper identification of and accounting for community and public sector obligations.

Many state-owned enterprises will require deeper restructuring, including ones created from failing private sector companies. These state-owned enterprises will need proven and professional management to place the restructured state-owned enterprise into a sustainable recovery plan, and independent board members qualified to oversee this process. Non-core functions should be shut down or spun off, and transparency and accountability will be essential for the entire restructuring process, including in the sensitive disposal of impaired and other assets.

For state-owned enterprises undergoing restructuring, provisions will also have to be made for employees who lose their jobs, including retraining, separation packages, and other steps. Consideration will also have to be given to private sector creditors, how much of a loss they can absorb, and the wider impact of such a loss on the financial system. There may also be scope to consider broader stakeholders and policy changes, as long as these are consistent with restoring financial viability, such as removing (implicit) subsidies for fossil fuels and tapping cheaper renewables, or ending costly regional flights when cleaner rail or other options are available.

Crucially, successful reform requires going beyond state-owned enterprise governance and restructuring. It requires a fundamental change in how the state acts as an owner of assets. This function must be professionalized, depoliticized, and separated from policy making and regulation. This usually involves the creation of a holding company or other specialized entity.

It also requires developing a two-sided balance sheet for public commercial assets. This process can help identify new assets, like real estate, that are undervalued and underutilized. The IMF has estimated that better utilization of public assets in this way can add additional public revenue equal to 3% of GDP.

Part of this reform includes the correct classification of state-owned enterprise debt and borrowing. State-owned enterprise borrowing often has an implicit or explicit sovereign guarantee, making it part of the government's overall debt burden. Sometimes governments claim that there is not a guarantee, but push social programs and spending through state-owned enterprises. This is just hiding the debt. However, financially viable state-owned enterprises can legitimately borrow without guarantees, reducing the overall national debt burden.

Better management of public sector assets and correct categorization of debt can facilitate careful privatization and other forms of private sector participation. Crucially, they can help avoid a post-COVID-19 investment crash, probably the greatest long-term economic threat from the pandemic. Without these tools, borrowing for this investment is simply treated as an increase in public sector liabilities and debt-burdened governments are likely not to make those investments.

Together with better state-owned enterprise governance and necessary restructuring, these tools will preserve necessary infrastructure investments; reduce risks from public debt; and preserve— and in many cases enhance— the financial viability and service delivery of the state-owned enterprises that still supply energy, transport, and water to so many people in Asia and the world.

3. Supporting Micro, Small, and Medium-Sized Enterprises

Micro, Small, and Medium-Sized Enterprises: Policy Measures for COVID-19

Cyn-Young Park and Shigehiro Shinozaki

Stringent containment measures including lockdowns, travel restrictions, and social distancing adopted to arrest the coronavirus have also slowed economic activities and hurt businesses of all sizes and their employees.

Micro, small, and medium-sized enterprises (MSMEs) are at particular risk due to a combination of broken supply chains and tightened credit conditions. While definitions of MSMEs vary considerably across borders, these firms make up 97% of all businesses and employ 72% of workers on average in developing Asia, according to the latest ADB study.[1] As economies slow, MSMEs have faced immediate cash flow constraints to cover their working capital, including taxes, wages, payments to suppliers, and debt-servicing payments. MSMEs face declining revenues, rising business and financial costs, and greater risk of default as liquidity has dried up. They may also opt to cut wages/benefits and lay off employees under the circumstances, thus reducing incomes for households during the pandemic. Keeping MSMEs in business and their employees on payrolls is thus crucial for cushioning the COVID-19 impact on people and economies.

Potentially massive defaults and mounting job losses pose considerable risks to economic and social stability and call for well-targeted public support to provide essential financial relief for MSMEs. Financial support should aim to ensure business continuity, preserve employment, and provide sufficient liquidity for doing business during the COVID-19 outbreak and recovery afterward. It is also important to ensure these measures are timely and time-bound, and delivered through relief packages accessible for MSMEs.

---

[1]   Asian Development Bank. 2020. *Asia Small and Medium-sized Enterprise Monitor 2020.* Forthcoming.

Practical and Feasible Options

Many countries have introduced measures to financially support MSMEs (Table 3.1). Based on these experiences, a financial assistance framework for MSMEs can be made in three broad channels:

- *Direct financial support* can include special/emergency loan programs (US, France), provision of new credit with lower/near zero/zero interest rates (Japan) with or without collateral, and faster/simpler loan processing and approvals (Australia, Italy). Direct funding support can provide immediate relief and be effective. But it may be relatively more costly and translate directly into fiscal burdens. This can therefore be targeted at specific industries (such as transport, travel, and tourism) or heavily affected businesses to limit the impact on fiscal sustainability.

- *Guarantees* can help MSMEs access credit indirectly. Some countries offer new public guarantees (Austria, Israel, Japan, the Republic of Korea), accounts receivable insurance (the Republic of Korea), and credit mediation services for small and medium-sized enterprises (SMEs) wishing to renegotiate credit terms (France). For MSMEs involved in international trade, supply chain and trade finance can also benefit from guarantees based on accounts receivables and letters of credit. The cost of guarantees per company will be less than direct funding, hence similar fiscal budgets can cover more companies. However, administration may be more complicated, with additional time and cost for implementation, unless there are credit guarantee agencies in the countries that already have credit histories of the MSME applicants.

- *Moratoriums or forbearance* on existing debts and repayment have been announced in Indonesia, the Republic of Korea, Malaysia, the People's Republic of China, and Singapore. Earlier, banks in some countries took voluntary debt holidays or moratorium periods for their household and business clients. But increasingly across the region, a large-scale moratorium on loan payments and restructuring of MSME debt is provided within fiscal packages. These measures mitigate some cash flow constraints for MSMEs and help them avoid a liquidity crisis. But a moratorium also requires relaxing regulatory requirements for banks on nonperforming loan classification and liquidity and reserve requirements, which may impinge on banks' balance sheets and liquidity. Therefore, central banks need to provide adequate liquidity to the banking system while ensuring that these measures do not jeopardize long-term banking stability.

Challenges and Risks

Financial assistance should be provided as temporary relief to solvent enterprises. Eligibility criteria of MSMEs for various facilities should be carefully reviewed and monitored. But there is a certain trade-off between complex eligibility criteria and urgency for these facilities. For the short term (say 3 to 6 months), it may be more appropriate that simpler eligibility criteria are applied to MSMEs. For example, all MSMEs that are heavily affected by COVID-19 can be eligible if they meet certain criteria, such as number of employees, asset size, type of business, or subject to losses incurred to the sales income due to the pandemic. After the first time period, eligibility can be reviewed for a possible rollover of the program.

These facilities should have clear time-bound measures. For each facility, details of repayment plans and schedules have to be clearly communicated with these enterprises, whether it is for new credits or for a moratorium.

After the initial stage, the government may need to consider the worst-case scenario of defaults and debt forgiveness. In such cases, creation of funds/ mechanisms for business and debt restructuring for MSMEs in financial distress might be worth consideration.

The role of central banks is key by maintaining accommodative monetary policy (and quantitative easing through repo and purchasing commercial paper). Monetary and macrofinancial policies can support MSME access to banks and nonbank financial institutions by injecting liquidity into commercial banks; cutting the reserve requirement ratio to help banks to expand credit to MSMEs (e.g., the People's Republic of China); and granting regulatory forbearance, including reclassification of nonperforming loans.

Table 3.1: Financial Assistance to Micro, Small, and Medium-Sized Enterprises in Response to COVID-19 in Select Asian Countries

Country	Capital Buffer Safeguards	Deferral of Debt Repayments	Relaxation of Lending Conditions	New Lending	Credit Guarantees	Regulatory Forbearance
Brunei Darussalam		✓ • deferred principal payments				
Cambodia	✓ • capital injection • base rate reduced	✓ • debt restructuring for priority sectors		✓ • a new public bank for MSMEs		✓ • banking sector stimulus
Indonesia	✓ • capital buffer on banks required	✓ • debt restructuring	✓ • interest rate reduced by 25 bp	✓ • max p10 bn loans for MSMEs		✓ • banking sector stimulus
Lao People's Democratic Republic		✓ • debt restructuring				✓ • loan classification
Malaysia	✓ • RM3 bn for MSME loans with 3.5% interest rate cap	✓ • 6-month moratorium on repayments • debt restructuring	✓ • interest rate reduced by 50 bp	✓ • COVID-19 Special Relief Facility (working capital loans for MSMEs)	✓ • RM50 bn guarantee scheme (80%)	✓ • waiver of listing fees on capital markets for SMEs
Myanmar				✓ • COVID-19 Fund for MSMEs and affected sectors (1% interest)		
Philippines	✓ • base rate reduced • capital req relaxed	✓ • 0-day grace period for debt repayments	✓ • interest rate reduced by 25 bp			

continued next page

Table 1 continued

Country	Capital Buffer Safeguards	Deferral of Debt Repayments	Relaxation of Lending Conditions	New Lending	Credit Guarantees	Regulatory Forbearance
Singapore	✓	• deferred principal payments		✓ • enterprise financing scheme expanded		
Thailand	✓ • B0.9 tn liquidity support measures	✓ • deferred principal payments • debt restructuring	✓ • interest rate reduced by 25 bp	• soft loans/credit lines for MSMEs		✓ • banking sector stimulus
Viet Nam	✓ • base rate reduced • transaction fees scrapped	✓ • deferred principal payments • debt restructuring	✓ • interest rate and transaction fees reduced/waived	• soft loan packages • zero interest loans for wage payments		
Japan				✓ • emergency loans for MSMEs with low/zero interest rate	✓ • 100% guarantee scheme for firms decreasing sales	
Republic of Korea	✓ • base rate reduced	✓ • deferred loan repayments	✓ • interest payments for MSME loans suspended (6-month)	✓ • emergency funding for business with low interest rate • W29 tn MSME loans	✓ • W5.5 tn guarantee scheme for MSMEs • 100% guarantee for small merchants	
People's Republic of China	✓ • liquidity support • CNY800 bn extra funding by FIs for MSME loans	✓ • deferred principal and interest payments for MSMEs	✓ • interest rate reduced by 10 bp	✓ • refinancing facility for MSMEs with 2.5% interest rate • special credit quota for MSMEs		✓ • NPL definitions

bn = billion, bps = basis points, CNY = yuan, COVID-19 = coronavirus disease, FI = financial institution, MSME = micro, small, and medium-sized enterprise, NPL = nonperforming loan, RM = ringgit,
Rp = rupiah, THB = baht, tn = trillion, W = won.
Source: Recomposed from World Bank Map of SME Support Measures in Response to COVID-19. 14 April 2020.

The COVID-19 Impact on Micro, Small, and Medium-Sized Enterprises: Evidence from Rapid Surveys in Indonesia, the Lao People's Democratic Republic, the Philippines, and Thailand

Shigehiro Shinozaki

Prolonged containment of COVID-19 increases the risk of business failure and bankruptcy. In particular, micro, small, and medium-sized enterprises (MSMEs) are at greater risk due to supply chain disruptions and financial difficulties.[2]

To assess the initial impact of COVID-19 and related containment measures on MSMEs, ADB's Economic Research and Regional Cooperation Department (ERCD) conducted rapid online business surveys in Indonesia, the Lao People's Democratic Republic (Lao PDR), the Philippines, and Thailand during March and May 2020.[3]

A total of 3,877 complete responses from MSMEs were collected: 525 in Indonesia, 364 in the Lao PDR, 1,804 in the Philippines, and 1,184 in Thailand. MSMEs were defined using the employment threshold set by national definitions. The study adopted non-standard sampling procedures, given that responses were not based on random or representative samples.[4]

---

[2]   This section summarizes the findings from Asian Development Bank. Forthcoming. *Asia Small and Medium-Sized Enterprise Monitor 2020—Volume II*: Special Chapter: Impact of COVID-19 on Micro, Small, and Medium-sized Enterprises in Developing Asia. Manila.

[3]   The surveys were done in partnership with the Department of SME Promotion of the Ministry of Industry and Commerce in the Lao PDR; the Bureau of Small and Medium Enterprise Development of the Philippine Department of Trade and Industry and the Philippine Chamber of Commerce and Industry; and the Office of Small and Medium Enterprise Promotion in Thailand, the Thai Credit Guarantee Corporation, and the Thai Chamber of Commerce, as well as through ADB's Facebook channels. For Indonesia, only ADB's Facebook channel was utilized to collect responses from MSMEs. Throughout the article, references to specific months (for example, March and April) refer to 2020 unless otherwise indicated.

[4]   The extent of data bias between ADB surveys and existing country sampling frames are explained in the forthcoming report.

This summary presents the key findings from the surveys using aggregate MSME data.[5]

The survey findings show how the COVID-19 pandemic and associated quarantine measures instantly affected MSME business operations. Of the MSMEs surveyed, 70.6% in the Philippines and 61.1% in the Lao PDR, along with nearly half in Indonesia (48.6%) and Thailand (41.1%), suspended operations a month after the virus outbreak and national quarantine measures were imposed (Figure 3.1). The rest had to deal with supply disruptions, while they continued to operate. Supply disruptions were experienced by about one- third in Thailand and the Philippines, and less than one-fifth in Indonesia and the Lao PDR.

Figure 3.1: MSME Business Environment after the COVID-19 Outbreak

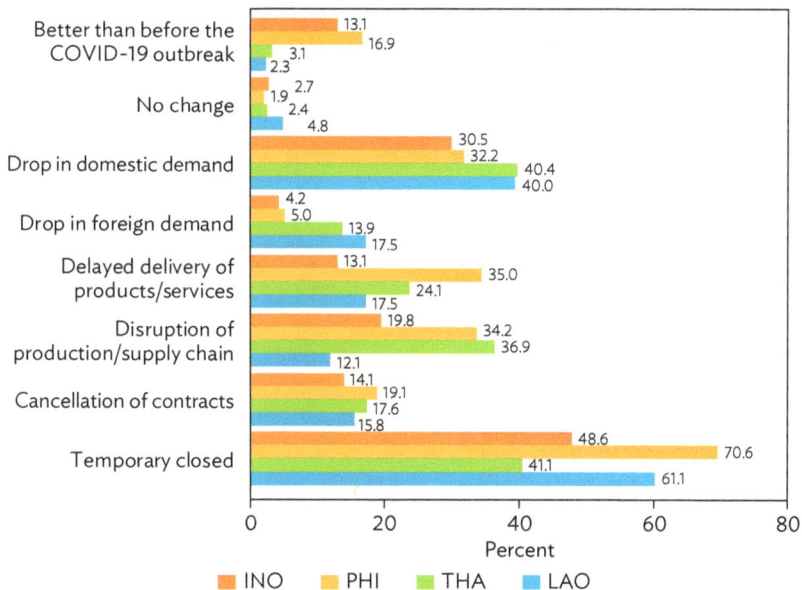

Category	INO	PHI	THA	LAO
Better than before the COVID-19 outbreak	13.1	16.9	3.1	2.3
No change	1.9	2.7	2.4	4.8
Drop in domestic demand	30.5	32.2	40.4	40.0
Drop in foreign demand	4.2	5.0	13.9	17.5
Delayed delivery of products/services	13.1	35.0	24.1	17.5
Disruption of production/supply chain	19.8	34.2	36.9	12.1
Cancellation of contracts	14.1	19.1	17.6	15.8
Temporary closed	48.6	70.6	41.1	61.1

INO = Indonesia, MSME = micro, small, and medium-sized enterprise, PHI = Philippines, THA = Thailand, LAO = Lao People's Democratic Republic.
Note: 525 valid samples in INO, 1,804 in PHI, 1,147 in THA, and 355 in LAO.
Source: Calculated based on data from the rapid MSME surveys in Indonesia, the Philippines, Thailand, and the Lao PDR, April–May 2020.

---

[5]   Detailed analyses by firm size and industrial sector are included in the forthcoming report.

MSME sales and revenue dropped sharply in March and deteriorated further in April, with increased business closures leaving no sales or revenue, especially in micro and small firms, and also across all industrial sectors (services, manufacturing, and agriculture). Domestic demand for MSME products fell for 40% of MSMEs surveyed in Thailand and the Lao PDR, and 30% in the Philippines and Indonesia. Accordingly, in Indonesia, Thailand, and the Lao PDR, monthly sales volumes fell over 30% for many MSMEs in March, with a larger number in April attributing no sales to the rising number of temporary closures. Worse in the Philippines, most of the MSMEs had no sales in March, immediately after strict lockdown measures were imposed. Monthly MSME income followed the same trend as sales.

Revenue decreased sharply in March, but there were more MSMEs with no revenue in April, caused by the temporary business closures in Indonesia, the Lao PDR, and Thailand (Figure 3.2). In particular, in April, the Lao PDR had a very sharp increase in MSMEs that did not generate revenue.

Figure 3.2: MSME Monthly Income during the COVID-19 Pandemic

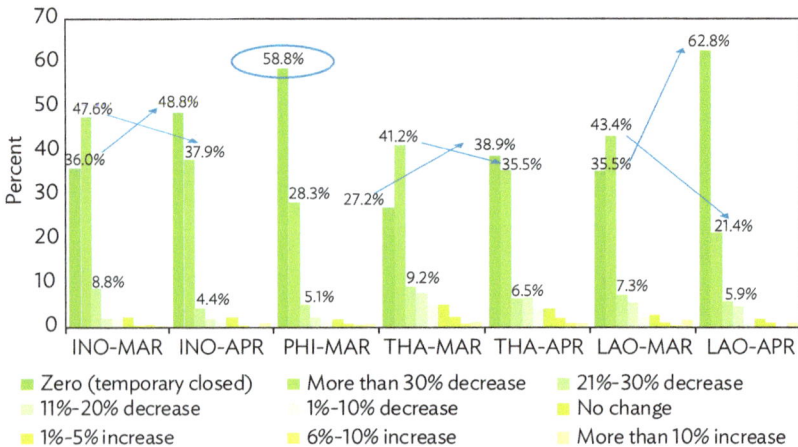

INO = Indonesia, MSME = micro, small, and medium-sized enterprise, PHI = Philippines, THA = Thailand, LAO = Lao People's Democratic Republic.
Note: 525 valid samples in INO, 1,804 in PHI, 1,147 in THA, and 355 in LAO.
Source: Calculated based on data from the rapid MSME surveys in Indonesia, the Philippines, Thailand, and the Lao PDR, April–May 2020.

These trends largely follow the "stringency index," prepared by the University of Oxford, to measure national containment policies. The survey results support that strict lockdown measures from March in the Philippines and April in the Lao PDR contributed to higher proportions of zero revenue among MSMEs in the Philippines in March and the Lao PDR in April. Combining the stringency index with the Google's "extent of mobility" measure[6] explains how the stringent Philippine and Lao PDR policies accelerated the decline in consumers' mobility outside the home, which in turn contributed to depressing MSME sales and revenue.

In terms of employment during the pandemic, across the Lao PDR, the Philippines, and Thailand, about 60% of MSMEs saw no change after the outbreak, while 40% reduced their workforce. By contrast, in Indonesia some 60% reduced staff in both March and April, especially for micro and small firms, with reductions more pronounced among manufacturers. This suggests that more MSME workers lost their jobs during the first 2 months after the virus outbreak in Indonesia. The survey findings revealed that the temporary staffing cuts were how most MSMEs across all countries coped with the revenue crunch, followed by reduced working hours (Figure 3.3).

Figure 3.3: Changes in MSME Employment after the COVID-19 Outbreak

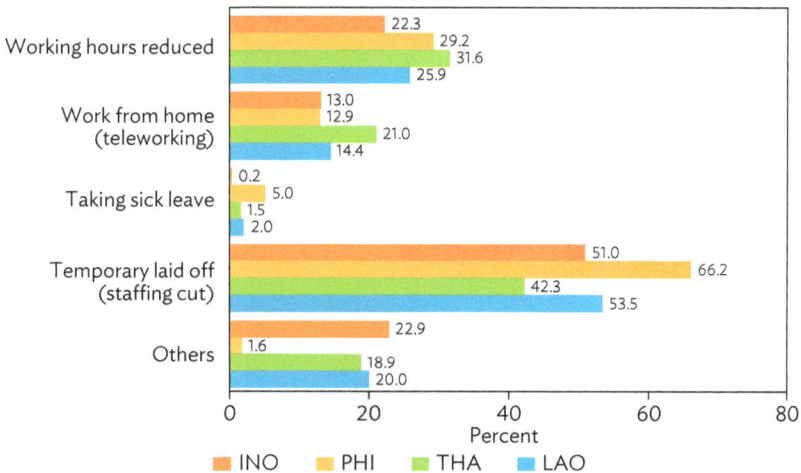

INO = Indonesia, MSME = micro, small, and medium-sized enterprise, PHI = Philippines, THA = Thailand, LAO = Lao People's Democratic Republic.
Note: 525 valid samples in INO, 1,804 in PHI, 1,147 in THA, and 355 in LAO.
Source: Calculated based on data from the rapid MSME surveys in Indonesia, the Philippines, Thailand, and the Lao PDR, April–May 2020.

---

6   Our World in Data; Community Mobility Reports, Google.

Also, the surveys found "work-from-home" was not a serious option for MSMEs (only 13%–21% adopted work-from-home measures), even as each country's government promoted the practice. When data are broken down by firm size, more micro and small firms cut staff, while medium-sized ones kept workers on by encouraging them to work from home and adjusting working hours. Temporary staffing cuts were a major coping response for MSMEs across all industrial sectors.

As for wages, after COVID-19 outbreaks, most MSMEs have either suspended (nearly 60% of the MSMEs surveyed in Indonesia and the Philippines) or cut them. The severity is a bit less in Thailand and the Lao PDR and more than one-third of their MSMEs reported no change in monthly wage payments (Figure 3.4). Suspended wage payments were more pronounced for microenterprises across all industrial sectors.

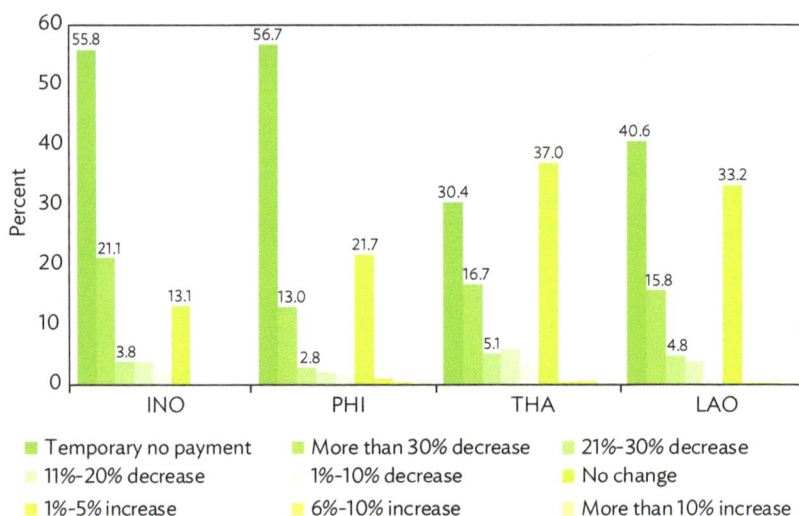

Figure 3.4: Wage Payments by MSMEs during the COVID-19 Pandemic
(%)

INO = Indonesia, MSME = micro, small, and medium-sized enterprise, PHI = Philippines, THA = Thailand, LAO = Lao People's Democratic Republic.
Note: 525 valid samples in INO, 1,804 in PHI, 1,147 in THA, and 355 in LAO.
Source: Calculated based on data from the rapid MSME surveys in Indonesia, the Philippines, Thailand, and the Lao PDR, April–May 2020.

MSMEs surveyed in all four countries reported a serious lack of funds to retain business (Figure 3.5), especially in Indonesia where 88% of microenterprises said they had no cash or savings or would run out funds within a month—with high proportions of small firms (77%) and medium-sized firms (63%) reporting the same shortages. Further, most MSMEs across all countries had to resort to borrowing fund to overcome the shortage of working capital. They did not change their normal approach to raising funds even during the crisis—relying mostly on their own funds or borrowing from family, relatives, and friends (Figure 3.6). The number of MSMEs which obtained bank credit remains limited, although several government measures—such as special refinancing facilities, soft loan programs, and special guaranteed loans—were launched in all countries.

Figure 3.5: MSME Financial Condition during the COVID-19 Pandemic

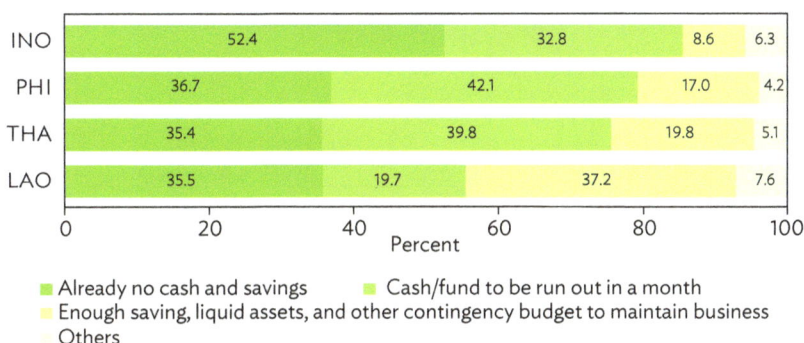

INO = Indonesia, MSME = micro, small, and medium-sized enterprise, PHI = Philippines, THA = Thailand, LAO = Lao People's Democratic Republic.
Note: 525 valid samples in INO, 1,804 in PHI, 1,147 in THA, and 355 in LAO.
Source: Calculated based on data from the rapid MSME surveys in Indonesia, the Philippines, Thailand, and the Lao PDR, April–May 2020.

Immediate working capital is critical for MSMEs to survive, but most had problems raising even local currency amounts equivalent to $1,000. This problem was more prevalent in microenterprises, and those in services and agriculture. In all countries, a large number of micro and small firms relied on borrowing from close relatives. But medium-sized firms relied on their own funds or retained profits to survive the pandemic, and they could usually apply for bank credit or nonbank financial institution loans. This suggests that the ability to raise funds varied greatly according to firm size.

Figure 3.6: MSME Funding during the COVID-19 Pandemic

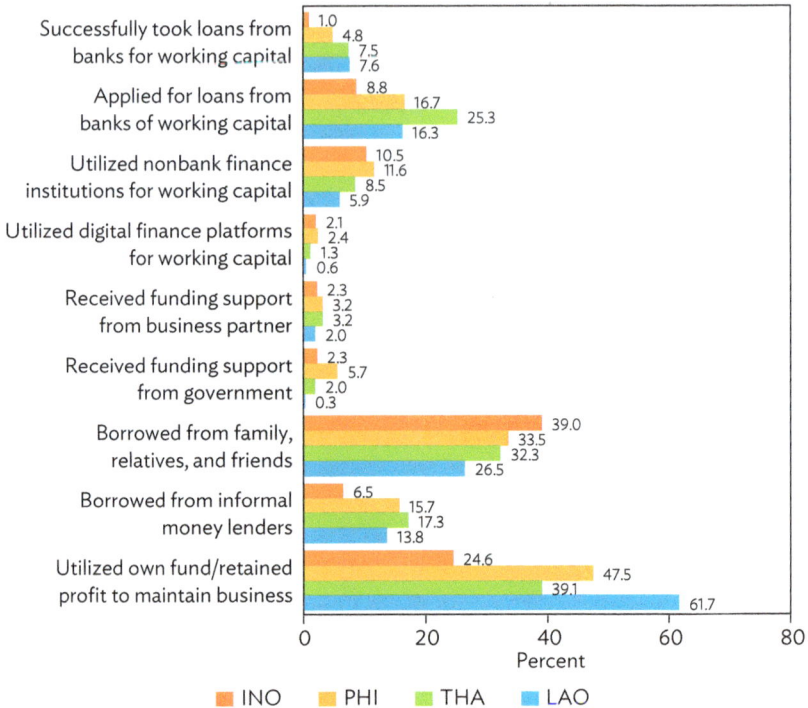

INO = Indonesia, MSME = micro, small, and medium-sized enterprise, PHI = Philippines,
THA = Thailand, LAO = Lao People's Democratic Republic.
Note: 525 valid samples in INO, 1,804 in PHI, 1,147 in THA, and 355 in LAO.
Source: Calculated based on data from the rapid MSME surveys in Indonesia, the Philippines, Thailand,
and the Lao PDR, April–May 2020.

The survey also asked what main concerns and obstacles MSMEs would have if the pandemic continued beyond the end of June, more than a month after the survey. Shortage of funds was the top concern for 60%–77% of MSMEs when considering how to maintain or restart their businesses. Following this was concern about further drop in domestic demand for the Lao PDR and Thailand, a supply chain disruption for the Philippines, and loan repayments for Indonesia. More concretely, considering a pandemic lasting beyond June, half or more of the MSMEs surveyed said they would seek deferral of loan repayments. This was true across all countries but more pronounced in the Lao PDR (Figure 3.7). More than half in the Philippines and the Lao PDR wanted deferred tax payments. In Thailand, nearly half were considering further layoffs and wage cuts. And in Indonesia, one-fifth were considering having to apply for bankruptcy, the largest share among countries surveyed.

Figure 3.7: MSME Responses

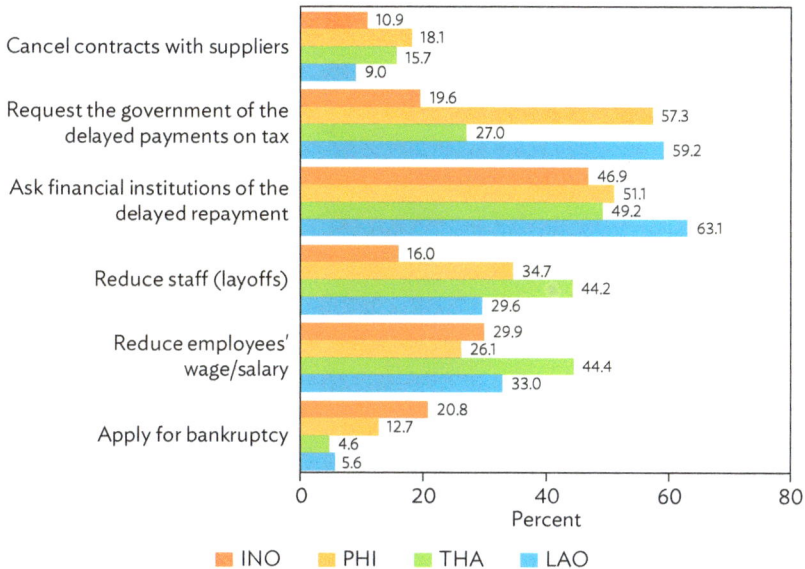

INO = Indonesia, MSME = micro, small, and medium-sized enterprise, PHI = Philippines,
THA = Thailand, LAO = Lao People's Democratic Republic.
Note: 525 valid samples in INO, 1,804 in PHI, 1,147 in THA, and 355 in LAO.
Source: Calculated based on data from the rapid MSME surveys in Indonesia, the Philippines, Thailand,
and the Lao PDR, April–May 2020.

Most MSMEs strongly wanted further assistance from governments, especially financial support, regardless of size and business sector. Of the 21 policy options listed in the survey, more than 90% desired zero interest rates and/or collateral-free loans, which was followed by subsidies, cash transfers, and grants for business recovery in Indonesia, the Philippines, and Thailand, with refinancing in the Lao PDR (Figure 3.8). Interestingly, 90% of Indonesian MSMEs suggested exit finance to restart their business, signaling a large number of bankruptcies looming.

In sum, the surveys identified seven policies that could support MSMEs during and after the pandemic. First is to further outline and disseminate **assistance to focus groups** to encourage effective use of limited budget and support for the most devastated firms in sectors such as manufacturing, traditional wholesale and retail trade, accommodation, tourism, and transportation, among others. Governments of countries surveyed already provided economic stimulus packages, but if the pandemic continues, as it

Figure 3.8: Policy Measures Desired by MSMEs

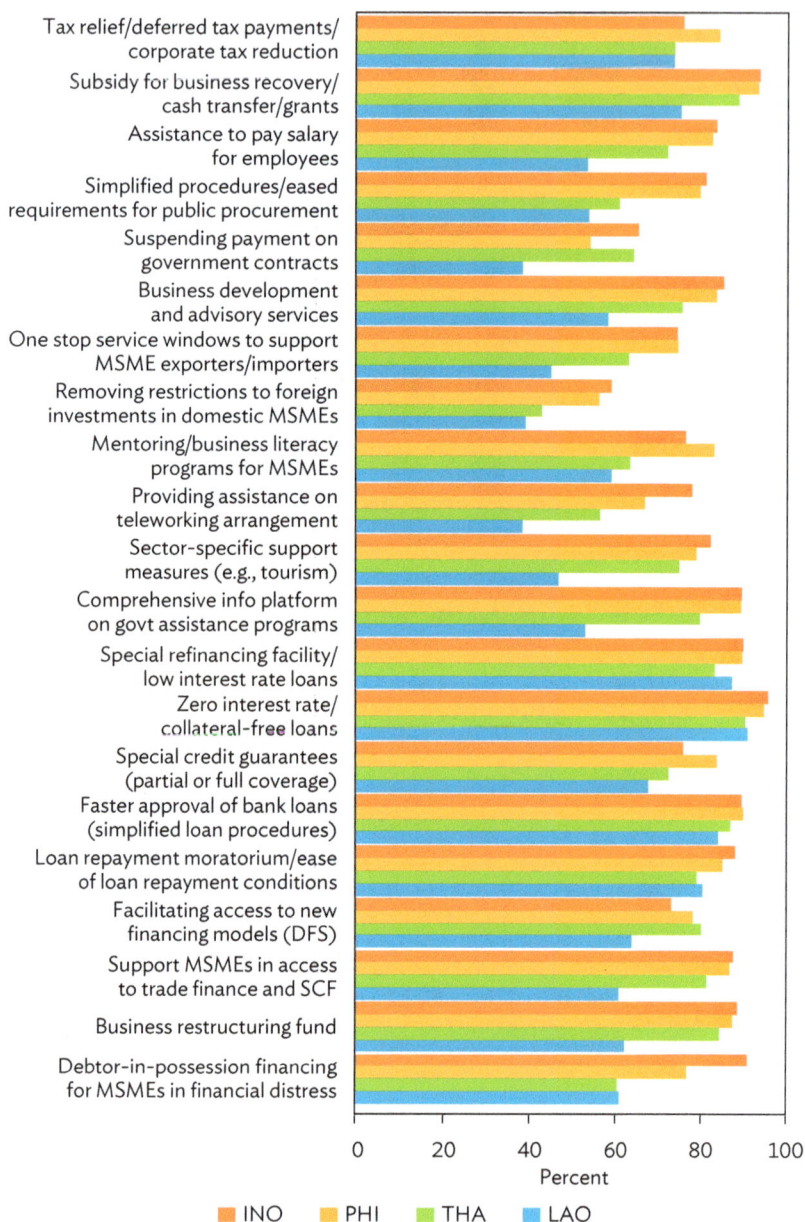

Tax relief/deferred tax payments/corporate tax reduction

Subsidy for business recovery/cash transfer/grants

Assistance to pay salary for employees

Simplified procedures/eased requirements for public procurement

Suspending payment on government contracts

Business development and advisory services

One stop service windows to support MSME exporters/importers

Removing restrictions to foreign investments in domestic MSMEs

Mentoring/business literacy programs for MSMEs

Providing assistance on teleworking arrangement

Sector-specific support measures (e.g., tourism)

Comprehensive info platform on govt assistance programs

Special refinancing facility/low interest rate loans

Zero interest rate/collateral-free loans

Special credit guarantees (partial or full coverage)

Faster approval of bank loans (simplified loan procedures)

Loan repayment moratorium/ease of loan repayment conditions

Facilitating access to new financing models (DFS)

Support MSMEs in access to trade finance and SCF

Business restructuring fund

Debtor-in-possession financing for MSMEs in financial distress

Percent

■ INO   ■ PHI   ■ THA   ■ LAO

INO = Indonesia, MSME = micro, small, and medium-sized enterprise, PHI = Philippines,
THA = Thailand, LAO = Lao People's Democratic Republic.
Note: 525 valid samples in INO, 1,804 in PHI, 1,147 in THA, and 355 in LAO.
Source: Calculated based on data from the rapid MSME surveys in Indonesia, the Philippines, Thailand,
and the Lao PDR, April–May 2020.

has, a more detailed budget allocation for those most affected by COVID-19 and lockdown measures is needed.

Second is to adopt **a phased approach** so governments can flexibly redesign policy support, given the uncertainty over containing the spread of the pandemic. Third is to **differentiate policy measures** by firm size, given the different time horizons between micro and small enterprises and medium-sized firms with distinctive differences in their abilities to cope with the impact. Fourth is to help promote **a shift to digital transactions**, given that many small businesses generally require personal contact, and assist the transition to **work from home** to avoid layoffs. This includes improving skills training for MSME owners and employees.

Fifth is to strengthen **the distribution** of government support programs, especially **financial support**, to ensure it reaches target beneficiaries (as most MSMEs still rely on informal sources for funds during the pandemic). Sixth is how to **keep businesses running and employees secure**, given the potential for a large number of MSME bankruptcies and high unemployment. And finally, one must periodically **monitor MSME business conditions** to fine tune the direction of government policy support—in this, ADB can help developing member countries design evidence-based policies through follow-up MSME surveys.

Three Ways to Support Businesses and Their Workers During a Pandemic

Paul Vandenberg and Matthias Helble

Travel restrictions, store closures, and social distancing, prompted by COVID-19, is causing an economic slowdown that may last to the end of 2020 and possibly beyond. Businesses are experiencing a precipitous fall in demand, which is reducing revenue and making it difficult to pay bills, including wages. Layoffs have started. Workers without wages means households without income and that, in turn, leads to difficulty buying food and other essentials.

Keeping businesses operating—which helps to keep workers employed—is thus essential in cushioning the impact of the slowdown on households. In this way, policies that support small and medium-sized businesses, and other affected enterprises, are an indirect but critical means of providing social protection. They are not a substitute but a complement to more direct social protection measures.

How can governments support businesses, particularly small and medium-sized enterprises that collectively employ an average of 60% of the workforce in Asian countries and are particularly vulnerable to a demand shock? We suggest three measures.

Provide credit. With reduced revenue, enterprises are running short of working capital. At the same time, banks and other financial institutions will be reluctant to lend, in part because they predict some businesses will not survive and the loans may never be repaid. Nonetheless, lending can be encouraged in several ways. One is to use state-owned banks, of which there remain many in Asia.

For private banks, more funds can be provided by the central bank for on-lending to businesses. This can be further encouraged by the expanded use of credit guarantee schemes which exist in an increasing number of economies. The coverage ratio on loans (i.e., share of the loan that is guaranteed), which is usually set at 50%–80%, can be increased to 100%, as is being done in Hong Kong, China, and was done for emergency loans in Japan to cushion the negative impacts of the Great East Japan Earthquake in 2011.

Governments can also encourage the delay of payments on existing credit, as Italy has recently announced. Such a mid-tenure grace period means that interest and principal can be deferred for 3 to 6 months, taking some pressure off businesses. This measure will no doubt impinge on the liquidity of banks. They can be encouraged through extra liquidity provided to them, moral suasion, and the idea that a delayed payment is better than no payment should the business collapse. Tax breaks or deferments for banks will also ease liquidity constraints.

Reduce business transfers to government. Payments remitted by businesses can be deferred by governments. This includes taxes on income, property taxes, excise duties, employers' contributions to social security programs, and others. This will help to conserve needed operating capital in the short run. Several countries have already announced such measures. For example, Viet Nam will allow a delay in tax payments for 5 months. It will also delay land use fees until October 2020. Thailand will extend the deadline for corporate income tax payments by 3 months. Excise payments required by entertainment and service businesses will also be extended for 3 months.

Maintain employment. Government, along with chambers of commerce, should encourage enterprises to maintain employment, where possible. Certainly, quarantine restrictions and government-mandated lockdowns will leave businesses shuttered and people unable to get to work. Where businesses can remain in operation, firms might reduce work hours but still allow workers to earn some income.

For example, if the enterprise reduces operations by 50%, it would be better to reduce the work hours of all workers rather than laying off half of them and keeping the others all full hours. In countries with unemployment benefit schemes, the lost income from reduced hours can be made up from unemployment insurance benefits.

Reduced hours and partial use of unemployment insurance were methods used during the global financial crisis to cushion the employment impact. Governments in some countries, including the United Kingdom and Denmark, are providing businesses with 75%–80% of the wages for workers who would otherwise be laid off during the pandemic.

These measures will be costly for the government and for lenders. The number of nonperforming loans, even with a grace period, will rise. Banks will become more highly leveraged. Payouts on credit guarantees will increase and the credit guarantee fund likely need replenishment. Government revenues, from income and other transfers, will tighten. This is to be expected as government has a role to play in the intertemporal reallocation of resources to cushion the effects of an economic crisis. The idea is to reduce the severity of the slowdown on households and businesses during the pandemic by shifting some of the support costs to the post-pandemic period. Businesses, banks, and governments will be better able to bear those costs as the economy revives. For its part, the central bank can allow some regulatory forbearance in terms of loan classification.

It is important for an economy that businesses survive during a temporary crisis. When businesses collapse, assets are sold off and workers are let go. An entity that generates output and employment is lost. The loss of value has a scarring effect on the economy as there is an element of irreversibility in the loss of business investments, and liquidations are costly to the broader economy. It is also costly to reconstitute businesses after the crisis, not only for firms themselves but also their employees. Workers face costs in finding jobs and may need to be retrained. Avoiding bankruptcy will help recovery and give it a better chance to be V-shaped instead of U- or "bathtub"-shaped.

Evidence from the global financial crisis showed that business support can be a valuable investment. While costly during the crisis, it allows many firms to continue operating and then fully reboot once the crisis is over. Equally important is the fact that business support measures are valid instruments of social protection. They can protect workers from the loss of employment and the coincident loss of income to support their families.

There is little doubt that many workers will be displaced as a result of the slowdown and many businesses will collapse. But support to businesses gives some of them a fighting chance to weather the storm.

Five Ways Banks Can Help Asia's Smallest Businesses Survive COVID-19

Susan Olsen

Before COVID-19, poverty rates were the lowest in recorded history and businesses were looking for profits at the "bottom of the pyramid" as the poor increased their spending power. Micro and small enterprises—vastly informal, but the key to creating 70%–95% of new jobs in Asia—were helping drive growth through improved access to finance.

This rise in socioeconomic status is now being crushed by COVID-19. The International Labour Organization (ILO) reports that 1.6 billion workers in the informal economy—nearly half of the global workforce—are in immediate danger of having their livelihoods destroyed.

The banks that could throw a lifeline to these businesses and their workers are also under stress. They are being asked to give loan moratoriums to customers while there is no guarantee that their own debt payments will be waived. Governments have tried to help the banks, with lowered cash reserve requirements and bond purchases, with more measures likely to come.

How can banks weather the pandemic and serve the micro and small businesses that create most of Asia's jobs?

Get strong. Banks cannot serve the neediest customers without being strong themselves. In an era of "survival of the fittest," being fit means rapid deployment of business continuity plans, boosting cash in hand, and avoiding the debt trap of borrowing short to lend long. Shareholders are vital partners now to bolster confidence and boost capital in order to weather an expected wave of bad loans ahead. This is the time when public and private sector credit guarantee programs are most needed to pool risk and help restart businesses.

Cash is golden. Micro and small enterprise lenders have always known this, especially for those active in the challenging unsecured business loans segment. Serving informal markets relies on an ability to assess cash flow net of hard-to-track debts that often lie outside the formal financial system. While in-person assessment methods have fallen somewhat out of favor in an era of social distancing, they are key to restarting the credit engine. When it comes time to unlock micro and small enterprise disbursements, credit officers are the essential workers on the front lines to perform business health checks and unlock prudent lending decisions.

Go digital. While cash is still golden, that does not mean banking should depend on the exchange of bills, especially given the shift away from touch-related exchanges. The G20 push for innovative and digital financial inclusion is ongoing, but it took nationwide lockdowns to break many of the cash-dependent collection methods in microfinance. Yet, some micro and small enterprise lending models still rely on paper-based records and post-dated checks, which are slow to process as banks work with skeletal staffing. Markets such as India have strongly enabled frameworks for digital payments, and India has set a target to reach 15% transaction turnover as a share of GDP by 2021. COVID-19 should hasten the transition, particularly relating to the flow of mobile money payments and to the digitization of micro and small loan applications. Upfront investments in tech architecture could pay off through lower credit review costs, more accurate cloud-based records, better remote access for clients, and minimized operational risk going forward.

Alternative channels. Regulators have allowed mobile wallets, web services, and nonbank agent networks, but more alternative partnerships are needed. This includes bank alliances with "fast-moving consumer goods" companies, telecom providers, and other non-traditional actors with strong distribution channels to reach the last mile, such as India's *kirana* (local neighborhood) stores, where more than 90% of retail sales take place. Banks need to improve their consent-based use of digital and supplier credit data to better serve the millions of neighborhood stores reaching more than a billion low-income consumers. The old proverb "If you want to go fast—go alone. If you want to go far—go together" still holds true.

Add value. Well before COVID-19, banks needed to create higher-value add-on experiences to retain customers. Even in developing markets where only 20% have access to formal loans, banks need to provide more than access to finance. With micro and small enterprise debt service capacity directly impacted by frozen economic activity, finding other value propositions is key. One important timely add-on is "government-to-person" digital transfers to subsidize livelihoods. Banks can also work with women's groups to mobilize savings and industry associations to foster cluster-based learning and business skills upgrades. Insurance distribution is another value proposition that banks can offer. While bank accounts have become more universal, only one-third of adults in India have life insurance. Even fewer have affordable health or business risk products. In times of crisis, clients will reward the banks who help them recover and emerge stronger in the face of business challenges ahead.

Banks know that the road to recovery post-COVID-19 is full of risk. In the eye of the storm, they need to innovate and expand their services to help rebuild the small businesses that provide a lifeline to Asia's poor.

Small Business Solutions for Pandemic Challenges

Lotte Schou-Zibell

The COVID-19 pandemic is hurting small enterprises globally. But socioeconomic pressures are particularly severe in developing countries, where resources are limited and economic activity is weak, and small business frequently the backbone of growth. The pandemic threatens to throw economies into recession and push tens of millions of households back or even deeper into poverty.

The pandemic's impact will be disproportionate in least-developed and small-island developing countries, notably in Africa and in the Pacific, which are especially vulnerable to economic volatility and shocks. Their health systems and economies are less able to cope with challenges, leaving their poor and vulnerable groups at increased risk.

Exogenous trade shocks are transmitted through the global value chain. Large retailers have closed stores, hurting factories and workers locked into just-in-time supply chains in countries including Bangladesh and Cambodia. Many micro, small, and medium-sized enterprises (MSMEs) are fighting for survival as a result. Yet, they must cover salaries, rent, and other operating expenses; debts to financial institutions; and taxes.

Many will see letting go of workers as the best solution. This could transform economic crisis into social calamity. Fortunately, the focus of most businesses for now is on protecting employees, understanding the risks to their business, and in managing supply chain disruptions. This will be important for safeguarding jobs and incomes, preserving financial stability, and reviving growth by minimizing disruptions to trade and global supply chains.

Quick recovery of these businesses can mitigate the direst consequences. But beyond the immediate recovery, we need to ensure the medium- to long-term survival of small businesses by removing impediments to their growth.

The key challenges will be to improve access to finance and investment for small enterprises; give them more freedom to expand into new sectors; and promote their use of new technologies to better connect with producers, suppliers, and consumers.

The first challenge is the biggest. Banks are often reluctant to lend due to a lack of market information, concerns about risk, and poor-quality loan applications. Unless investors, entrepreneurs, and viable businesses can be financed, opportunities will be wasted and growth potential squandered.

Business laws and regulations can be overhauled to suit the needs of modern commerce. In many countries, starting a business involves high costs and long delays, compromising investment and business growth. This is a key reason behind the large informal labor markets of some countries. Efforts must be made to remove bureaucratic red tape to allow businesses to open and operate as quickly as possible when COVID-19 restrictions are eased.

A second step is to rethink the role of state-owned enterprises to provide extra space for small enterprises to grow. In many countries, state-owned enterprises provide essential services such as power generation, water, sewage, and telecommunications. But they can be inefficient, drain government resources, and generate low returns. Many are monopolies. The pandemic might provide governments with opportunities to allow MSMEs to provide some of these essential services.

In tandem, competition and consumer protection frameworks can be improved, especially in markets where participation of governments may be extensive and a few firms dominate key sectors. This reduces consumer choices, keeps prices high, and constrains small businesses. Better consumer protections would reduce the scope for price controls and gouging, which distorts markets and impacts heavily on consumers.

A priority is also to give women the tools to realize their potential to run businesses, broadening avenues to contribute to community welfare and economic growth. Female-led businesses can be encouraged through training in business processes, access to finance, and addressing customary practices that favor men over women. To promote female entrepreneurs in Armenia, for example, such programs resulted in more business registrations by women, improved skills, and better access to finance, while financial institutions were guided on hiring more female loan officers.

Finally, small businesses can be supported to reinvent their business models using new technologies.

A potentially promising sector is health care, currently a global priority as the world battles COVID-19. Instead of having to travel to the nearest major city to see a specialist, tele-health platforms provide virtual diagnosis, treatment, preventive, and curative services, as well as training for health care professionals in areas such as epidemiology and pandemic influenza risk communication. These services are becoming indispensable and seem tailor-made for MSMEs with sufficient expertise and capital.

Support for the agriculture sector innovations can provide further fertile ground for these businesses. Already, small-scale farmers are using innovative technologies and practices to raise yields, manage inputs more efficiently, introduce new crops and production systems, and enhance product quality. With well-targeted support, such practices can be crucial to business survival in the current crisis.

For instance, governments can invest in satellite-based earth observation technology to provide smallholder farmers with continuous data on land and water resources. Satellite information on water levels and weather forecasts can help smallholder farmers reduce water stress and consumption while raising yields by as much as 200%–250%.

Tailoring these approaches to specific country circumstances could help save millions of livelihoods in poor communities and fortify economies against future shocks.

4. Mitigating the Impact on the Poor and Vulnerable

Photos on previous page: [From the top] The poor in Asia were already dealing with major challenges even before the COVID-19 health crisis; Small and micro business operators are particularly vulnerable to fraudulent offers and often need financial education; Women and girls face challenges unique to their gender during the pandemic; Direct contact is needed in order to make a living.

Mind the Gap in Combating COVID-19

Juzhong Zhuang

A public health crisis like the COVID-19 pandemic destroys economic growth and pushes millions into poverty. Without policy interventions, it will also worsen income inequality.[1]

As of 23 July 2020, there have been more than 2.3 million reported cases of COVID-19 and about 54,000 deaths in 33 out of the 45 economies in developing Asia. The pandemic is inflicting tremendous human, social, and economic pain on society at large. As countries implement social distancing and lockdown measures, economic growth has stalled and unemployment has surged.

If the pandemic lasts for 6 months, it could reduce the region's GDP by $2.5 trillion, destroy an equivalent of 167 million full-time jobs, and push 140 million people into poverty. Without policy intervention, the pandemic will worsen the region's income inequality as well. Reducing income inequality is a major challenge many countries in Asia and the Pacific face and it forms a key part of the region's sustainable development goals.

COVID-19 is likely to worsen the region's income inequality at least five ways.

First, unskilled workers will be hit harder than skilled workers. Skilled workers are more difficult to replace and so the unskilled are more likely to lose their jobs or experience wage cuts. The possibility of working from home is also greater for high-skilled occupations than for low-skilled ones.

---

[1] This article originally appeared in East Asia Forum as part of a special feature series on the novel coronavirus crisis and its impact. https://www.eastasiaforum.org/2020/06/18/mind-the-gap-in-combating-covid-19/#more-263701.

Second, the economic contraction caused by the pandemic affects both labor and capital, but workers, on average poorer, are likely to be hurt more severely. It is easier for capital-intensive production, such as manufacturing, to manage containment measures than labor-intensive production like the service sector. This is because the former involves working with machines, while the latter involves directly serving people. Firms also have the option of substituting workers with machines and technology.

Third, the pandemic will have a disproportionate impact on vulnerable groups such as women, the elderly, and micro, small, and medium-sized enterprises (MSMEs). MSMEs are more vulnerable to economic shocks than large firms and often provide informal employment with inadequate social protection and lower wages.

Women are more likely to work in labor-intensive industries than men and also get paid lower average wages. The elderly are the most vulnerable to the epidemic, earning less than the working age population. Those working on the frontlines to deliver food and medicine, and provide paid care services face the greatest risk of infection.

Fourth, the pandemic could increase regional income inequality, as poor regions often have less capacity to implement containment measures and provide adequate health care services. Poor regions also face greater constraints in providing fiscal support to local economies and affected groups. When poor regions rely on remittances from migrant workers, they also become affected by job losses in rich areas.

Finally, government stimulus measures could exacerbate income inequality if they are not well designed and insufficiently targeted at protecting the jobs and livelihoods of low-income households and vulnerable groups. MSMEs might be unable to apply for liquidity support programs made available by the government or central bank.

Historical experience shows that income inequality often falls in the aftermath of catastrophic disasters such as wars, earthquakes, and stock market crises because they involve large-scale wealth destruction. But a study of five pandemics, including SARS (2003), H1N1 (2009), MERS (2012), Ebola (2014), and Zika (2016), shows that health disasters increase income inequality as they involve large-scale job destruction that disproportionately affects lower-income groups.

Worsening income inequality can intensify social tensions and constrain consumption, and poses a risk to economic recovery. But the following policy measures can help dampen the devastating impact of COVID-19 on growth, poverty, and income inequality in Asia and the Pacific.

The first is to contain the outbreak as quickly as possible. This requires the effective implementation of testing, contact tracing, social distancing, and lockdown measures supported by necessary social protection measures. For those countries that have successfully reduced the number of daily infections to very low levels, vigilance is needed to prevent multiple waves of infections. This should happen alongside investment in health care systems to build the capacity to treat severe cases and reduce fatalities.

The second is to protect jobs, those who have lost their jobs, and the most vulnerable in society. The policies to achieve this vary according to in-country circumstances, but include support for firms (especially MSMEs) through tax cuts, wage subsidies and credit guarantees, extending unemployment and social assistance to those severely affected, and fiscal transfers to poor regions to combat the outbreak.

The third is to support the economic recovery in an inclusive manner. Countries should combine short-term stimulus with long-term strategies for sustainable and inclusive growth. This requires policy packages with a focus on investment in education and health, building sustainable public transport, providing basic social services, and supporting rural development. Social protection should also be strengthened through the provision of social safety nets for the informal sector and by working toward universal health coverage.

Governments in Asia and the Pacific are taking action. More than 40 developing Asian economies have announced income support and job protection measures amounting to more than $1.5 trillion or 5.6% of regional GDP.

The COVID-19 pandemic will worsen income inequality in Asia and the Pacific. But well-designed policy responses can avert it.

To Survive the Pandemic, Indonesia's Urban Poor Need Economic Support and Basic Services

Joris van Etten and Tiffany Tran

Indonesia is at a critical juncture with how it responds to the needs of its millions of urban poor. By now, it is clear that urban poor populations could disproportionately suffer from—and contribute to—the spread of COVID-19 due to their lack of adequate housing and basic services.

With large-scale social restrictions still in place in many cities, those who earn daily wages as informal workers face dual blows to health and livelihood. Without a sufficient response that addresses their basic needs, these urban poor and near-poor Indonesians—who will likely fall deeper into poverty—are most at risk. Policies to support vulnerable populations are thus more urgent than ever.

To enhance the resilience of Indonesia's urban poor, two complementary areas of intervention are needed: one that cushions the economic impact of the pandemic, and one that provides the basic services needed to stay safe and healthy.

Increase Local Government Capacity for Data Collection, Entry, and Verification

Roughly 60% of all working Indonesians are employed in the informal sector. Of those, 40% who are engaged in non-agricultural work live in cities. Their income varies widely depending on social interactions with the community—increasingly uncertain with the continued lockdown measures.

The government has already disbursed direct cash assistance (BLT), a temporary unconditional cash transfer program previously disbursed in

2005, 2008, and 2015 to help poor households cope with economic shocks. It will also restart its pre-employment training program and has extended its non-cash food assistance program (BPNT), its conditional cash transfer program (PKH), and another cash transfer program (BST) through the end of 2020.

These initiatives, though promising, have been plagued by unreliable data, making disbursement of assistance particularly challenging. A recent study by the SMERU Research Institute found that in one district surveyed, 20% of recipients listed should have been ineligible because they were either above the poverty line or deceased.[2] In another case of mistargeted funds, 1,500 beneficiaries received double the amount of social assistance because of duplicate entries in separate databases. As of July 2020, only 113 of 514 districts had updated their beneficiary data in the Integrated Social Welfare Database (DTKS).

To support the rapid expansion and long-term resilience of these social protection programs, the central government should prioritize investments in capacity building for program administration, especially for local governments. Increasing administrative capacity for data collection, entry, and verification at this critical time could improve targeting and delivery of benefits while also helping to refine the DTKS. This would enable the government to optimize coverage and help close the last-mile gap in poverty reduction.[3]

Increase Access to Water Supply, Sanitation, and Health Care

An estimated 30 million city residents—one in five—in Indonesia do not have access to handwashing facilities with soap and water. In Jakarta, poor households may already spend about 10% of their monthly income on bottled drinking water. For the millions who live in slum areas, the overcrowded, unsanitary conditions are kindling for a swift and sudden wildfire of disease.

As a short-term response, the government should provide water subsidies and temporary basic infrastructure for slum communities. In many neighborhoods, community groups have already set up handwashing

---

[2] D. F. Rahman. 2020. Data fiasco causes delays in disbursement of social assistance: Study. *The Jakarta Post*. 20 July.

[3] OECD. 2020. Social Protection System Review (SPSR) of Indonesia... in 60 seconds.

stations like those used to contain the 2014-2016 Ebola outbreak across West Africa. These can be equipped with foot pumps that activate the flow of water, preventing transmission from touching surfaces.

Supporting community-driven awareness and action is also increasingly critical, especially as people reduce visits to health centers. Many neighborhoods have already instated their own lockdown measures to limit travel. Governments could leverage this community mobilization and form systems for community health delivery and contact tracing in these hard-to-reach communities.[4]

The longer it takes to contain the virus, however, the more challenging it will be to ensure community compliance with handwashing, physical distancing, and face-covering regulations. To build long-term resilience, the central government should prioritize investments in water supply and sanitation as well as community health centers (*puskesmas*), where most of the urban poor receive primary health care. Economic incentives could help retain nurses and midwives while entrepreneurial models of community health delivery could increase the effectiveness of community health volunteers.[5] Investments in health care delivery and infrastructure at this critical time will also further the government's goals to reduce maternal mortality and deliver clean water and sanitation to households by 2024.

Whether through earthquakes or disease, history shows us that disasters present critical opportunities for transformative change in societies. Life-saving advancements in public health, such as water supply and sanitation systems, have sprung from the urgent need to curb outbreaks of infectious diseases.

Today, the COVID-19 crisis presents a pressing opportunity to rethink public health, infrastructure provision, and social protection systems. With an eye toward the future, we must find ways to make our cities more resilient without compromising the interdependence that holds our society—including the urban poor—together.

---

4   UNFPA. 2020. UNFPA Indonesia COVID-19 Response Situational Report 1 May–30 June.

5   D. Yanagizawa-Drott et al. 2020. An Entrepreneurial Model of Community Health Delivery in Uganda.

We Need Better Social Protection to Safeguard the Poor from COVID-19

Amir Jilani

As I write this blog post, a global pandemic has spread across countries and territories with daily reports of new cases and deaths. Although cases of COVID-19 are being reported in both developed and developing economies, many low-income economies in Asia and the Pacific continue to face bottlenecks in effectively diagnosing the virus. Consequently, understanding of the actual incidence and prevalence of COVID-19 infections in developing countries remains unclear.

Despite this uncertainty, we know that the COVID-19 crisis is devastating economies and leaving lasting scars across the developing world. We also know well from the region's past experiences that shocks hit poor and vulnerable groups the hardest and that these groups often take the longest to recover. To protect them effectively, governments can expand social protection, and especially social assistance, to provide vital support and strengthen resilience.

Before turning to the policy options available to governments, it is important to recognize that disease outbreaks have both direct and indirect impacts resulting from sickness, death, and preventive measures to contain the spread of the virus.

The direct economic impacts of sickness and death are higher costs and lower incomes for families affected by the virus. Rising health care costs coupled with lost wages and jobs can trigger spikes in poverty. Direct impacts also include a substantial increase in risk for vulnerable groups. Unlike a one-time shock, such as an earthquake, contagious health epidemics can quickly multiply, particularly in densely populated areas. This is precisely what happened in the case of Ebola, where researchers found that urban slums in

Liberia became hotspots for the spread of the disease, infecting 3.5 times as many people as those in less densely populated and richer neighborhoods. In developing Asia, many migrant workers similarly live in crowded dorms without access to health insurance, increasing the risk of infection and forcing others to return home.

Disease outbreaks also have indirect impacts, disrupting production and consumption across the economy. These impacts disproportionately affect poor workers and families, particularly in the informal sector. On the supply side, business closures (either due to government orders or firm decisions) affect workers' ability to earn wages. We have already seen such closures across most economies impacted by the virus. On the demand side, people are spending less. This is hurting workers in many sectors in developing countries, especially tourism which provides a vital source of income and sustains small businesses and communities with limited access to alternative livelihoods or social protection. In the food and agriculture sector, panic purchases, illness-related labor shortages, transport interruptions, and limited access to markets may break supply chains and cause localized price hikes or result in food loss and waste.

These channels of disruption and economic impact can translate into significant GDP losses for countries. According to ADB estimates, the potential economic impact of COVID-19 on Asia and the Pacific could range from $1.7 trillion to $2.5 trillion in lost output (or 6.2%–9.3% of regional GDP), with some countries experiencing larger GDP losses and certain sectors such as trade, tourism, and transport affected more than others early on.

So how can governments strengthen social protection to minimize the economic impact of COVID-19?

Poverty in Asia and the Pacific has fallen dramatically, but the region was still home to more than 264 million people living in extreme poverty in 2015 and 1.1 billion people living on less than $3.20 a day. Many of the region's governments have already been investing in social protection systems to mitigate chronic poverty, reduce vulnerability, and nurture inclusive growth. But in the face of the COVID-19 crisis, governments will need to radically expand social protection to cushion the shocks and combat both existing and new poverty. Based on promising global evidence, here are three ways that can do exactly that.

Strengthen social assistance. Expanding cash assistance can support poor and vulnerable households during a crisis. Temporary expansion of an existing program can be horizontal (adding more people) or vertical (increasing benefit amounts). In a crisis, it is also essential to disburse funds faster by setting up or strengthening digital payments and relaxing the eligibility criteria or conditions of existing programs that already have the cash delivery infrastructure in place.

In the Philippines, conditional cash transfer program beneficiaries will receive full grants without having to comply with program conditions (school attendance, health center visits) during the quarantine. Similarly, the Government of Pakistan undertook unprecedented steps to expand both horizontal and vertical coverage under the Ehsaas Emergency Cash program, providing an estimated 16.9 million families at risk of falling into extreme poverty (approximately half the country's population) with PRs12,000 (about $75) to meet subsistence requirements. Cash transfers have the double benefit of helping people in need while stimulating consumption, which in turn strengthens the economy. In expanding social assistance, governments should find effective ways to reach informal settlers and urban migrant workers, since these groups face unique challenges in terms of livelihoods and access to government services.

Provide social insurance. Unemployment insurance should be temporarily expanded by extending its duration, increasing benefits, or relaxing eligibility. Where paid sick leave is not offered by employers, governments may fund it to allow unwell workers and caregivers to stay home without losing their jobs. Measures such as emergency employment for informal sector workers and financial support to affected workers in private enterprises are now in place in the Philippines. Subsidizing health insurance to expand coverage and/or waiving fees may also become necessary to help the most vulnerable, including support to enterprises that serve these populations.

Upgrade labor market policies and programs. With COVID-19 likely to affect all workers, governments should review passive and active labor market policies and programs, including protective labor rules. Given the inevitable impact on workers in terms of temporary or permanent layoffs, governments need to think about ways to support workers in the short and medium term, including through job facilitation, training, and other interventions during and after the crisis. Although Europe's social policies and protection are often seen as too generous, they are shielding workers from some major disruptions caused by the virus.

Many of us will be feeling anxious about restrictions being implemented to limit the spread of COVID-19. But the millions of families who were already poor and vulnerable before this began will be facing impossible decisions about food, health care, and survival. More than ever in the face of this unprecedented crisis, we have a responsibility to act immediately and protect those most in need.

How to Protect Asia's Rapidly Aging Population from COVID-19

Meredith Wyse

COVID-19 has become a global health crisis with significant human costs that are rising at an alarming rate. The risks of this virus for older persons have been amply highlighted, with mortality rates increasing rapidly with age, especially for those with underlying chronic conditions. A study from the National Health Commission in the People's Republic of China (PRC), suggested that about 80% of people who died from the virus in the country were over the age of 60, and 75% had preexisting conditions.

People in Asia and the Pacific are rapidly aging: 58% of the global population, or 614 million persons, over the age of 60 years old live in the region. In many countries, more than half of older people are affected by underlying conditions, with the prevalence rising sharply with age. Many conditions, such as hypertension and diabetes, which increase complications of COVID-19, are undiagnosed. It is estimated over 60% of hypertensive cases and 30% of diabetic cases in India are not diagnosed, and poverty is strongly associated with a lack of diagnosis and treatment, increasing risks and complications in dealing with this pandemic.

Overstretched health services and nascent care systems in most Asian countries create substantial challenges for governments to address the needs of the at-risk populations in the region. Understanding the circumstances of older persons and designing specific actions in COVID-19 responses will be critical.

The design of COVID-19 response programs must recognize the situations and diversity of the older population. In the rush to protect older people we can overlook this. There is significant diversity in health status across all age groups, in the range of contributions made on a daily basis to their own families and the multiple roles they have in society as workers, carers, volunteers, and community leaders. That extends to the ability of older men and women to be resilient and withstand shocks. These differences need to be recognized to ensure older people are not discouraged from contributing to the collective response as well as ensuring that specific individual vulnerabilities are reduced.

Participation in the informal labor force for many older people is a necessity with approximately 40% of persons over 60 years old working in countries such as Bangladesh, the Philippines, and Viet Nam, increasing to 66% in Nepal. The widespread economic impact of the COVID-19 pandemic will also affect them. Social protection programs must recognize this and ensure initiatives to protect against economic shocks for informal workers include older people.

For people over the statutory retirement age in Asia and the Pacific, 55% currently receive a pension although the value is small compared with other regions. Countries without social pensions tend to have old-age poverty rates higher than average poverty rates. Expanding coverage of social pension schemes to reach older persons and injecting additional cash through these programs in response to this crisis can help.

This has already happened in Argentina, Colombia, and Peru. It particularly helps older women who are less likely to have other sources of income to take better preventive precautions, access health care if needed, and mitigate against a loss of income for themselves and those in their care. Often pensions are collected at designated communal pension points. Now is the time to ensure appropriate and safe distancing measures are implemented or alternative distribution channels are in place to facilitate older persons receiving their pensions.

Beyond the urgent strengthening of health systems and measures to ensure income security, aged care including social and community services serving older persons needs to be included in the response plans. The importance of focusing on these services is vividly demonstrated by the tragic infection cluster spikes in residents and staff in nursing homes reported in Australia, Italy, and the US, and reports of older people dying unattended in care homes in Spain.

Strong infection control protocols, testing and personal protective equipment, and other supplies are needed to protect staff and those in care. This needs to target residential facilities, such as nursing homes, care homes, and social welfare institutions, and organizations providing home and community services on which people rely on. Agencies responsible for overseeing care and other social services need to be supported and not overlooked in the response so they can ensure appropriate services are provided.

In Asia and the Pacific, as across the globe, most day-to-day care is provided by family members, often spouses and daughters. This makes up a significant portion of the care burden in households. Self-isolation is not an option when providing personal care, and even less so in larger households. Education on how to protect family caregivers and those they care for must be disseminated quickly and widely as well as access to testing, hygiene kits, and personal protective equipment secured. Additional financial support to allow family caregivers to stay home should be considered. Global practitioners and academics are pooling technical expertise and resources as well.

Every day we heard inspiring stories of how communities rallied together to ensure the well-being of all their members and governments from Thailand to India called on armies of volunteers to support over stretched services. Across the region there were many networks of community health workers and social and community-based organizations, such as older people's associations, often led by older persons themselves, which were mobilized to support these efforts.

Over the past months, older peoples associations in Shaanxi Province, PRC were involved in enforcing community quarantine measures and provided cleaning supplies and personal protective equipment to older persons. And in Viet Nam and Cambodia they delivered public health messages and food packages, especially to those living alone.

These organizations established systems to provide members of their community with basic needs, psychosocial assistance, and support plans if they fall ill. These and other community groups and organizations played a key role in ensuring communities stay socially connected, safe, and ensure that no one was left behind. Resources to build on their capacities, networks, and skills will help strengthen responses at the community level for those who are ill but not in need of hospital care.

Governments in the region are gradually adapting as they transition to aging societies. The COVID-19 crisis highlights the urgent need to strengthen programs and policies affecting older persons; the importance of developing targeted approaches in the areas of health care systems; income; and building on the strengths and assets of the community organizations which are already operating on the ground and serving this population.

Helping Women and Girls Survive COVID-19 and its Aftermath

Malika Shagazatova

With COVID-19 imposing new challenges on women and exacerbating the numerous other difficulties they already face in their daily lives, a gender-sensitive response is crucial to this global health emergency. So, what do we know about the impact of COVID-19 on women and what would a gender-sensitive response look like?

Historically, women played three key roles in households, communities, and societies—mothers, nurses, and teachers. This continues today as gender stereotypes prevail in our societies and they influence career choices made by women and men. The World Health Organization (WHO) estimates that women make up almost 70% of health care workers around the world. Moreover, women continue to make up the majority of health facility service staff (cleaning and housekeeping, laundry and food services).

These health care workers and service staff are on the front lines of the fight against COVID-19 and, as such, are at a greater risk of being infected. As highlighted in the recent report co-published by WHO and Women in Global Health (2019), women continue to be mostly engaged in the lowest-paying jobs, underrepresented in decision making and higher-paid roles, and the health care sector continues to exhibit systematic gender bias.

As we already know, women health care workers experience a different set of needs and challenges from those experienced by men. The problem is not simply in the lack of the essential products for women such as smaller-sized personal protective equipment and menstrual hygiene products, but rather the lack of understanding and accommodation of female workers' needs. Therefore, meaningful consultations with women health care workers to understand their needs and prepare for the challenges that they may face are essential for development of COVID-19 response programs.

We also know that many women around the world bear much of the responsibility for child and elderly care, and on average perform three times more unpaid care work than men. With offices being shut down, many women around the world are losing their jobs and income, as many of their professions prevent them from working remotely. As it generally takes longer for women to recover their income, they are at a greater risk.

On top of that, juggling domestic responsibilities and child and elderly care is a challenge in itself, but with schools shutting down, the pandemic exacerbates these challenges. With many women expected to take the responsibility for taking care of family members infected by COVID-19, these social and economic burdens will only be intensified. There are other numerous challenges that arise during a global health emergency. Much of the research shows an increase in domestic violence associated with isolation and lockdowns.

There are other numerous challenges that arise during a global health emergency. Much of the research shows an increase in domestic violence associated with the isolation especially during a period of increased amount of stress. With the pandemic presenting more challenges, victims of gender-based violence may be unable to receive the life-saving care and treatment, report such cases, or even escape, as hospitals, police stations, and other institutions are overburdened with handling cases related to the virus or not operating.

In its 2018 report, the United Nations Children's Fund (UNICEF) highlighted that women and children are at greater risk of exploitation and sexual abuse during public health outbreaks, as was seen during the Ebola outbreak in West Africa. With more governments implementing lockdowns, we must pay attention to the sex-disaggregated data when developing a gender-sensitive response.

The decision makers need to be mindful of gender issues and ensure that they are considered as we seek solutions in response to, and recovery from, the COVID-19 pandemic. It is clear that pandemics worsen existing inequalities experienced by women and girls. As such, there is a need for immediate solutions and policies that will prevent the worsening of gender inequalities and widening of the gender gap.

Women and Girls Need Targeted Assistance

For starters, ongoing problems and issues experienced by women health care workers need to be addressed. At a minimum, women caregivers and frontline responders should be provided proper personal protective equipment, including feminine hygiene products for those working longer shifts. Additionally, during this pandemic, it is crucial that women and girls have access to adequate maternal and pediatric care, reproductive health services, and essential information.

Moreover, as more women continue to lose their jobs and steady sources of income as a result of the pandemic, it is critical that necessary targeted support is provided to ensure food security to prevent these vulnerable individuals from succumbing to negative coping mechanisms. And last but not least, the issue of increasing incidents of gender-based violence which have been reported by many countries is vital to be addressed.

Some countries have recently introduced policies and special measures to address this phenomenon including by introducing alternative reporting mechanisms, remote services delivered through mobile phone or messaging apps, and supporting shelters for gender-based violence survivors. It is crucial to continue developing and adapting such measures to ensure that the most vulnerable receive necessary support.

As policies and recovery plans are developed, it is imperative that long-term targeted economic and gender empowerment strategies are embedded to mitigate the impact of this pandemic and future outbreaks. To do so, data related to the outbreak must be disaggregated by sex, age, and other criteria, to accurately reflect the different challenges in different demographics arising from the pandemic.

Policy makers need to be mindful of ways to support further economic development and post-pandemic recuperation. Lastly, as more small businesses collapse and demand for informal work arrangements decreases, women will continue losing financial independence, affecting their empowerment in the short term, with potential longer-term impacts on children's schooling (particularly for girls). This could result in adverse effects on female labor force participation for the next generation.

Providing support through targeted social assistance schemes for women during this pandemic and ensuring women's access to finance is pivotal for a speedy recovery and long-term economic and social improvements. In the efforts to restore the economy, the inspiration should be to use this opportunity and develop a socioeconomic system that is capable of delivering gender parity.

The Informal Sector Needs Financial Support

Junkyu Lee and Arup Chatterjee

COVID-19 has attacked societies at their core, as it threatens to swamp health care and economic systems. Governments in Asia and the Pacific are quickly introducing a series of measures to help workers and small and medium-sized enterprises (SMEs) to cope with the lockdowns and other disruptions, but this is proving difficult in the informal sector.

In a region where on average 70% of the employment is informal, the financial impact of COVID-19 on poor households is enormous. Many in the sector are domestic workers, street vendors, rickshaw pullers, small farmers, fishers, and landless laborers. They are hit hardest by the crisis.

Governments have limited levers at their disposal for mitigating the negative impact of the COVID-19 pandemic on the informal sector compared to the formal sector. Yet, failure to help informal workers and businesses can reverse a decade of hard-won progress in reducing poverty in the region. Innovative ways of extending financial support to the sector is urgently needed.

Social Protection for the Most Vulnerable

Cash transfers for sustenance. Informal sector workers slog away without any written contract, paid leave, minimum wages, and access to social safety nets. Most face "no work, no pay" conditions, and with joblessness extended over several days, they are in imminent fear of slipping below the poverty line.

Emergency cash transfers to the vulnerable sector should form an essential component of COVID-19 relief packages. It should provide the flexibility to respond to the immediate financial needs of the informal workers, including families below the poverty line, women, senior citizens, and people with disabilities.

India is among the few countries that is better placed to successfully roll out direct benefit transfers with its digital national identity card, *Aadhaar*. The key elements to make payments work include a universal digital identity system to authenticate a person linked to socioeconomic data on households, a bank account to receive money, and a mobile phone to access cash. In one of the largest-ever cash transfers, the Indian government last April disbursed $3.9 billion to the bank accounts of more than 320 million individuals.

In the Philippines, conditional cash transfers are credited to the cash cards of beneficiaries, which can be used for cashless purchases of groceries and medicines through point-of-sale machines at cashiers or check-out counters.

The electronic transfer of funds is generally faster, cheaper, safer, and more secure than in-person cash distribution. Given the digital divide and infrastructure gap in the region, most countries are deploying a combination of conventional methods for delivery like in-person cash transfer, branchless banking, and digital technology. With the demonstration effects of the success of e-payments, this is an opportune time to nudge governments to switch to digital payments.

Social assistance. Lack of adequate social security has exacerbated economic insecurity among poor households. The stimulus packages also include wage support to low-income workers, unemployment benefits, and discounts on food and utility payments. Some governments have also provided social pension advances to senior citizens, widows, and persons with disabilities.

Health insurance. In countries where universal health insurance exists, testing and treatment for COVID-19 are now covered. The governments of Bangladesh, India, Indonesia, and Nepal have provided life and health insurance coverage to frontline health workers, including sanitation staff, paramedics, nurses, and community health workers. However, universal insurance coverage is inadequate for informal workers in terms of out-of-pocket expenditure, availability, accessibility of services, quality, and financial sustainability. The COVID-19 pandemic is a timely reminder of the importance of investing in health care and social protection for the informal sector.

Financial Support for Microenterprises

Microenterprises are disproportionately affected as business orders are stalled by restrictions on mobility, delays in payments, and pricing distortions. They urgently need a mix of financial aid and loans to restart production and services and resume cash flows.

Commercial banks and nonbank financial institutions regard lending to the informal sector as risky due to their inability to furnish collateral and expensive due to the small size of loans. Uncertainty and increasing delinquencies have also shaken the ability and confidence of microfinance institutions to finance them, as they need to manage liquidity and honor commitments to their funders.

Governments need to come up with creative solutions and enable the adoption of financial technologies to assist microenterprises in pursuing their income-generating activities. For example, authorities can set up a pandemic grant stabilization facility to provide urgent financial support to microenterprises with digital access tools using financial technologies to enhance transparency. Coordinated policy responses that can help in garnering complementary social assistance funding from local governments can also be useful to support business activities in the informal sector.

Equity Considerations in Post-Crisis Fiscal Responses

The real impact of the crisis will depend on the duration of the lockdowns as well as the effectiveness of policy responses for mitigation. Due attention is needed for the risks and equity implications of reducing the economic vulnerability of informal workers. Research and evidence suggest that the crisis will likely deepen poverty and income inequality, especially among vulnerable groups, while proper response mechanisms including credit availability to the vulnerable sector affect income distribution. Without tailored actions, income gaps are bound to widen, resulting in a larger economic cost in the future. Asian governments therefore must leverage on the COVID-19 momentum to make rapid progress toward collectively financed, comprehensive, and reliable social protection systems for the informal sector.

Strings Attached: Financial Education Is Needed to Judge Pandemic Assistance

Arup Kumar Chatterjee

COVID-19 has created an overwhelming sense of uncertainty about health, jobs, and finances. Sustaining livelihoods and servicing financial commitments are principal concerns after the sudden loss of income in the aftermath of disruptions in agriculture, industrial, and services sectors. Economic pressure arising from sickness, disrupted schooling and unemployment due to layoffs, furloughs, and job losses are forcing people to adjust their spending, defer payment of rentals and loan installments, and seek new loans or even financial assistance.

Governments and central banks have unleashed several stimulus measures to keep businesses afloat, protect jobs, and cushion economies, though many of them encourage more lending rather than bail out the already indebted borrowers.

Financially stressed households and small businesses are making critical financial decisions, often without adequately weighing the pros and cons based on financial knowledge of their options. Due to a lack of awareness and low financial literacy levels, many are likely to regret their decisions once the pandemic subsides. Many will face increased unsecured household debt.

The responsibility for prudent financial decisions is increasingly being transferred from government to individuals. Some of the financial choices facing families and trades during the pandemic involve programs such as:

- *Emergency cash transfers* by governments offer a rapid and cost-effective means to recover and rebuild after the crisis. It is a one-time benefit for a specific period. The decision to divide the money received between immediate and long-term needs lies with the recipients based on their individual circumstances.

- *Government guarantee-backed schemes* include business loans, overdrafts, and additional credit for eligible individuals and firms. Since these are not grants, even with backstop, banks remain cautious and are reluctant to take on additional risks. Financial knowledge can help businesses understand the eligibility conditions.

- *Deferred interest options* are not financially prudent, even though postponement does not affect the credit standing of individuals and enterprises who enjoyed good standing before COVID-19. If the balance remains unpaid, either partially or fully, at the end of the period, interest is chargeable on the entire original balance after backdating. With mortgages, there is negative amortization, with the loan's principal balance increasing because of deferred interest. As a result, borrowers will either be paying more in the long run or carrying the risk of increased monthly installments once payments resume.

- *Deferred repayment on loans and lines of business credit* needs careful examination. In the case with the former, interest continues to accrue with the deferred payment amount added to the end of the loan. For credit lines, interest continues to accrue and is added to the principal balance when the deferral period ends. Extended payoff periods will increase costs to the consumer. And even with no adverse credit reporting, some lenders may view a deferred account as risky (though it might still be better than a late payment).

- *Extensions to trade finance and working capital loans* help manage cash and liquidity by enabling stock to be held for longer to customers with a sound track record. Financial education can help companies understand the terms of their credit facilities, their ability to access capital, avoid being in default, and address financial covenants' related issues. Defaults in payment of principal and interest under the loan or under any specified material agreements can deny a company access to a credit facility due to the acceleration of outstanding debt.

- *Withdrawal of a specific portion of the pension and provident funds* recognizes that accessing some of the savings today may outweigh the benefits of maintaining them until retirement. However, accessing retirement savings should happen under extenuating circumstances, and people should only withdraw what they need. Financial awareness can explain why retirement savings need to grow over the long term. By taking out more than what is necessary now, they might miss an opportunity for future growth, thus undermining their post-retirement incomes.

- *Deferring insurance premium payments and premium loans* is not without consequence. Not all insurance policies will be eligible for this insurance premium deferment. The policy holder will continue to be covered under the insurance policy during this period and still be able to make claims should the need arise. However, the outstanding premiums need to be paid in full before the deferment period ends to prevent policy and coverage lapse.

Governments and financial institutions are also prioritizing digital channels and platforms as they grapple with the logistical challenges of delivering financial services to consumers and businesses through digital devices. Online apps are handling a growing volume of government-to-person (G2P) payments, money transfers, mobile payments, remittances, insurance, and investments safely and securely.

E-commerce and social media platforms are slowly being integrated into the life of everyday consumers and small businesses for business-to-business (B2B) and business-to-consumer (B2C) commerce. In some cases, this is excluding vulnerable populations, such as those without access to technology, women, the elderly, the disabled, and people in remote areas.

Digital financial literacy, along with consumer protection, should accompany the "digital first" push. This should include helping them avoid excessive borrowing, mis-selling, and financial abuse related to pandemic fears. Discrimination, unauthorized use of data, and fraud such as phishing and hacking should also be avoided.

To address these concerns, financial education needs to include concepts like credit rating, debt accumulation, mortgage borrowing, retirement savings, risk diversification, data security, financial planning, and wealth accumulation for crisis-proofing of a person's financial future.

Governments and financial institutions should prioritize financial education for young people, women, and the less educated as they offer financial assistance and digital solutions to consumers. Financial literacy should become a graduation requirement for high school in the times ahead.

5. Ensuring Food Security and Sustainable Agriculture

Photos on previous page: [From the top] Many of the world's food producers are struggling to get their products to market during the pandemic; Throughout Asia, countries are grappling with food supply disruptions and other challenges brought about by COVID-19 (photo by Debbie Molle); Digital solutions are offering new ways to produce and distribute food (photo by Omer Rana).

COVID-19 Highlights the Need for Safe, Nutritious, and Affordable Food

Akmal Siddiq

Global hunger and malnutrition have been rising for the past 5 years. Lockdowns imposed to combat the coronavirus pandemic have disrupted the local and international food trade, as well as production and distribution. Tens of millions of urban and migrant workers have lost their jobs, many perhaps permanently—pushing them into a hunger trap.

Efforts to end hunger and malnutrition (Sustainable Development Goal 2) now seem in jeopardy. Even after full lockdowns are relaxed, continued disruption in food production and distribution will likely increase consumer prices. With lost livelihoods for tens of millions of households, increased food insecurity and malnutrition will become a grim reality without focused measures to support food production and marketing.

Food insecurity and malnutrition should have been headline news before the COVID-19 pandemic. Despite impressive economic growth in Asia and the Pacific over the past 4 decades, endemic food insecurity and malnutrition have persisted. The number of people living in extreme poverty (under $1.90 a day) declined from 53% in 1990 to about 9% in 2013. Still, 326 million people lived below the poverty line. Poverty is inextricably linked to food insecurity, and accordingly the number of food-insecure people in the region has remained high.

Feeding these hungry and malnourished millions is a daunting challenge. Malnutrition affects people of all ages—ranging from severe undernutrition to obesity—but children bear the heaviest burden. Over 86 million, or 25% of children younger than five years old suffer from stunting, and 34 million children are wasting. A further 12 million suffer from acute malnutrition with high risk of death. The income penalty of stunting amounts to 7%–10% of

GDP in the region. But governments allocate only 1% of public expenditure for nutrition programs.

The widespread loss of employment and income triggered by the COVID-19 pandemic will make the situation much worse.

Take the example of unsafe food. Even before the COVID-19 pandemic, the impact of unsafe food on human health was staggering. In 2018, the WHO estimated that globally over 600 million fall ill and 420,000 die every year after eating contaminated food. Children under five years old carry 40% of the foodborne disease burden with 125,000 deaths every year. If loss in employment and disruptions in food production and distribution continue and safe food becomes even harder to find for poor communities, this toll of sickness and death could escalate in the COVID-19 era.

There's no easy fix for these pressing challenges. But there is a single step, albeit a large one, that will have immediate beneficial impacts on the region's food security.

Governments need to devote at least as much attention to the rural sector as they do to their urban communities. Rural development and the farm sector have been largely neglected in most of the region. The resulting underinvestment has taken a significant toll on the agriculture sector, and on the food security and health status of societies.

Smallholder farmers provide 80% of the region's food. When they do not make a profit, they cannot invest in modern technology and higher quality inputs. As a result, farm productivity across the region is low, cost of production is high, and consumers pay higher prices.

Poor quality and contaminated food undermine public health. Malnourished people have weak immune systems, making them more vulnerable to diseases like COVID-19. This vicious cycle can only be broken by focused government attention at senior policy making levels.

What can governments do to help farmers produce safe, nutritious, and affordable food in the region?

The first priority is to provide smallholders with access to quality seeds, fertilizers, and pesticides. Often, these are not available on time and are adulterated. Governments either do not have adequate quality and safety regulations or do not enforce them. Three actions will bring significant improvements: (i) expand smallholders access to input financing, especially for women; (ii) improve marketing of key inputs by easing constraints on imports and distribution; and (iii) improve compliance with quality standards, especially for seeds and chemicals.

Second, the region desperately needs functional markets for perishables and nutritious food such as fruits and vegetables, meat, fish, eggs, and dairy. Post-harvest losses amount to 30%–40% of production due to a lack of cold chain facilities and proper market infrastructure.

In the short term, governments should improve hygiene and compliance with food quality standards at existing wholesale markets. In the medium term, there's a need for investments in modern wholesale and retail market infrastructure through public–private partnerships. An ADB study estimates that in order to achieve SDG 2 in Asia and the Pacific, annual investments in agricultural research and development, market infrastructure, irrigation, and water use efficiency must increase from the current $42 billion to as much as $79 billion. Given the unfolding toll of COVID-19 on the food sector, this investment requirement will be even higher.

The third way governments can head off pandemic-induced food shortages is to improve their own capacities. Ministries dealing with agriculture in most governments are sometimes the weakest link in the system. Their capacity to make evidence-based policies require significant |improvement immediately.

Due to COVID-19, unemployed urban migrant workers are heading home to rural areas. It's safer there, as social distancing is easier in households with larger living spaces than in cramped urban communities. Improved rural development and profitable farming will also generate plentiful non-farm jobs. Increased income in rural areas will also generate higher demand for city jobs. The pandemic is a threat, but also an opportunity to reap dividends as workers return to farms and rural areas—but only if governments invest more in agriculture and rural development and take helpful and decisive policy actions.

Decent on- and off-farm rural incomes and jobs will deliver safe, nutritious, and affordable food that societies—especially poor communities—and economies need to survive and thrive in the COVID-19 era.

Keeping Asia and the Pacific Fed during the Pandemic

Kijin Kim, Sunae Kim, and Cyn-Young Park

The COVID-19 pandemic has raised food security risks in Asia and the Pacific as lockdowns and export restrictions have affected food supply chains.

The pandemic is hitting the entire food value chain from farm to fork (Figure 5.1). Farms and small and medium-sized agricultural businesses face labor shortages due to lockdown measures and a decline in migrant workers. Transporting harvests quickly to markets has become a challenge as well. Large amounts of unsold seasonal vegetables and fruits have been wasted in farms as restaurants, hotels, and schools have been shut down.

While disruptions in food production, processing, and distribution caused farm-gate prices to fall for perishable products, retail prices of staple food, fresh vegetables, and fruits rose sharply due to panic buying (at least temporarily) and higher transportation costs. Altogether, they are adversely affecting consumers' choice of food and posing immediate threats to food security for the poor and vulnerable.

The sudden closure of borders, and trade restrictions, add strain on food security for import-dependent countries. The retail prices of rice and wheat have risen sharply in several developing economies in the region as more than 20 countries including major rice and wheat exporters in Asia have adopted temporary trade restrictions to stabilize domestic food supply.

Across the region, the pandemic has turned a spotlight on stark inequalities and its impact on the most vulnerable. The pandemic-induced economic slowdown has already dealt a devastating blow to vulnerable jobs in developing countries in Asia. According to the ILO, Asia and the Pacific—where 7 in 10 workers are employed informally—suffered the greatest

Figure 5.1: Lockdown Impact on Food Supply Chain

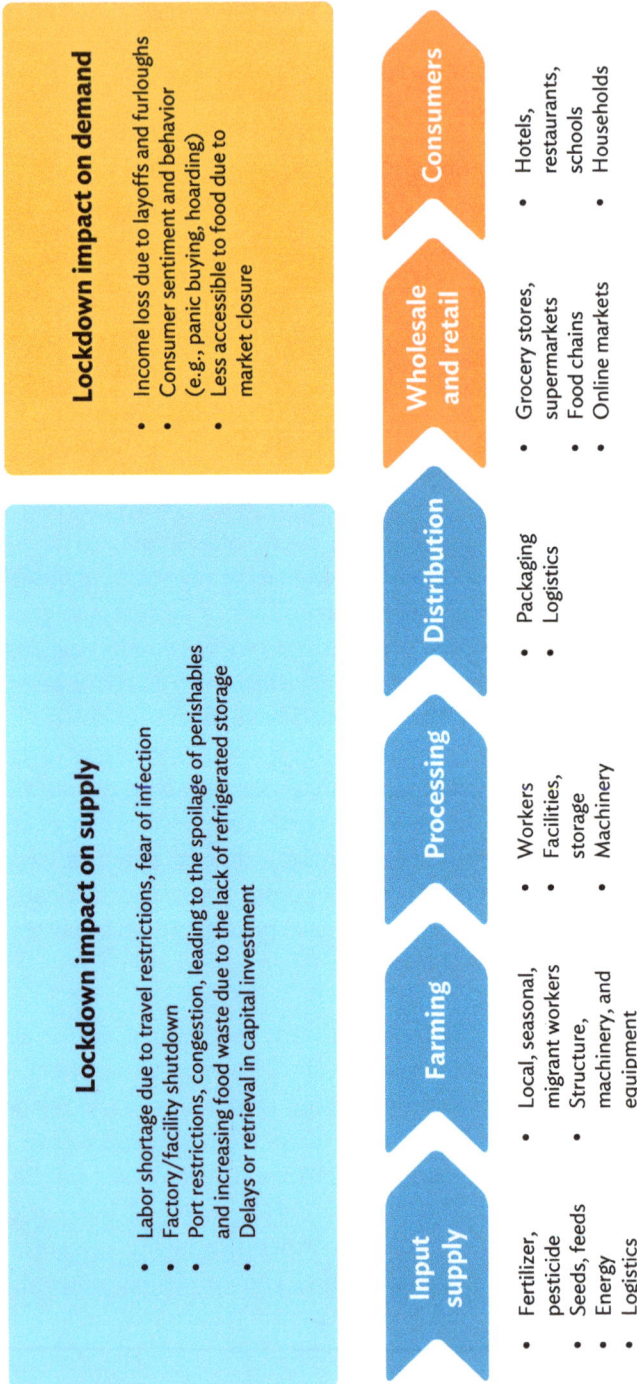

Lockdown impact on supply

- Labor shortage due to travel restrictions, fear of infection
- Factory/facility shutdown
- Port restrictions, congestion, leading to the spoilage of perishables and increasing food waste due to the lack of refrigerated storage
- Delays or retrieval in capital investment

Lockdown impact on demand

- Income loss due to layoffs and furloughs
- Consumer sentiment and behavior (e.g., panic buying, hoarding)
- Less accessible to food due to market closure

Input supply	Farming	Processing	Distribution	Wholesale and retail	Consumers
• Fertilizer, pesticide • Seeds, feeds • Energy • Logistics	• Local, seasonal, migrant workers • Structure, machinery, and equipment	• Workers • Facilities, storage • Machinery	• Packaging • Logistics	• Grocery stores, supermarkets • Food chains • Online markets	• Hotels, restaurants, schools • Households

Source: Authors.

impact in terms of lost working hours (Figure 5.2). There was an estimated 7.2% reduction in working hours or an equivalent of 125 million full-time jobs lost in the second quarter.

A particular concern is the nutrition status of those most exposed and vulnerable to the COVID-19 crisis. As schools close due to the pandemic, school meal programs have been suspended, significantly affecting low-income children's access to healthy and balanced diets. Pregnant women, lactating mothers, and young children should have access to micronutrient-rich food such as fresh vegetables, fruits, fish, and milk, but those foods are highly perishable, thus more vulnerable to supply chain disruptions.

Figure 5.2: Informal Employment
(% total employment, latest available years)

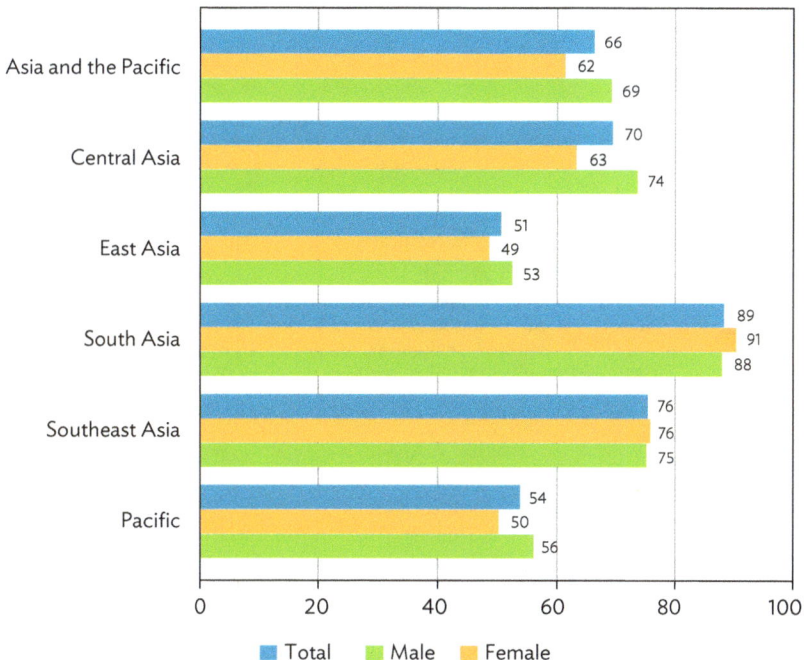

Region	Total	Female	Male
Asia and the Pacific	66	62	69
Central Asia	70	63	74
East Asia	51	49	53
South Asia	89	91	88
Southeast Asia	76	76	75
Pacific	54	50	56

Legend: ■ Total ■ Male ■ Female

Note: Employment figures include both agriculture and non-agriculture activities.
Source: International Labour Organization. ILOSTAT. https://www.ilo.org/ilostat/ (accessed May 2020).

Compared to the 2007–2008 food crisis when poor harvests drove the global prices of major cereal crops significantly higher, international prices of rice and wheat have not risen to alarming levels (Table 5.1). Driven largely by disruptions in food supply chains and trade restrictions, the current food security concern can be broadly manageable as long as the pandemic can be effectively contained soon. Stock-to-use ratios of rice and wheat, which measure the extent of downward pressure on prices have remained well above 2007–2008 food crisis levels for the past several years (Figure 5.3). Policy responses to COVID-19 in Asia's developing countries have so far focused more on social protection and production support than on banning food exports.

Table 5.1: Major Factors Contributing to Higher Food Prices in the 2007–2008 Food Crisis and the COVID-19 Pandemic

	Food Price Crisis, 2007–2008	COVID-19 Pandemic (2020, as of 22 May)
Main factors	• **Supply:** Poor harvests, lower grain stocks, higher oil prices ($86/barrel on average; 2007–2008) • **Demand:** Rapid growth of global economy, inflation, crop (maize) demand for biofuels • **Policies:** Export bans and restrictions, lowering import tariffs, restocking • **Other:** Weak United States dollars	• **Supply:** Lockdowns and movement restrictions create logistics problems, low energy prices ($39 on average, Jan-Apr 2020) • **Demand:** Panic buying • **Policies:** Export bans and restrictions
Trade restrictions	• Adopted by 33 countries • Share in world market of calories: 19% • On rice: 17 countries including CAM, PRC, IND, INO, PAK, THA, and VIE. • On wheat: 13 countries including RUS, KAZ, PRC, UKR, and ARG • On maize: 6 countries including IND, PRC, and UKR	• Adopted by 22 countries (13 are active) • Share in world market of calories: 5% • On rice: 3 countries (VIE, CAM, MYA) • On wheat: 6 countries including RUS, KAZ, and UKR
Food policies in Asian developing countries	• Total number of policies: 132 (35 in 2007 → 97 in 2008) • Consumer-oriented: 20% (22% → 19%) • Producer-oriented: 43% (53% → 39%) • Trade-related: 34% (17% → 40%) • Macroeconomic: 4% (18% → 2%)	• Total number of policies: 153 • Consumer-oriented: 42% • Producer-oriented: 45% • Trade-related: 8% • Macroeconomic: 5%

ARG = Argentina, CAM = Cambodia, PRC = People's Republic of China, IND = India, INO = Indonesia, KAZ = Kazakhstan, MYA = Myanmar, PAK = Pakistan, RUS = Russian Federation, THA = Thailand, UKR = Ukraine, VIE = Viet Nam.
Note: Average oil prices are calculated using West Texas Intermediate spot prices; Consumer-oriented policies mainly include social protection, market management, and nutrition and health assistance; Producer-oriented policies mainly include production support and market management.
Source: Wiggins, Keats, and Compton (2010); Laborde and Parent (2020); Food and Agriculture Policy Decision Analysis database (accessed May 2020).

Figure 5.3: World Stock-to-Use Ratio and Prices of Rice and Wheat

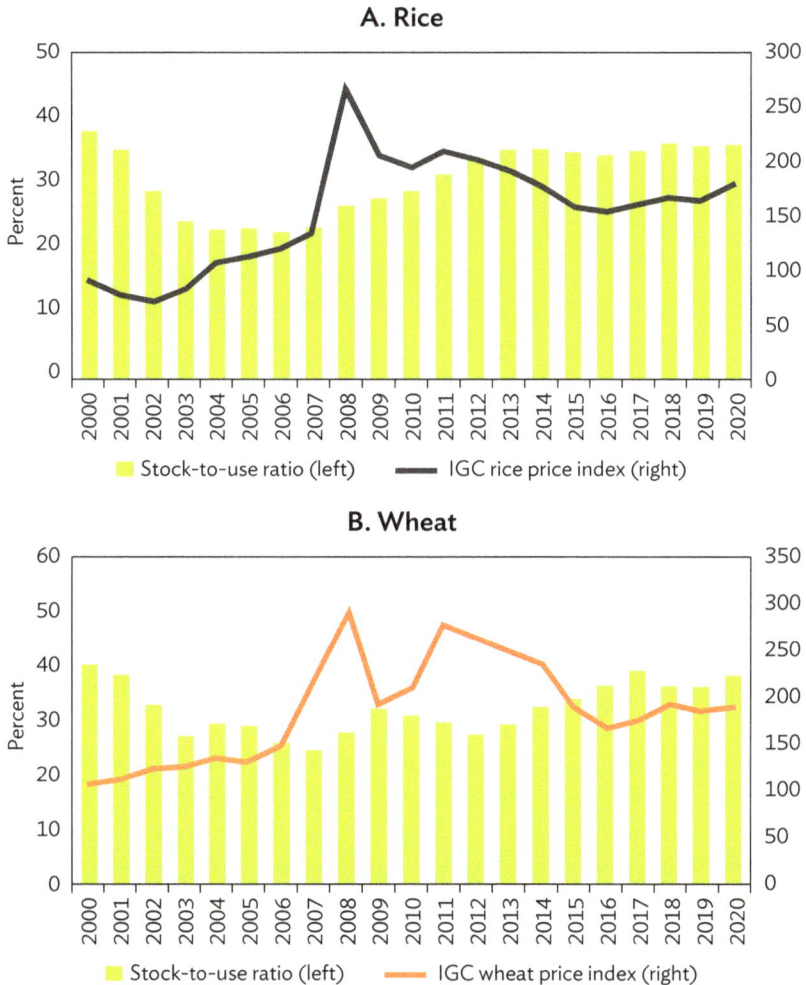

A. Rice

Stock-to-use ratio (left)   IGC rice price index (right)

B. Wheat

Stock-to-use ratio (left)   IGC wheat price index (right)

FAO = Food and Agriculture Organization of the United Nations, IGC =International Grains Council, USDA = United States Department of Agriculture.
Prices for 2020 are averages of January–July 2020; Stock-to-use ratios for 2020 are projections as of 2 July 2020.
Sources: FAO Agriculture Market Information System (see http://www.amis-outlook.org/amis-about/en/); International Grains Council, USDA PSD Production, Supply and Distribution (accessed in July 2020).

Current low energy prices will also keep the likelihood of food price inflation low. However, economic slowdowns and rising job and income losses will inevitably hit vulnerable countries and communities hard, leading to deterioration of people's real income. Further, should the lockdowns be extended, shortages of labor and input supplies could also reduce the scale of crop production. Prolonged disruptions in food supply chains and higher costs in logistics would also limit smallholder farmers' choices of better-priced markets, negatively affecting farm incomes.

Swift, bold, and innovative policy interventions are needed to secure food supply chains and mitigate the immediate impact of the crisis on the most vulnerable groups. Effective policy interventions should be comprehensive, covering a wide range from protecting consumers and public health, securing supply chains for producers, fair labor, trade, macroeconomic policies, and regional cooperation.

First and foremost, the authorities should increase coverage, relax eligibility criteria, and enhance the benefits of social protection programs such as food transfer schemes so that vital support reaches the poorest of the poor and the most vulnerable.

Immediate support should be also provided to enhance smallholder farmers' access to markets, for example, by arranging food transportation. During lockdown, farmers have difficulties in locating the markets they can access. Even when they know, it is challenging to arrange transportation.

In the same context, it is critical to provide financial relief and liquidity support to farmers, agri-businesses, and food processors who fall under financial stress due to COVID-19. Many governments in the region have been rolling out fiscal measures aimed at cushioning the immediate impact on farmers, agri-firms, and other stakeholders along the food supply chain by providing loans and subsidies for working capital and allowing for debt rescheduling or restructuring under immediate liquidity stress.

Lessons from the 2007–2008 food crisis have taught the region's policy makers to be more careful this time not to impose trade restrictions on food and not to turn a health crisis into a food crisis. Enhanced regional cooperation mechanisms such as the ASEAN+3 Emergency Rice Reserve also help strengthen the food supply safety net.

Post-COVID-19 agriculture sector reforms should support a transition from a labor-intensive supply chain to a more resilient and efficient agriculture system, including smart agriculture and mechanization. Such a transition will help mitigate the impacts of climate change, environmental degradation, and shrinking natural resources on food security.

Wider adoption of agricultural technology such as remote sensing and geographic information system-based land and soil management will be needed to address long-lasting constraints to scaling up of agricultural production capacity with enhanced productivity, including lack of financing or public–private cooperation, cumbersome regulatory environments, and incoherence of policies across various economic sectors.

The COVID-19 crisis should be used as an opportunity for developing economies to initiate or start implementing long-sought agricultural reforms. A recent move by India may be a good example: India announced in May 2020 a long-awaited plan that deregulates the production, supply, distribution, and prices of key food commodities to help provide price assurance for farmers, and allow farmers to freely choose the market.

A shift toward digital agriculture and mechanization may accelerate in the post-COVID era, and Asia's developing countries will need to cope with this new environment to make the agriculture sector more competitive.

How COVID-19 Could Accelerate the Digitization of the Food Supply Chain

Qingfeng Zhang and Jan Hinrichs

The coronavirus outbreak has acted as a catalyst for an inevitable long-term trend: the increasing role of digital technology in the supply chain revolution.

Lockdowns across the world in the wake of COVID-19 have not only restricted people's movement but also their access to traditional sources of food. This has prompted the search for alternatives, especially in urban centers.

Consumption patterns have had to change, with consumers seeking out reliable food delivery services, as they try to shorten the supply chain and cut out bottlenecks. An Indian online grocery platform has moved to a community selling model where it is asking apartment complexes to put orders together for their residents. This helps the company meet consumers' demand despite having a smaller-than-usual workforce.

Out of town, farmers, seed and fertilizer suppliers, as well as food wholesalers and distributors have turned to online platform services as distribution and marketing channels. E-commerce and other smart logistic fulfillment services have been helpful in matching supply and demand for agricultural produce. As a result of lockdown restrictions, vegetables were being discarded by farmers in the Malaysian Cameron Highlands. An e-commerce platform connected vegetable farmers to last-mile delivery service providers and consumers in Kuala Lumpur.

With social distancing and quarantine measures not likely to be going away any time soon, food supply chains require further digital innovations to be ready.

The food value chain for staple commodities (rice, wheat, corn, soybeans) is less sensitive to labor shortages from movement restrictions. But the logistics in distributing the commodities from farms to consumers is heavily affected by such restrictions.

High-value commodities (fruits, vegetables, and livestock products) are perishable and sensitive to labor shortages at the production level on farms and in sorting, packaging, and processing. Besides the movement restrictions, limited labor availability can quickly derail these supply chains. A vivid example is the closure of meat processing plants in the US and Europe due to COVID-19 cases among staff.

In the PRC, disruptions to the flow of seeds, fertilizers, and temporary labor for the spring planting season threatened farming productivity. Regular distribution channels were disrupted at retail and wholesale points and hit by plummeting demand from shutdown of restaurants and canteens. Thanks to several policies targeted at keeping "green channels" open, overall food prices and availability remained stable. However, there have been shortages in some locations where lockdown measures resulted in large amounts of unsellable seasonal vegetables and fruits backlogged or even unpicked in farms.

E-commerce enterprises developed dedicated agricultural product or labor platforms, which helped reduce the mismatch of supply and demand in countries throughout the region. Thai durian was sold through an e-commerce platform to customers in the PRC during lockdown in Thailand.

Digitization has also helped to set up and optimize the logistics and fulfillment services required for distributing food during COVID-19 disruptions. At locked-down urban communities, COVID-19 has accelerated the trend toward the use of online platforms for food purchases.

In remote rural areas, digital infrastructure plays a critical role, making food accessible and reducing the risk of food perishing. Farmers with online marketing skills and simple food products that do not need complex processing and packaging have been able to sell their products directly to consumers. Most interventions have been targeted at delivering packaged food from retail outlets to consumers.

In some cases, this has shortened food supply chains for high-value commodities that are perishable and very sensitive to any movement restrictions. Digitally connected farms, farmer cooperatives, sorting, packaging, and processing enterprises have been able to connect directly to consumers through online platforms, shared sale points, and smart logistics.

Individual small-scale farmers cannot be expected to attend to production management issues and at the same time specialize in online marketing of their food products. A recent study among farmers in Southeast Asia and East Asia has shown that only a small fraction of farmers with smartphones are using dedicated e-commerce applications.

But giving farmers access to e-commerce requires support to standardize production, organize the farmers, and build logistics capacity in remote areas. The private sector has a comparative advantage in expanding and adapting e-commerce and other platforms into food supply chains.

Free two-way flow of information with direct feedback loops about food characteristics such as price, safety, and origin of production is essential for an effective food supply chain.

There is no doubt that digitization has helped improve existing supply chains and catalyzed supply chain restructuring. However, key enterprises and supportive government policies are the drivers for the evolution of food supply chains to be more robust to restrictions such as COVID-19.

More investment is needed in public sector food safety and quality certification to service decentralized and digitally connected food value chains. Investments into a more digitally connected and decentralized food processing supply chain with linkage to alternative logistics providers would increase resilience.

Only with further investments into cold chain logistics, warehouses, packaging, and processing capacity closer to production areas can we reap the benefits from digitization. Urban consumers would benefit from increased resilience of the food chain while rural areas would be provided services and income opportunities.

6. Building Resilient Trade and Supply Chains

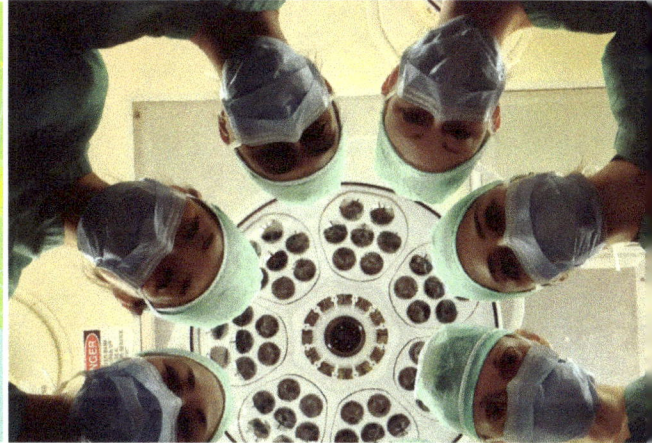

Photos on previous page: [Top] During the pandemic, the supply chains that move medical goods and keep the world fed are under duress (photo by iStock). [Bottom] There is a global struggle underway to get protective gear to medical staff and frontline workers.

Stringency of Containment Measures: Spillovers and Sectoral Effects through Trade and Production Linkages

Abdul Abiad, Mia Arao, Editha Lavina, Reizle Platitas, Jesson Pagaduan, and Christian Jabagat

Most global and regional analyses of COVID-19's economic impact apply same-sized shocks to pandemic-affected economies. In Abiad et al. (2020), country-specific information on outbreak severity, stringency of containment measures, and declines in mobility outside the home are used to calibrate the size of domestic demand declines that result.[1] Estimated domestic demand and external demand shocks—where the latter includes both tourism shocks and outbreak-induced declines in domestic demand in many of the world's economies—are fed through ADB's Multi-Region Input–Output Tables (ADB MRIOT) to capture spillovers through trade and production linkages. ADB MRIOT captures all domestic and international sectoral linkages across 62 economies (which account for 90% of global GDP), with each economy disaggregated into 35 sectors. We assess the impact of the pandemic economy-wide and by sector, under both a shorter-containment and a longer-containment scenario and present the summary of the impact assessment here.

Links between Containment Stringency, Reduced Mobility, and Economic Activity

Data on outbreak severity, proxied by COVID-19 cases per million people, comes from the COVID-19 Dashboard of Johns Hopkins University.[2] The stringency of various containment policies—including school and workplace closures, travel and transport bans, stay-at-home requirements,

---

[1] A. Abiad et al. 2020. "The Impact of COVID-19 on Developing Asian Economies: The Role of Outbreak Severity, Containment Stringency, and Mobility Declines. In S. Djankov and U. Panizza, eds. *COVID-19 in Developing Economies*. London: Centre for Economic Policy Research.

[2] COVID-19 Dashboard by the Center for Systems Science and Engineering at Johns Hopkins University. https://www.arcgis.com/apps/opsdashboard/index.html#/bda7594740fd40299423467b48e9ecf6

and restrictions on large gatherings and public events—comes from the University of Oxford's COVID-19 Government Response Tracker.[3] And measures of the decline in mobility outside the home come from Google's COVID-19 Community Mobility Reports.[4] All three indicators cover almost all developing Asian economies, are comparable across countries, and are updated daily.

Crowdsourced assessments are used to estimate the size of the COVID-19-induced domestic demand shock for all of 2020. Specifically, forecast revisions for 2020 consumption and investment growth from the May 2020 Consensus Forecasts reports are used, where the revision is measured against pre-COVID forecasts in December 2019 Consensus Forecast reports.[5] These forecasts incorporate all information available to forecasters, including data releases, severity of outbreaks, and policies (including lockdowns) in these countries.

Figure 6.1 shows how consumption and investment growth forecast revisions are correlated with outbreak severity, stringency of containment measures, and declines in mobility. The regression results suggest that a 10-point increase in stringency is associated with an additional downward revision of about 0.6–0.7 percentage point in consumption growth, and of 1.2–1.3 percentage points in investment growth. Similarly, a 10-percentage-point decline in mobility is associated with an additional downward revision of about 0.5 percentage points in consumption growth, and of 1.1 percentage points in investment growth. These regressions can then be used to generate predicted values for consumption and investment declines, for economies not covered by Consensus Forecast reports.

---

[3]   University of Oxford. Coronavirus Government Response Tracker. https://www.bsg.ox.ac.uk/research/research-projects/coronavirus-government-response-tracker.

[4]   Google. COVID-19 Community Mobility Reports. https://www.google.com/covid19/mobility/.

[5]   Consensus Economics surveys 250 prominent financial and economic forecasters—180 of whom cover Asia and the Pacific—for their estimates on a range of variables in Consensus Forecast reports. Forecasts for consumption and investment growth in 2020 are available for 37 countries, including 10 developing Asian economies.

Figure 6.1: Consumption and Investment Growth Revisions versus Restriction and Severity Measures

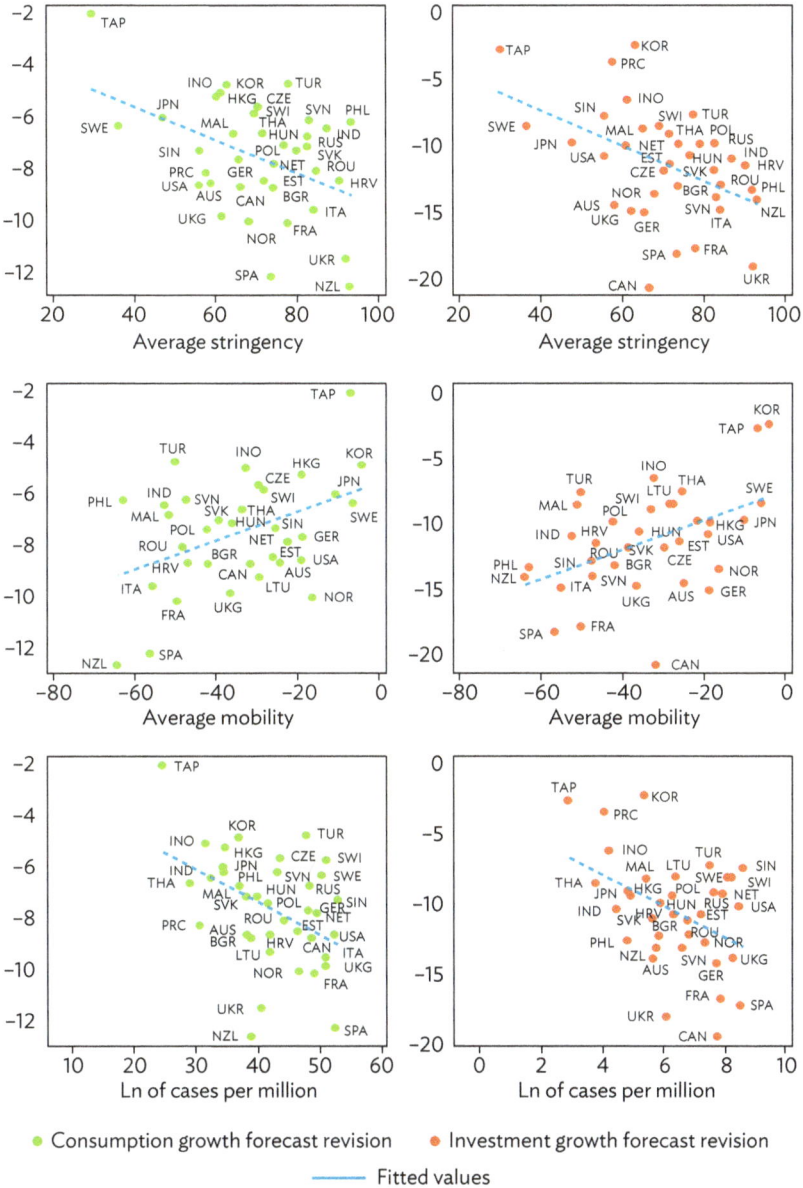

● Consumption growth forecast revision   ● Investment growth forecast revision

—— Fitted values

continued next page

Figure 6.1 continued

ARM = Armenia; AUS = Australia, AZE = Azerbaijan; BGR = Bulgaria; CAN = Canada; CZE = Czech Republic; EST = Estonia; FRA = France; GER = Germany; HKG = Hong Kong, China; HRV = Croatia; HUN = Hungary; IND = India; INO = Indonesia; ITA = Italy; JPN = Japan; KOR = Republic of Korea; LTU = Lithuania; MAL = Malaysia; NEP = Nepal; NET = Netherlands; NOR = Norway; NZL = New Zealand; PHI = Philippines; POL = Poland; PRC = People's Republic of China; ROU = Romania; RUS = Russian Federation; SIN = Singapore; SPA = Spain; SVK = Slovakia; SVN = Slovenia; SWE = Sweden; SWI = Switzerland; TAP = Taipei,China; THA = Thailand; TUR = Turkey; UKG = United Kingdom; UKR = Ukraine; USA = United States.
Note: Scatter plots chart revisions to consumption and investment growth due to the COVID-19 pandemic against measures of the average stringency of containment policies, the decline of mobility outside the home, and the severity of demand shocks across 31 economies.
Source: Consensus Economics; University of Oxford; Google; and authors' estimates.

Spillovers through Trade and Production Linkages

The effect of global spillovers on an economy can be quantified by running the model with no shock applied to domestic demand.[6] This can be calculated for each of the 24 developing Asian economies covered in the ADB MRIOT. Not surprisingly, the impact of global spillovers on each economy is closely related to how open an economy is to international trade. Using exports-to-GDP ratio as a proxy for openness and sensitivity to external demand, Figure 6.2 confirms that more open economies will experience larger spillovers from weak external demand, under both shorter-containment and longer-containment scenarios. A regression of global spillovers on country openness finds a statistically significant relationship, with about 68% of the variation in the magnitude of global spillovers accounted for by variation in openness.

The estimated impact of the COVID-19 pandemic on 45 developing Asian economies, under the shorter of two containment scenarios, is presented in Figure 6.3. We stress that these are estimated impacts relative to a no-COVID baseline and are not growth forecasts; neither do they reflect the views of ADB country teams, whose forecasts in ADB (2020) incorporate judgment on many factors not accounted for in this analysis—including effects through oil and commodity prices, remittances, capital flows, uncertainty, financial stress and volatility, and perhaps most importantly,

---

[6]   The effect on the tourism sector, which is particularly important for some developing Asian economies and which has been hit hard by travel restrictions, is analyzed separately and reported in greater detail in Abiad et al. (2020).

Figure 6.2: COVID-19 Global Spillovers and Exports to GDP
(% of GDP)

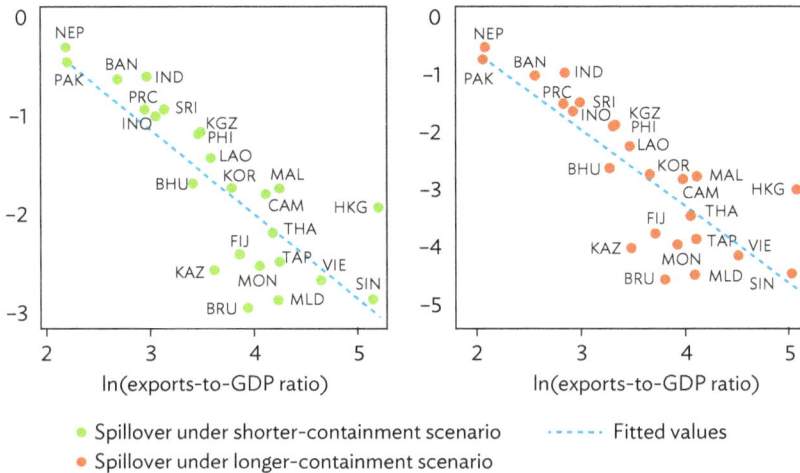

- Spillover under shorter-containment scenario
- Spillover under longer-containment scenario
- - - - - Fitted values

BAN = Bangladesh; BHU = Bhutan; BRU = Brunei Darussalam; CAM = Cambodia; FIJ = Fiji;
HKG = Hong Kong, China; IND = India; INO = Indonesia; KAZ = Kazakhstan; KGZ = Kyrgyz Republic;
KOR = Republic of Korea; LAO = Lao People's Democratic Republic; MAL = Malaysia;
MLD = Maldives; MON = Mongolia; NEP = Nepal; PAK = Pakistan; PHI = Philippines; PRC = People's
Republic of China; SIN = Singapore; SRI = Sri Lanka; TAP = Taipei,China; THA = Thailand;
VIE = Viet Nam.
Note: The length of the containment scenarios varies in both scatter plots. A shorter-containment
scenario assumes that it takes 3 months for economies to get their domestic outbreaks under control
and start to normalize economic activity and end travel bans (roughly consistent with the People's
Republic of China's experience). A longer-containment scenario takes 6 months, if for example there
are recurrent waves of outbreaks.
Source: World Bank; April 2020 Asian Development Outlook Database; and authors' estimates.

policy responses that in some countries will provide a substantial countervailing force to COVID-19's impact.[7]

The sectoral decomposition of impact in the 24 developing Asian economies covered by the ADB MRIOT is presented in Figure 6.4.

---

7   ADB. 2020. *Asian Development Outlook 2020 Supplement: Lockdown, Loosening, and Asia's Growth Prospects.* 25 June. Manila. https://www.adb.org/sites/default/files/publication/612261/ado-supplement-june-2020. pdf

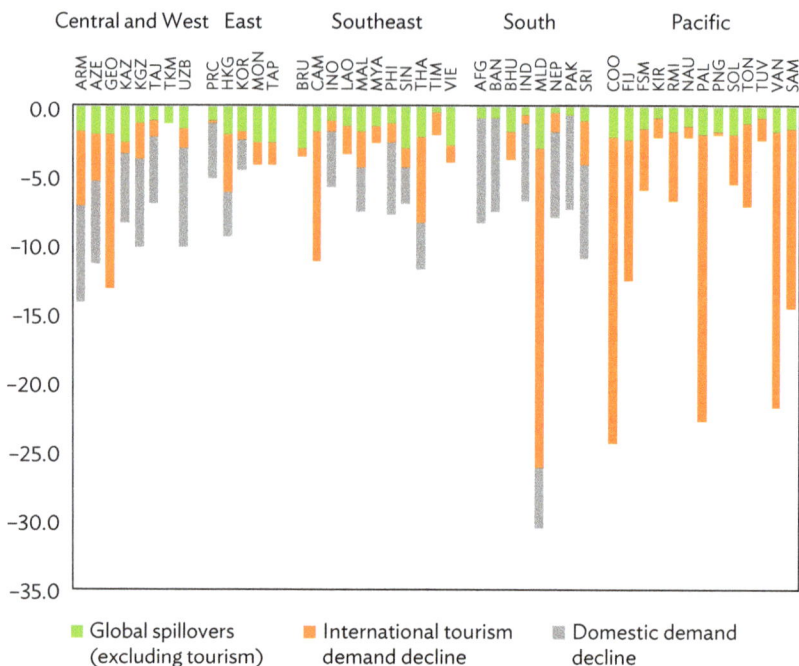

Figure 6.3: COVID-19 Impact on Developing Asian Economies

AFG = Afghanistan; ARM = Armenia; AZE = Azerbaijan; BAN = Bangladesh; BHU = Bhutan; BRU = Brunei Darussalam; CAM = Cambodia; COO = Cook Islands; FIJ = Fiji; FSM = Federated States of Micronesia; GEO = Georgia; HKG = Hong Kong, China; IND = India; INO = Indonesia; KAZ = Kazakhstan; KGZ = Kyrgyz Republic; KIR = Kiribati; KOR = Republic of Korea; LAO = Lao People's Democratic Republic; MAL = Malaysia; MLD = Maldives; MON = Mongolia; MYA = Myanmar; NAU = Nauru; NEP = Nepal; PAK = Pakistan; PAL = Palau; PHI = Philippines; PNG = Papua New Guinea; PRC = People's Republic of China; RMI = Republic of the Marshall Islands; SAM = Samoa; SIN = Singapore; SOL = Solomon Islands; SRI = Sri Lanka; TAJ = Tajikistan; TAP = Taipei,China; THA = Thailand; TIM = Timor-Leste; TKM = Turkmenistan; TON = Tonga; TUV = Tuvalu; UZB = Uzbekistan; VAN = Vanuatu; VIE = Viet Nam.

Note: Domestic demand declines are assumed only for economies with significant outbreaks (more than 1,000 cases).

Source: Authors' estimates.

Figure 6.4: Sectoral Impact on Developing Asian Economies

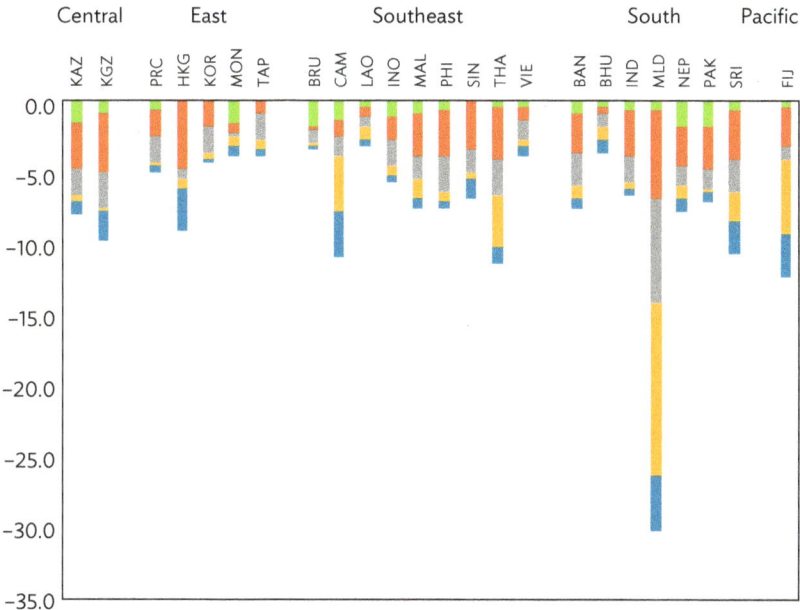

Agriculture, mining and quarrying

Business, trade, and public services

Light/heavy manufacturing, utilities, and construction

Hotel and restaurant, other personal services

Transport services

BAN = Bangladesh; BHU = Bhutan; BRU = Brunei Darussalam; CAM = Cambodia; FIJ = Fiji; HKG = Hong Kong, China; IND = India; INO = Indonesia; KAZ = Kazakhstan; KGZ = Kyrgyz Republic; KOR = Republic of Korea; LAO = Lao People's Democratic Republic; MAL = Malaysia; MLD = Maldives; MON = Mongolia; NEP = Nepal; PAK = Pakistan; PHI = Philippines; PRC = People's Republic of China; SIN = Singapore; SRI = Sri Lanka; TAP = Taipei,China; THA = Thailand; VIE = Viet Nam.
Note: Sectoral impacts are available only for 24 developing Asian economies covered by the ADB Multi-Region Input-Output Tables (MRIOT).
Source: Authors' estimates.

Even with Borders Closing, We Need to Keep Trade Flowing

Steven Beck

The global COVID-19 pandemic is a reminder that our world is an intimately connected place. Global issues need global solutions and clear thinking.

Physical borders can be closed to those who might pass on the virus, but the crisis underlines the need to streamline other important connections, such as trade. How can we maintain trade flows at a time when everyone's attention seems to be focused on tightening borders? How can we keep goods moving when the financial systems that companies rely on are under stress?

Apart from the everyday importance of global trade, countries need easy access to medicines, medical equipment, and other goods vital to the health of their populations. Few countries make everything they need themselves, which means the flow of trade in those goods needs to be through gates that are opened wider, not shut.

A recent study found that out of 164 members of the World Trade Organization (WTO), only 50 do not tax imported medical devices. Seventy-nine governments went into the crisis taxing imported soap at rates of 15% or more, noted in a study by Professor Simon Evenett of the Swiss Institute of International Economics and Department of Economics.

"A tax on soap is a tax on hygiene and hastens the spread of coronavirus," says the March 2020 study, which noted many governments were increasing the restrictions on trade in medical goods as the crisis intensified.

Governments should take action to eliminate trade barriers on goods and component parts for goods critical to fighting COVID-19.

Global economies and financial systems, plus intimately connected supply chains, are already under pressure. Factories are closed, movement has been restricted in many countries and worries are growing that the pandemic could spawn a repeat of the global financial crisis of 2008–2009 or worse.

The outbreak will have a significant impact on developing Asian economies through numerous channels, including sharp declines in domestic demand, lower tourism and business travel, trade and production linkages, supply disruptions, and health effects, according to a recent ADB study.[8]

The magnitude of economic losses will depend on how the outbreak evolves, which at this point is, of course, highly uncertain.

Still, this is not a repeat of the global financial crisis. That event resulted from burst financial bubbles coupled with mounting bad debts and undercapitalization.

This crisis is rooted in a short-term supply/demand shock, or at least it could be limited to that if well managed. We need to watch closely as it reverberates through the real and financial supply chains. Some adjustments are called for and some are already being made.

To help the financial and real sectors ride out a short-term shock without spinning off into a medium- and longer-term economic and financial crisis, the banking sector should consider a 3-month grace period for obligations, between banks themselves and between banks and their commercial and retail clients. Of course, the same would apply to trade loans.

And governments should consider a guaranteed minimum income for 12 months. That would help people ride this out and dampen a potentially devastating economic impact from extremely low demand, with consumers stuck at home without income.

It has been inspiring to see people rising to the challenge they now face. Compared with the financial crisis 12 years ago, the amount of coordination and oversight in trade finance today means problems can be spotted and attended to much more quickly.

---

[8] A. Abdul et al. 2020. The Economic Impact of the COVID-19 Outbreak on Developing Asia. *ADB Briefs*. No. 128. Manila.

ADB is working to support companies manufacturing and distributing medicines and other items needed to combat the virus. This support, working in partnership with commercial banks, will provide companies in Asia and the Pacific with additional working capital to meet expansion and other requirements.

ADB has pledged $20 billion for a range of measures to help its members through the crisis and has approved changes to streamline its operations for quicker and more flexible delivery of assistance.

As part of that, working in partnership with commercial banks, ADB is providing companies in Asia and the Pacific with additional working capital to meet expansion and other requirements.

That support includes an additional $200 million of supply chain finance to help companies in areas that are critical to fighting the virus to ramp up production of items such as test kits, N95 masks, and ventilators.

Given that a single pool of supply chain finance is typically used for a subsequent delivery over a period of 120–180 days, this facility could support more than $400 million of financing over the next 12 months. Fifty-fifty risk sharing from partner commercial banks could boost support under the facility to $800 million over the same period.

Combined trade and supply chain finance has amounted to almost $2 billion in transactions supported so far this year from ADB's Trade and Supply Chain Finance Program. Those deals have included 100 medical supply transactions including test kits, medical equipment, medicine, and other goods worth $35 million and 520 food security- and/or agriculture-related transactions valued at $455 million.

When it became clear that key medical items were becoming scarce and that alternate sources for those goods were hard to find, ADB began a project to map the supply chains for those products. The aim of this supply chain mapping tool is to identify blockages and other impediments to these critical goods being produced and distributed to where they're needed.

In May, the first phase of the project was completed—interactive maps that enable banks, investors, governments, and health care professionals to pinpoint key companies in the supply of portable ventilators, N95 respirators, face shields, goggles, aprons, surgical masks, and gowns. The maps consider the elements of each product down to its component metals and fabrics.

Since then, the supply chain maps have been extended to other products. We are looking at supply chain maps for vaccines, including the distribution channels required to administer the drug when it becomes available. Anyone can use the tool, free of charge, through the ADB website.

ADB's Trade and Supply Chain Finance Program has shown it is a powerful crisis response vehicle, as it was during the financial crisis 10 years ago, because of its many agreements with hundreds of banks in dozens of countries. That makes it a great channel to inject urgently needed support.

This is not the time to panic. Our actions now will make the difference between a short, sharp shock and an extended downturn.

The Case for Regional Cooperation in Trade and Investment Finance for Asia

Arup Kumar Chatterjee, Arjun Goswami, Jules Hugot, and Marianne Vital

Export credit agencies (ECAs) have played a significant role in supporting the expansion of trade and investment. Most of them are state-owned. They were established primarily to support their own companies seeking to export or invest in developing countries, by providing a combination of three products: trade credit insurance, investment guarantees, and direct lending to foreign buyers and third-party financial institutions.[9]

The precise institutional arrangements vary across countries, from the government directly serving as an ECA to a private company providing ECA services on behalf of the government (Table 6.1).

Private risk insurers emerged in the early 1980s, initially reinsuring ECAs by underwriting short-term political risk, before expanding to long-term risk coverage and lending.

In the 1990s, the ECAs widened their mandate beyond strictly supporting domestic exporters to adapt to the complex transaction risks associated with global value chains. Several ECAs also started to provide long-term project financing for investment projects. With this new role, the ECAs also gradually strengthened their developmental, environmental, and social safeguard standards.

With most developing countries having joined the World Trade Organization (WTO) by the end of the 1990s, the WTO's Agreement on Subsidies and Countervailing Measures became applicable. The agreement implies that ECAs shall not provide unfair support to domestic exporters by undercutting the market rates offered to foreign buyers. Most ECAs have thus found

---

[9] This is an abridged version of a *policy brief* published in May 2020.

Table 6.1: Export Credit Agency Models, by Degree of Government Intervention

Model	Description	Example countries
Government department	Department operating under the authority of a ministry/secretary	Switzerland, the United Kingdom
State-owned agency	Autonomous government-owned institution	Armenia, Canada, the People's Republic of China, France, India, Japan, Turkey, the United States, Uzbekistan
Virtual ECA	No formal institution, but the government is involved in decisions and risk taking	New Zealand
Private company acting on behalf of the government	Private company issuing policies on behalf of the government, as part of an exclusive arrangement	Germany, the Netherlands
Government provides reinsurance	Government provides reinsurance treaty to insurers holding the sole underwriting mandate	Australia, the United Kingdom

ECA = export credit agency.
Source: Compilation by the authors, building upon Smallridge (2006).

themselves in a position of lender of last resort—restricted to the segments that private insurers would find too risky, such as political risk—while still seeking to break even.

The Global Financial Crisis: Expansion of Action

During the global financial crisis, ECAs became insurers of last resort for cross-border transactions, with private insurers having left the stage. Governments collectively committed $250 billion in support to trade finance in April 2009, to try and reverse the trade contraction. To add to their countercyclical action, ECAs further expanded their operations to small and medium-sized enterprises (SMEs) and to direct lending. ECAs from industrial Asian countries also considerably expanded support to exporters, and investments in mega projects in developing countries, often as part of a broader geostrategic agenda.

Despite concerns about ECAs crowding out the private sector, public and private insurers have largely complemented each other. However, private insurers still rarely establish a local presence in smaller developing countries, where national ECAs often remain the only source of export credit insurance. In large developing countries, ECAs might attract private insurers as co-insurance and reinsurance partners as they can absorb larger losses through risk diversification.

Rationale for State-Backed Export Credit Agencies

ECAs are designed to compensate the market failures that limit the provision of trade and investment finance. These failures arise from information asymmetries which deters private insurers from providing risk coverage. Risky traders have more incentives to purchase insurance cover (adverse selection) and having purchased insurance also prepared to accept higher counterparty risks (moral hazard). The commercial risks affecting trade transactions, e.g., not honoring a contract, and delays and losses occurring during shipment are covered by conventional insurance policies. A unique feature of ECAs which are particularly relevant to cross-border transactions is that they also cover political risks, such as war, terrorism, government expropriation, restrictions on currency convertibility, trade embargos, and sovereign defaults.

Impact of export credit agencies on trade and investment

Even after a decade-long recovery, trade finance continues to remain under provisioned in developing countries, particularly for small and medium-sized enterprises. The 2019 Trade Finance Gaps, Growth, and Jobs Survey—a survey of financial institutions conducted by ADB—estimates the global gap in trade finance at $1.5 trillion, 40% of which is in Asia and the Pacific. Broadening access to trade finance in developing countries therefore remains a challenge.

Although export growth and the activity of ECAs are correlated, it does not necessarily follow that ECAs cause exports. Upon matching firm-level export data with bank-level data reflecting credit availability, one generally observes a positive and significant impact of trade credit access on trade. Positive impacts can also be drawn upon analysis of Berne Union data on trade credit commitments by ECAs. Interestingly, the effect of guarantees on exports to non-industrial countries is insignificant, suggesting that frictions might be so large that guarantees do not provide sufficient relief.

Impact of export credit agencies during crises

The volatility of international trade is amplified by its sensitivity to access trade finance, which is considerably reduced during crises. Bank-financed trade credits declined by about 50% in the Republic of Korea and 80% in Indonesia during the Asian financial crisis (1997–1998), while medium- to long-term trade finance contracted by 40% in the last quarter of 2008. Trade finance costs increased twofold to threefold during the global financial crisis because of an increase in the bank's own funding costs or to comply with regulatory capital requirements. Private insurers also increased premiums during the crises. Therefore, the positive effect of public trade guarantees on exports is larger during episodes of negative or slow export growth.

Potential Adverse Effects of Export Credit Agencies

ECAs also have potential adverse effects that need to be considered and possibly mitigated. Export credits add to the debt burden of developing countries as a significant proportion of the debt of developing countries arises from it, and not from development loans. As a result, debt to ECAs is now a subject to the sovereign debt sustainability criteria imposed by the IMF in exchange for emergency support.

State-backed export credit insurance is a form of indirect export subsidy. Although it is allowed under the WTO's Agreement on Subsidies and Countervailing Measures through a "safe haven" clause, it is regulated by the Arrangement on Officially Supported Export Credits of the Organisation for Economic Co-operation and Development (OECD), which stipulates that WTO members may not provide finance at interest rates below their own sovereign borrowing cost. The role of the OECD in ECA regulation, however, excludes developing countries from setting the rules.

In most developed countries, regulations prevent ECAs from covering marketable short-term risks to ensure ECAs do not crowd out the private sector. Some ECAs are able to avoid the burden of rigorous environmental and social safeguards for supporting investment projects. OECD has elaborated "common approaches" to due diligence to discourage such tendencies.

The Case for a Regional Export Credit Agency in Asia

Berne Union, Asian Exim Banks Forum. The Berne Union which comprises 85 institutions from 73 countries (only 15 from Asia) provides trade credit insurance for 13% of world trade. At the regional level, it has also encouraged interactions among Asian insurers, with the establishment of an Asian Regional Cooperation Group. Outside the Berne Union, nine institutions formed the Asian Exim Bank Forum in 1996—Australia, the PRC, India, Indonesia, Japan, the Republic of Korea, Malaysia, the Philippines, and Thailand, before expanding to Turkey and Viet Nam. The forum acts as an informal platform to facilitate bilateral agreements among institutions. Since many ECAs and Exim banks in Asia are not part of these arrangements, they are not affected by the informal standards they imply.

Existing sources of trade finance in Asia. A review of 45 ADB members in the region found that only 18 have a national ECA or an Exim bank. To fill market gaps in trade finance, the Trade Finance Program (TFP) of ADB has been providing support since 2004, through short-term guarantees and loans to commercial and state-owned banks. The TFP leverages ADB's AAA rating to finance cross-border transactions across Asia, through more than 240 partner banks located in more than 90 countries. From 2009 to 2018, the TFP has supported $36 billion worth of transactions, and provided cofinancing amounting to $22 billion.[10] To complement its trade finance business, ADB launched the Supply Chain Finance Program (SCFP) in 2014. The SCFP aims to close market gaps for SMEs operating in domestic and cross-border value chains.

New global developments require deeper regional cooperation. Global headwinds such as weak economic recovery in developed countries and increasing trade protectionism are causing uncertainties that affect trade and investment. Further, global rules to prevent money laundering and the financing of terrorism as well as prudential regulations such as Basel III present challenges to developing countries and their financial system. Trade finance could thus be further constrained, weighing down small players and even some state-backed insurers. Lastly, gaps in project financing may also constrain future economic growth and development.

Advantages of a regional ECA. A regional ECA would notably bring larger business volumes and the benefit from economies of scale by distributing

---

[10]   ADB. 2019. *Trade Finance Program*. Brochure. Available on www.adb.org (accessed 23 August 2019).

fixed costs over a larger turnover. It will also be better suited to finance large infrastructure projects due to its larger financial capacity. The large size will also make it more interesting for private insurers and multilateral development banks to partner with, including through reinsurance schemes. Risk diversification will also translate into cheaper financing in the form of lower funding and insurance costs. It will also help address governance issues that affect national ECAs. Banks across the world are gearing up to comply with Basel III standards. For meeting the prudential requirements, banks are increasingly willing to de-risk their portfolio for providing loans with a partial credit guarantee from an investment grade credit insurer, which can include a regional ECA.

Finally, a regional ECA could provide a platform for regional cooperation on policy and regulatory coordination and emergency response in times of crisis. It can carry the collective voice of the region in global regulatory discussions and the best practices can also be shared across member countries. It can also provide emergency trade finance support when a crisis affects one of its members by making full use of its risk mitigation tools.

Lessons from Regional ECAs in Asia

For establishing a regional ECA in Asia, one needs to consider the lessons learned from existing multilateral institutions as well as national ECAs in the region. To fully reap the benefits of scale, a regional ECA should rely on fully paid-in capital from its inception. While risk coverage limits of each country can be linked with the amount of the capital contributed by each country, in a regional ECA it must allow for pooling of capital, to make it eligible for a higher credit rating and leveraging its capital to issue more policies. For maximizing its effectiveness, it should also identify an appropriate product range including insurance, guarantees, and credit, with various maturities. These products can be used to mitigate counterparty risk or obtain financing from banks, notably for working capital.

More sophisticated products, such as factoring and securitization arrangements should also be considered. To enhance uptake there is a need to ensure product awareness by organizing information sessions, particularly targeting the SMEs.

Sustaining sound operations requires sufficient expertise, in-house and also through partnerships with private insurers. As partners in reinsurance agreements (or even shareholders), third-party public or private insurers can bring both expertise help in portfolio de-risking. A regional ECA should also limit political risk through the preferred creditor status, by which member countries guarantee to cover claims arising from the materialization of insured political risks occurring in their own country. Finally, it should address integrity risks through appropriate governance and monitoring.

The Way Forward

While national ECAs have played a significant role in developing countries in Asia, regional cooperation could be instrumental in optimizing their action. The establishment of a regional ECA, could take the form of a second-tier reinsurance and re-guarantee institution, to complement existing ECAs and private insurers.

Next steps regarding regional cooperation in Asia could go on two pathways, albeit not necessarily in a mutually exclusive manner. The first option would be to follow the Berne Union model and agree on harmonized standards to ensure healthy regional competition.

As a second option, an Asian multilateral ECA could also be created. It could be a new institution, with subscription from governments and support from international development partners, as was the case for the Islamic Corporation for the Insurance of Investment and Export Credit and the African Trade Insurance Agency. The corporation was established in 1994 and is owned by the Islamic Development Bank and 44 other countries. It provides *Shariah*-compliant trade credit and insurance. The African agency's membership comprises 15 countries and 9 institutions, including the African Development Bank, European ECAs, and private insurers. A regional ECA can address issues that commonly plague national ECAs.

Further, as with the case of the Islamic Corporation for the Insurance of Investment and Export Credit, a regional ECA does not need to compete with national ECAs, but rather, they can complement them through reinsurance and refinancing. Alternatively, it could build upon ADB's TFP, which is already backed by ADB's AAA rating and maintains relationships with a vast network of banks. Scaling up the TFP to take on the role of a regional ECA would require expanding the product range to provide a full suite of products in demand across Asia.

During COVID-19, Countries Need to Work Together to Ensure the Supply of Protective Equipment

Susann Roth and Jesper Pedersen

Those who are procuring supplies for COVID-19 preparedness and response these days realize why so many countries struggle to protect their frontline health workers and provide critical care for people who fall severely ill from the infectious disease.

Amid the uncertainties of the epidemiology of the disease, and a lot of media attention on worst-case scenarios, the market for personal protective equipment, ventilators, and medicine is failing. This is resulting in depleted stockpiles, order backlogs of 4–6 months, and significant price increases ranging from 50–100 times historical pricing. This ultimately leads to unprotected frontliners and high fatality rates.

The pandemic exposes the vulnerabilities of supply chains in many industries, as laid out in a recent policy brief.[11] For the last few decades, countries have failed to buy into the idea of pandemic planning and stockpiling, causing the lack of protective equipment stocks to meet the surge in demand during disease outbreaks. This affects health care workers most. In many developing countries, health workers are getting infected and among those getting severely sick and dying.

Interestingly, health security experts have predicted such a market failure for many years. Papers were published about the issue after the 2003 SARS outbreak. Many of us have urged governments and health facilities to build stockpiles and develop intelligent surge capacities to quickly deploy

---

[11] C. Park et al. 2020. *Global Shortage of Personal Protective Equipment amid COVID-19: Supply Chains, Bottlenecks, and Policy Implications.* ADB Briefs No. 130. April. Manila.

supplies and equipment where needed. What we are experiencing now is an eye opener.[12]

It shows us that money alone will not fix the interconnected political, technical, and public health problems, which are fueling the pandemic. If we cannot protect our health workforce and ensure infection, prevention, and control in our health facilities, we fail our populations and patients. We force people into prolonged lockdowns to ease the burden on already fragile health systems. A sustainable and scalable approach is required. This includes:

- Political solutions with support from the highest levels of governments, UN agencies and the private sector to ease export bans and other government restrictions.

- Evidence-based solutions to ensure allocations of supplies are based on epidemiological trends, country capacity, and country risk profiles.

- Focus on prioritizing frontline health care workers.

- Technical solutions utilizing demand forecasts to ensure proper visibility and transparency of needs and allocation of supplies, including deployment of products to the appropriate countries.

- Alignment of harmonized, evidence-based policies for masks and the use and disposal of other personal protective equipment.

An absence of price and market transparency also encourages a "hot market" with lots of shady offers from agents in the middle who ask for 100% upfront payments and hide their supply sources, leaving quality in question. This increases the risk that countries and agencies are exposed to low-quality products which give a false sense of protection.

To respond to the need for better global coordination, the UN set up the UN COVID-19 Supply Chain Task Force in April 2020, led by the WHO with the support from the greater UN system. The priority actions of the task force to achieve the sustainable and scalable approach described above include:

[12] S. Donato, S. Roth, and J. Parry. 2016. Strong Supply Chains Transform Public Health. *ADB Briefs No. 72.* November. Manila.

- Through WHO, develop a dynamic understanding of required supplies through a bottom-up assessment of needs from country-based modeling and to provide a robust forecast of overall needs. This will result in validated and aggregated requests funneled up through a digital portal to the task force for procurement and distribution.

- Through partners within the task force, identify all available global sources of supplies and negotiate with suppliers the necessary quantities and pricing. The sourcing mechanisms will be managed by three separate consortia convened by WHO for personal protective equipment (supported by UNICEF), diagnostics equipment, and oxygen and oxygen-based clinical care.

- Manage a transparent allocation mechanism based on WHO clinical protocols, epidemiological needs, available market supply capacity, and available funding.

- Through the World Food Programme, establish and manage a global logistics distribution system.

The international community of development partners needs to support this newly set up task force and coordinate supply and demand at the country, regional, and global level. A new online supply chain coordination portal set up by the UN COVID-19 Supply Chain Task Force will aggregate demand and supply data to inform procurement and logistics arrangements. It aims to be the one platform for development partners and countries to assess their needs and procure supplies. This requires that everybody commits to transparency and data sharing. It is time for UN agencies and multilateral development banks to come together and invest in the public goods of pandemic supply chain management and market shaping.

For a better global coordination to be successful, the UN agencies need to agree on fair administrative charges for procurement services. Many UN agencies need to raise their own income to fund their development programs and serving as procurement agent generates significant income that can be used for these programs. But in the case of emergencies, donors, countries, and development partners are then double paying without the security that supplies get delivered in time.

We have all the tools to establish and maintain such a platform and we have the leadership at the UN. What we need now is collective action across development partners and countries to collaborate with this online supply chain coordination portal and share actionable information about supply and demand. In this way, we can all work together toward a fair and timely distribution.

New ADB Tool Offers Road Map to Unblock Supplies of Life-Saving Products

ADB

The COVID-19 pandemic has exposed deep and dangerous fault lines in global supply chains. A telling impact is the shortage in many countries of life-saving medical equipment such as ventilators. As countries entered lockdowns to contain the virus, health care authorities and governments were left scrambling to find the products they needed.

Those efforts have been hampered by a lack of readily accessible information on supply chains for these crucial products. ADB's Trade Finance Program and Supply Chain Finance Program is helping resolve this through a new online tool which maps these supply chains, allowing governments, banks, investors, and health care professionals to pinpoint companies making these products and intervene to clear any blockages.

"This way, a fault somewhere along the supply chain can be fixed," said ADB's Head of Trade and Supply Chain Finance Steven Beck. "Banks or investors can fund a company struggling to meet increased demand."

Shining a Spotlight on Blocked Supply Chains

In the early days of the virus as health systems, governments, and international organizations realized they needed to start ramping up their stocks of goods like portable ventilators, it soon became clear that a key obstacle was a lack of clear understanding of who made what in the supply chains for those products.

Even the banks did not have a full picture of whether the companies they worked with were involved in the supply lines.

"That kind of information wasn't available in a way that would make it easy for someone to address problems that might arise," said Beck. "We decided to see if that was something we could do."

The solution was an interactive mapping tool for the supply chains of products vital to health care workers and others on the frontlines of the battle. The tool, launched in May, enables governments, banks, investors, and health care professionals to trace the companies that make every component in products such as portable ventilators, down to the metal and rubber that goes into each part.

As well as ventilators, the mapping tool includes the entire supply chains for N95 respirators, face shields, goggles, aprons, surgical masks, and gowns. Previously, the information on who makes which part for which product was available in piecemeal fashion. But this information had never been brought together in one database that would allow a quick search.

Since then, the supply chain maps have been extended to other products. We're looking at supply chain maps for vaccines, including the distribution channels required to administer the drug when it becomes available.

"When we heard about the issues with the supply chains, we started asking our bank partners which companies in their portfolios were involved in the supply chains for these products," said Beck. "The idea was that we could help shine a spotlight on these supply chains and get help to where it was needed."

A Few Clicks Can Pinpoint the Problem

ADB's trade and supply chain finance businesses are uniquely placed to address the economic and financial impacts of the pandemic, as they are in constant contact with banks and other stakeholders involved in global trade.

ADB has pledged $20 billion for a range of measures to help its members through the crisis and has approved changes to streamline its operations for quicker and more flexible delivery of assistance.

As part of that working in partnership with commercial banks, ADB is providing companies in Asia and the Pacific with additional working capital to meet expansion and other requirements.

That support includes an additional $200 million of supply chain finance to help companies in areas that are critical to fighting the virus to ramp up production of items such as test kits, N95 masks, and ventilators.

Given that a single pool of supply chain finance is typically used for a subsequent delivery over a period of 120–180 days, this facility could support more than $400 million of financing over the next 12 months. Fifty-fifty risk sharing from partner commercial banks could boost support under the facility to $800 million over the same period.

Combined trade and supply chain finance has amounted to almost $2 billion in transactions supported so far this year from ADB's Trade & Supply Chain Finance Program. Those deals have included 100 medical-supply transactions including test kits, medical equipment, medicine, and other goods worth $35 million and 520 food security/agriculture-related transactions valued at $455 million.

The supply chain mapping initiative represents a new type of support from ADB's Trade & Supply Chain Finance Program. It leverages the reach and agility of ADB's financing operations to give unprecedented insights into problems along the supply line and speed their resolution.

For example, if a shortage of rubber gaskets is holding up production of ventilators, someone using the ADB tool could quickly look up the companies making those gaskets. With a few clicks, they could see information detailing the size and turnover of those companies, their location, and how many people they employ.

They could tell whether those companies only make one particular gasket or whether gaskets are just a small part of their production. They could also see which banks the companies use, providing further information on how to dismantle barriers to financing.

"This mapping tool helps fill in the information deficit around supply chains and provides a template to ensure supply chain blockages do not hold up responses to future outbreaks," said Beck.

COVID-19 has exposed the shortcomings of global supply chains. The mapping tool is one way for countries to bridge these fault lines with information that can save lives.

7. Accelerating Digital Transformation

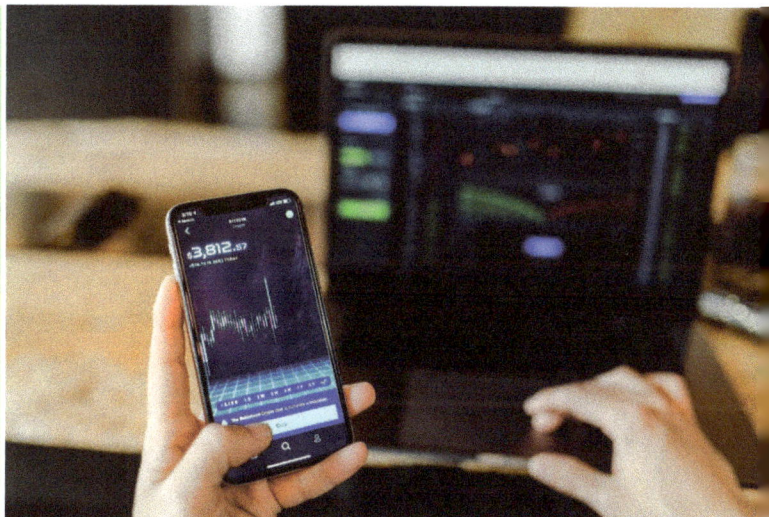

COVID-19: There's an App for That

James Villafuerte

Digital platforms—such as Apple, Google, Microsoft, Facebook, Amazon, Alibaba, and Tencent—are transforming the way we work, socialize, and create economic value. In the time of COVID-19, these platforms have proven to be useful and provide necessary tools to monitor and manage the crisis.

Digital platforms have also been used to find solutions to the pandemic, protect people, and get societies back up and running. For example, Google and Apple collaborated to use Bluetooth technology to launch a COVID-19 contact tracing app. E-commerce, food delivery, and digital payments have also stepped up.

Tight restrictions on mobility have triggered an abrupt shift to remote work, online video conferencing, massive open online courses for education, and online streaming for entertainment. As of mid-April 2020, the International Labour Organization (ILO) notes that 59 countries had implemented teleworking for non-essential publicly employed staff.

In terms of schooling, worldwide, more than 1.2 billion children in 186 countries are affected by school closures and most are studying remotely. Online education platform Tencent Classroom saw a meteoric rise of users after the Government of the People's Republic of China (PRC) instructed a quarter of a billion full-time students to go online.

As countries around the world respond to the COVID-19 outbreak with huge fiscal stimulus packages, many governments in developing economies also face the challenge of quickly and safely disbursing large amounts of cash to vulnerable people. Globally, 30% of all government packages after

COVID-19 are cash transfers and for some countries such as Argentina, Pakistan, and Peru, transfers go to a third of their populations. For others, such as the Philippines, transfers cover 70% of households. And the use of biometric identification and digital payment could help make these transfers more efficiently.

There is no denying that digitalization is a critical component of building a pandemic resilient world. Presently, depending on the definition, the size of the digital economy can range from 4.5%–15.5% of global GDP. Within the digital economy, the digital sector may account for 1%–6% of GDP and 0%–5.5% of direct exports. Use of digital technology and the size of the digital sector will likely increase further as physical connectivity is replaced with digital connectivity to makes our lives safer.

A forthcoming ADB study notes that a 20% expansion of the global digital sector could spur a productivity increase that would reduce global consumer prices by 2%, stimulate a $400 billion rise in global exports, and increase global GDP by $2 trillion.[1] Depending on the scenario used, this is about a third or a quarter of the estimated short-term impact of the COVID-19 pandemic on the global economy. These gains come from both the direct expansion effect from the digital sector and the indirect productivity enhancement effect that would reduce prices across the board.

While digital platforms continue to emerge at great speed, their success is not preordained. How policies and regulations respond to new challenges will be a key to leveraging the potential of digital platforms to accelerate economic growth after COVID-19.

In this regard, six policy areas will determine the readiness of countries to maximize the benefits of this innovation: (i) robust information and communication technology (ICT) infrastructure and services; (ii) efficient trade and logistics networks; (iii) an efficient payment system; (iv) an efficient and internationally compatible legal and regulatory framework, including effective implementation and enforcement of rules and regulations, both internally and externally; (v) a conducive business environment to promote start-ups for greater innovation and digital entrepreneurship; and (vi) the sufficient digital skills and literacy for workers, business, civil society, and governments.

---

[1]   Asian Development Bank. Forthcoming. Technology, Digital Platform, and Productivity Growth in a Post-COVID World. *ADB Briefs*. Manila.

At the same time, digital platforms also bring disruptions to markets, their participants, and the wider economy by reinventing market arrangements and creating new business models to generate and capture value. For example, the growth of e-commerce in many countries has cut retailers' profit margins and put some out of business. Platform technology has also affected labor market arrangements through independent contracts, with little employment protection and social security. It is important therefore to consider appropriate regulations to manage undue and unfair disruptions posed by the emergence of digital platforms, including:

*   **Competition.** Digital platforms are characterized by a "double-edged" nature. Numerous micro-businesses around the globe can potentially gain from unprecedented opportunities provided by the platforms, but they also have the tendency to create one or very few 'winners' due to the presence of strong network effects. Authorities should craft policies that encourage more competition and ease barriers to entry, while maintaining the network effect benefits that large platforms can bring about. Governments should promote interoperability which could help market players collaborate and innovate to the benefit of consumers.

*   **Labor security and social protections**. Governments should roll out emergency health and social services and expand the coverage of social protection systems to cover workers who may fall into the poverty trap, regardless of working arrangements. They should also provide adequate income security for those in the informal sector, migrant workers and their families, and other vulnerable members of society. Strengthening the grievance and feedback system to give voice to the vulnerable will also help.

*   **Data access, privacy, and security**. As the new data value chain rests on the access, use, and sharing of data, platforms should exercise caution and maintain transparency in using, sharing, and creating value from the intrinsic power of data. Policies and regulations should uphold individual privacy and ensure that access to data and information is secure and not used to discriminate against different groups, that effective security policies are built, and that regulations ensure information helps create more evenly distributed benefits. Cybercrime must also be addressed.

*   **Taxation**. Taxing digital platforms is challenging due to regulatory issues, difficulties in classifying digital activities, lack of cross-border

harmonization on tax matters, and many other problems. Internationally, as digital-enabled transactions become increasingly cross-border, greater international cooperation, stronger dialogue, and policy making on taxation issues for digital platforms is critical.

Countries in Asia and the Pacific, and around the world, are using digital platforms to address COVID-19. They need to take the next step and use these platforms to open up and propel their economies into recovery.

The Global Economy Will Emerge Stronger if COVID-19 Drives Digitization

Steven Beck

We may be nearing the end of the beginning for the crisis caused by COVID-19. From the viewpoint of global trade and supply chains, however, the hard work starts now.

The next phase will not be easy. A wave of nonperforming loans and bankruptcies is rising, and economic bulwarks need to be strengthened. In terms of infections, the pandemic seems to be leveling off in many countries, but history and medical experts say a second wave may occur.

It now looks unlikely that this will be a short and sharp crisis followed by a quick return to normal. But if it is properly handled, the financial system can use the experience as an opportunity to enact necessary changes, and not just an exercise in crisis management.

We have a historic opportunity, an imperative, to make global trade and supply chains more secure. To do this, we need to drive digitization through all component parts of the ecosystem: from exporters and suppliers to shipping, ports, customs, warehousing, finance, transport, buyers, and importers. And interoperability between these component parts is required to realize seamless digital trade and supply chains.

The entire financial system has been offsetting the severe economic impact caused by shutting down of millions of businesses and sending home hundreds of millions of workers. Governments have been quick to come up with programs to aid those hit hardest. Central banks have added liquidity. Banks and their customers have adapted as best they can.

Multilateral institutions have stepped in. To keep trade moving, the program limit for support from ADB's Trade Finance Program (TFP) was boosted by $800 million to $2.15 billion. Given the program's ability to attract cofinancing from the private sector and the short-dated nature of trade transactions—142 days—it is expected to support over $5 billion in trade this year.

The trade finance market, which is critical to supporting the flow of trade and supply chains, has been surprisingly resilient so far. ·

Had this pandemic occurred even 3 years ago, the situation would have been much worse. In just a short time, the move toward digitization has gained pace and advanced far enough that a full-on disaster—banks not being able to function during lockdown—has been avoided.

It has been a challenge to adjust from a system that in many instances is based on hand-to-hand delivery of signed paper documents. For the most part, flexibility has prevailed, and we know of no material credit and operational risk events in traditional trade finance instruments such as letters of credit.

That is true not just for the banking system.

Beyond trade and supply chains, consider the situation in countries where entire populations have joined the digital ranks—digital identifiers, electronic banking, and accounts—versus those which have been slow to adapt.

Moving the digitization agenda forward is critical to creating more robust and resilient global trade and supply chains. It will also help drive efficiency and productivity gains that will be important component parts for us to rebuild the global economy.

Despite progress in recent years, the process of digitizing trade is far from finished. We need to create a harmonized digital infrastructure—standard identities, laws, and technical protocols—of which digitization can really take hold through the global trade and supply chain ecosystem.

The first step should be global adoption of the Legal Entity Identifier (LEI), so that everyone agrees on a common method to easily identify the players involved. Global trade would benefit in a big way from having a single trusted global entity that could verify the identity of companies that banks finance, showing who is who, and who owns whom, and what.

The LEI is a 20-digit, alpha-numeric code based on a standard developed by the International Organization for Standardization (ISO). The Global LEI Index provides open, standardized, and high-quality legal entity reference data. Countries without an ID system do not need to create one. Governments can simply encourage, or require through legislation, companies to acquire LEIs. Countries that do currently have ID systems should consider mapping these to LEIs for global harmonization.

Second, the model digitization laws proposed by the UN Commission on International Trade Law and the International Chamber of Commerce need to be adopted globally. Global adoption of these model laws will render digital commercial documents legally enforceable. Without these laws, digitization will not advance materially. It has been coming anyway, but it needs to come faster.

Third, to drive interoperability of systems to create seamless digital trade, we are working with the International Chamber of Commerce and Government of Singapore to create digital standards and protocols. This important initiative will get underway in the third quarter and will need to involve all component parts of the trade and supply chain ecosystem: buyers and sellers, ports, customs, shipping, logistics, and finance.

Going forward, close coordination will be key. Now that we are beginning to see the scale of the problems we face, the entire trade and supply chain ecosystem needs to up its digital game.

If we are driven by this crisis to aggressively digitize global trade and supply chains, we can make the economic recovery stronger and the future economy more robust.

Will the Pandemic Speed Up Workplace Automation?

Sameer Khatiwada

The threat of automation taking away jobs due to new and emerging technologies has faded from public discussion lately, but COVID-19 might be speeding up the process in an "organic way."

Take the example of small robots and drones that are now deployed in COVID-19 infected areas to check if residents are maintaining social distancing. This is a job that would be done typically by police or security services. In warehouses, robots are deployed in greater numbers than before. In the months ahead as countries reopen, we are likely to see more of these changes due to COVID-19. This is happening to adhere to the public health guidelines on social distancing.

Even before COVID-19, automation was taking place across Asia and the Pacific, particularly in capital-intensive manufacturing sector where labor costs are much higher. In 2018, How Technology Affects Jobs, a chapter in ADB's *Asian Development Outlook,* showed that technology was impacting routine jobs. The pandemic is likely to hasten some of these trends.[2]

The experience of living through the pandemic could provide impetus to automate jobs in sectors even where the labor cost is not as high, because preferences might change. But that will depend on how the cost of doing business will alter after COVID-19.

Whether or not a business will automate depends on the economic feasibility of such measures. Just because it is technically feasible to automate a set of tasks done at work, this does not necessarily lead to

---

[2] ADB. 2018. Asian Development Outlook (ADO) 2018: Theme Chapter - How Technology Affects Jobs. Manila. https://www.adb.org/sites/default/files/publication/411666/ado2018-themechapter.pdf.

automation. Businesses will weigh labor and other costs associated with hiring workers against the cost of acquiring and maintaining new machinery or an artificial intelligence-enabled service delivery system.

Whether automation is driven by the pandemic or by increasing labor costs, evidence shows that once businesses replace humans with robots, it is unlikely they will go back to hiring a worker for that role. Industrial robots, which are increasingly more sophisticated, are difficult to create and integrate into businesses. Once adopted, they are cheaper than human workers to maintain and operate.

It will take time for businesses to adjust to the new reality. In advanced countries, where lockdown measures have been eased, governments have put in place new restrictions and measures to be followed by businesses as they reopen. These will add to the cost of doing business but are also essential to maintain public health and safety. Interestingly, this has also created new work opportunities for people in public health and logistical services.

Some jobs will disappear forever and others will emerge due to these changes. For example, if people's preference for buying goods online increases, then we might not need as many workers working on shop floors in the big malls. Many large retailers are already using self-checkout lines in their stores, which has increasingly been adopted due to COVID-19. Many of these retail jobs will not come back.

The retail sector accounts for large shares of employment across developing countries in Asia. In the Philippines, it accounts for 16.5% of total employment; and in India 8.0%, in Indonesia 15.9%, in Thailand 11.4%, and in Viet Nam 9.1%.

The impact of digitization on actual employment levels will depend on consumer preferences for the digital shopping experience. Surveys show that Asian consumers are more than twice as likely (19%) as the global average (8%) to shop using a smartphone, according to research by KPMG. Early evidence shows that Asia's retail sector is ripe for a digital transformation.

We can expect the demand for highly skilled workers—those who perform mostly nonroutine cognitive tasks at work—to increase steadily in the coming decade. The education sector thus faces the dual challenge of helping countries embrace technologies of the Fourth Industrial Revolution while addressing fundamental educational needs to ensure no one is left behind.

New technologies are to be welcomed, as technological change is the ultimate driver of economic growth and better standards of living. However, advances in robotics and computing power are enabling a higher degree of automation than ever before. With new restrictions on social gathering, the push for automation has gotten stronger. Although this poses some challenges for job creation, we should not be pessimistic. New and better jobs will also be created.

Governments have an important role to play in preparing the workforce by aligning education and training with the changing labor demand. COVID-19 is likely to cause the first increase in global poverty since 1998, so it is important for social protection systems to be strengthened to avoid reversing significant gains in poverty reduction.

Automation is not a new phenomenon. In fact, through history, much technological change has involved the replacement of human labor with machines of some sort. COVID-19 will certainly hasten the process in some sectors but less so in others. The key is to prepare for the inevitable change with the right set of policy interventions.

Blending Education and Technology to Help Schools through the Pandemic

Brajesh Panth and Jeffrey Jian Xu

The COVID-19 pandemic is forcing governments around the world to find innovative and practical approaches to improve teaching and learning. An unprecedented surge in online learning provides opportunities to reimagine ways of teaching and learning. But the big question is: what are the best ways to do it?

The pandemic has exacerbated the existing learning crisis for low-income and middle-income countries in Asia and the Pacific. This will likely translate into loss in lifetime opportunities and earnings. Prior to the outbreak, physical access was not a key contributing factor to the learning crisis; rather, children were not learning despite going to school. The pandemic has amplified concerns of access as well as poor learning. Basic literacy and numeracy skills of the next generation in these countries are likely to decline unless there is immediate and meaningful intervention.

Due to massive school closures, there is huge interest in distance learning and solutions through education technology or EdTech, the use of technology and digital innovations to improve teaching and learning. How can countries link short-term solutions to challenges triggered by the pandemic with their medium- and long-term education objectives?

There are five key areas where EdTech solutions might help countries make this link: government policies, infrastructure, schools and teachers, parents and students, and private EdTech providers. For EdTech to be equitable, enduring, and efficient, these areas should work in tandem during the pandemic response, recovery, and rejuvenation phases.

The *response phase* in most countries is best suited for low-tech solutions that provide distance learning to students without internet access at home while schools are still closed. According to United Nations Educational, Scientific and Cultural Organization (UNESCO), more than 75% of households in most countries have access to either a television or radio, so these are a quick and efficient way to broadcast lessons and continue schooling. To support possible interactions between teachers and students, students can be given short messaging service or social media-based instructions and printed learning materials to accompany the broadcasting services. Without requiring heavy technical infrastructure, this phase serves as a practical short-term solution before schools reopen.

The *recovery phase* offers a medium-tech solution for students with mobile phones but with limited or low bandwidth internet connections. These students will have better access to learning resources through a large variety of quality open educational resources made available by digital content providers such as Kolibri from Learning Equality and Khan Academy.

These open source platforms can provide underprivileged communities with 24/7 access to learning content with targeted guidance. Blended learning in this phase allows face-to-face teacher/student interactions when schools start to reopen with tighter health and attendance monitoring. Teacher training and teacher development can also be based on blended learning to fully utilize the best online learning resources in curriculum instruction and digital literacy to manage blended learning.

This could be complemented in two ways. First, through technology upgrades in school management systems to integrate student/teacher health monitoring and upgrades in assessment systems to enable more effective blended learning throughout this phase, which may span 2 years. Second, it is equally important to promote apps to encourage parents, guardians, and government to invest in devices and connectivity to keep children engaged in learning outside of schools.

Building on the above two phases, the long-term rejuvenation phase could lead to a high-tech solution that allows far more effective blended learning including livestreaming with interactive distance learning and the use of different smart devices and platforms for students and teachers. These can include systems for learning management, assessment, teacher support, school management, and parents and student support.

Tracking the progress of students through enhanced digitization—before, during, and after classes—will help schools adapt and personalize the learning experience for students while improving their performance. This will require greater investments in digital infrastructure (e.g., high-speed internet in schools and homes), content, and teacher preparedness to allow live streaming, virtual classes, and immersive learning anywhere and anytime.

Each country's situation is unique, and countries should plan their activities based on their specific needs, aligned to different phases of readiness.

COVID-19 Has Created Digital Opportunities in the Pacific

Lotte Schou-Zibell and Nigel Phair

When a teacher on Vella Lavella Island in Solomon Islands needs to access the money she's earned teaching or received as remittances from a relative, she needs to take a day off work and, at considerable expense, travel by boat to Gizo Island. Frequently, bad weather, even cyclones, causes delays, as does poor internet access.

People in the Pacific have long needed more convenient digital solutions for payments and other financial services. This will not only give more people access to the financial system, it will make life much easier for those already using the system. COVID-19 has intensified the need to address these issues.

This sense of urgency increased in March when the World Health Organization (WHO) advised countries "to use contactless payments to reduce the risk of transmission." Although possibly a low risk, a psychological fear exists that money may pass on infection. Many businesses stopped accepting cash and moved to either online or contactless tap-and-go payments. Cashless payments, when the basic infrastructure is in place and the recipient has a bank account, are faster and easier.

Like many places, Pacific island countries reacted quickly to the viral threat with measures to prevent its arrival and physical distancing rules to limit its spread. What's more, many countries announced fiscal packages to counter its impact on economic growth and household incomes. These include additional health spending, temporary cash transfers for displaced workers, and credit support to small, liquidity-strapped enterprises and affected sectors.

However, setting up cash transfer programs is constrained by limited infrastructure, databases, registries, identification systems, and the number of people who have bank accounts. This results in authorities and program managers facing challenges in identifying beneficiaries, setting up effective payment mechanisms, and promptly disbursing much-needed money.

Digital payments are convenient but only as effective as their underlying infrastructure. What happens when power shuts down and the credit card reader is out of service? What if you lose your card and have to travel long distances to find a cash machine or have to wait days or longer for a replacement?

Going cashless also risks excluding some of the most vulnerable members of society, like the aged. Many people remain unbanked—66% of the population in Indonesia, 75% in Solomon Islands, and 85% in Papua New Guinea.

Data connectivity, mobile technology, digital banking, and financial technologies (fintech) can help overcome these challenges.

The Pacific islands are already undergoing fundamental changes as the result of new technologies. The many benefits include greater financial inclusion, lower transaction costs, less cash to physically manage and secure, real-time payments, and enhanced budgeting. Pacific island businesses—particularly small enterprises—can also enjoy the technologically driven economic growth experienced in advanced markets as e-commerce regulations are established and online payments are embraced.

The payments industry has a track record of innovation that can help solve the development challenges in the finance sector of emerging economies. This includes everything from "chip and pin," digital wallets, virtual card issuance, and tokenization, which enhances the security of "card-not-present" transactions. It can also include payments made using mobile devices, wearable tech, or internet-of-things devices.

Distributed ledger technology, cloud computing, and artificial intelligence have the potential to support these innovative services. That is why we have seen big technology companies also entering the payment space utilizing their technical capabilities and customers' data to provide payment services aiming to solve the financial inclusion challenge.

Innovation is taking place that allows people to transact between themselves, with businesses and government, often using mobile smart devices that can work both online and offline. Not only are incumbent banks seeking new business opportunities in fintech, but start-ups are disrupting markets seeking to expand financial inclusion by using technology to cut operational costs. A recent trial of a digital access tool in Papua New Guinea, for example, will allow citizens without ID to participate in the banking sector with savings accounts and loans.

Digital payments are cost-effective and convenient. Indeed, with innovations such as digital wallets, the user may not even have to enroll at a physical bank branch, thus enabling rural or otherwise remote citizens to participate. In Solomon Islands for example, a mobile wallet product called EziPei, was launched in February this year. While still at an early stage, it holds promise for citizens to send money; receive money; top up airtime; and pay for electricity and water from anywhere using any smartphone or feature phone, and on any network.

However, there are challenges that come with innovative products and services and entering new markets. Consumer and investor protection, compliance costs associated with anti-money laundering/combating the financing of terrorism laws, enforcement of tax laws and international sanctions, as well as circumvention of capital controls and securities laws, to name a few, are areas of concern for industry stakeholders. Building consumer trust and confidence in new financial technologies is also an area of utmost importance in order to achieve scale and success.

If managed, the coronavirus pandemic can serve as an important catalyst to further accelerate the adoption of non-cash payments. But for this to happen, central banks will need to consider their own innovation as well as enabling that fintechs and techfins (technology firms such as Google, Amazon, and Alibaba) deliver innovative financial services. This may include digital currencies and application program interfaces (API) for open banking.

Efforts will need to:

- Rationalize cash and promote and design digitization programs for commerce and the economy.

- Ensure universal access where merchants and consumers, irrespective of finances and education, will have access to the tools of the future.

- Support omni-channel payments. The rapid build-out of omni-channel capabilities will become an essential requirement for all payment companies in most geographies.

- Make payments contactless. The fear of contact with contaminated surfaces has given a real boost to the use of card and wallet-based contactless payments.

- Explore the use of data and technology to protect against fraud and cybercrime. Consumer education is also key as individuals are often the target in online crime.

- Provide financial and technical literacy to ensure consumers know how to use digital products wisely, safely, and securely. They need to have the skills and confidence to manage their money soundly, and to understand the risks.

- Redesign the regulatory model. In today's technology-driven financial sector, we need to enable innovation to expand access to finance while ensuring stability, consumer protection, and competition.

COVID-19 is changing consumer behavior and expectations. It will be imperative to balance short-term crisis management today with thinking ahead to restarting economies. Innovative products provide opportunities to support the unbanked and under-banked at a time when traditional banks have been forced to adjust business models and strategies. Policy makers should seize the opportunities this pandemic has created.

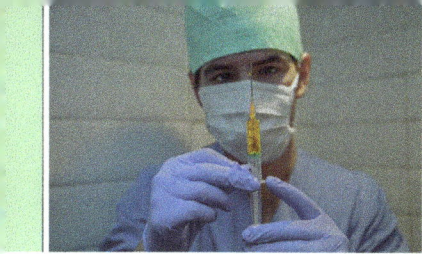

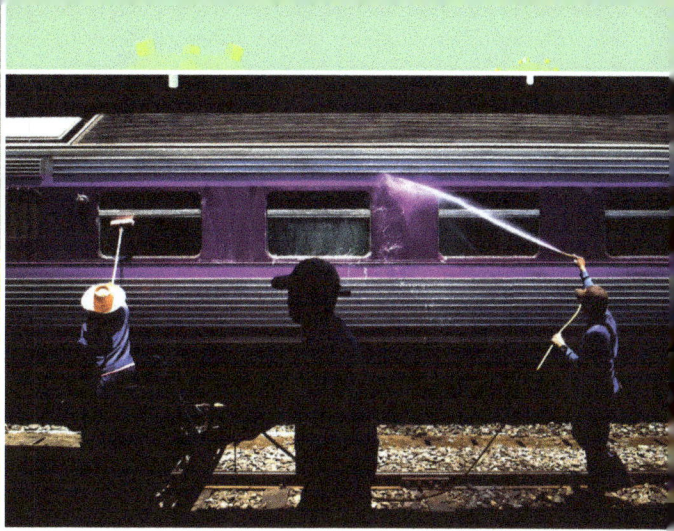

8. Rebooting Asia after COVID-19

Photos on previous page: [From the top] More than a third of the
world's COVID-19 vaccine developers are in Asia; Through the region,
nations in Asia and the Pacific are finding ways to cooperate on a
regional basis to overcome crises; Many leisure travelers are looking to
less crowded destinations in their home countries to visit during the
pandemic (photo by Sylwia Bartyzel); Terminal 2 of The Mactan Cebu
International Airport was built using a PPP contract; Asia's towns and
cities are waiting to spring back to life (photo by Benjamin Wong).

Rebooting the Economy during COVID-19

Patrick Osewe

Economies across Asia and the Pacific—like in much of the world—have been hit hard by the coronavirus outbreak. To slow the spread of the virus, many governments have chosen to impose lockdowns and travel bans. While vital, these measures have also had severe economic impact. ADB estimates that Asia is likely to lose 68 million jobs if the pandemic goes on until September.

With vast uncertainty about the possible health and economic outcomes of the virus over the coming months, experts in public health and epidemiology are urging countries to prepare for a second wave of infection. This means that countries must grapple with how to balance virus containment with national economic interests—not only now, but possibly again in the future.

Drawing on a rapid review of recent evidence, we have summarized below key issues for countries to consider as they restart their economies. They can be categorized into two main priorities: when to restart and how to restart. Applied early enough, the findings below may help some countries in the initial stages of an outbreak to avoid the need to shut down and restart their economy altogether.

While no country can expect zero new coronavirus infections in the foreseeable future, the WHO suggests six conditions that countries should aim to meet before they end their lockdowns.[1] These include: (i) having sufficient capacity to ensure that COVID-19 transmission is under control; (ii) diagnose, treat, and isolate all cases; (iii) protect vulnerable populations

---

[1] World Health Organization. 2020. 2019 Novel Coronavirus (2019-nCoV): Strategic Preparedness and Response Plan. Geneva. https://www.who.int/publications/i/item/strategic-preparedness-and-response-plan-for-the-newcoronavirus

from potential outbreaks; (iv) establish preventive measures in schools, work settings, and other essential places; (v) manage imported cases; and (vi) empower communities to live under a "new normal"—including maintaining social distancing, wearing face masks, and staying at home when sick with flu-like or COVID-like symptoms.

With countries in the region at different stages of the pandemic, several useful lessons have emerged about when to end a lockdown and reboot the economy:

- **Rebooting too early.** A number of countries are considering dialing back their restrictions, ending a lockdown prematurely—or without appropriate plans in place. This can start a cycle of new infections.

- **Rebooting while keeping disease at bay.** Some countries gained an early edge and managed to keep the virus under control by acting swiftly. Both Thailand and Viet Nam used their early start to slow disease transmission through extensive surveillance, monitoring, contact tracing, and isolation strategies.

- **Rebooting after an extensive outbreak was controlled.** The People's Republic of China (PRC) was able to stabilize COVID-19 infections after an extensive outbreak by identifying (i.e., testing) and quarantining infected individuals as quickly as possible.

For those coronavirus-stricken economies grappling with how to lift their lockdown, many experts in public health and economics also agree that a gradual or phased approach that embraces flexible strategies for different regions or sectors (depending on their readiness) is best. Some early findings from the PRC indicate that a systematic and phased approach in easing lockdown and restrictions—including classifying areas according to risk (low, medium, and high)—has so far maintained efforts to curb the pandemic and keep a second wave of infections at bay.

The following seven questions were designed to help governments think about how best to prepare for a phased reboot of their economies:

1. Are there fiscal policies in place to provide income support, ensure access to safety net programs, and/or support small business needs? For example, the Republic of Korea increased allowances for home

care and job seekers, while the PRC temporarily waived social security contributions for businesses.

2.   Which sectors should be reopened first? For example, does the country start with the sector with most value to the economy like manufacturing and farming—while still maintaining public health measures? Do they keep closed those sectors with potential risk of infection such as entertainment and sports activities?

3.   What areas/subregions/communities/cities should be opened first? For example, is there a strategy in place for areas and communities with crowded living conditions in order to avoid an outbreak?

4.   What kind of travel will be allowed upon opening? For example, does the country allow domestic travel within the country or restrict domestic travel (e.g., urban to rural) to avoid outbreaks in previously COVID-19-free areas?

5.   When and how should transport be reopened? For example, in Istanbul, local government provides free public transport for health care workers and pays the fuel and staff costs of privately-owned buses to subsidize public transport.

6.   What social restrictions should be lifted and when? For example, does the country ban public gatherings or limit them in size (e.g., 10 or 50 people) in public and private places?

7.   When should schools open (nurseries, schools, and universities)? Does the country open schools sooner as this will influence when parents are able to resume work?

Because of the unprecedented nature of the COVID-19 pandemic, governments will continue to grapple with tremendous uncertainty—and considerable social and economic turmoil. Using these considerations as a guide, policy leaders can make better, more informed decisions when it comes to getting their economies—and their countries—back on track.

Two Ways to Help Revive Tourism in Asia and the Pacific

Matthias Helble

Tourism in Asia and the Pacific has been hit hard by the COVID-19 pandemic. International tourist arrivals fell by over 90% in many countries during April to May 2020, compared to 2019—and the situation is likely to persist, with the UN2 World Tourism Organization forecasting a drop of up to 80% over the whole year. An International Air Transport Association survey in June 2020 suggested that half of respondents would wait 6 months or more before traveling again. Clearly, recovery will take time.

In the many countries where tourism is an important source of foreign exchange earnings, the sudden fall in demand is having severe economic and social consequences within and beyond the tourism sector. Two strategies are being tried to revive the sector in the short run: promoting domestic tourism and using "travel bubbles," an exclusive travel partnership among countries that have controlled the virus to allow tourism between them.

Promoting Domestic Tourism

The Philippines, for example, invested $8.5 million in a domestic tourism campaign in early 2020. In Viet Nam, domestic tourism has shown a clear upward trend after the lockdown was eased. Travel bans and the fear of infection have meant that redirecting tourists, who ordinarily travel abroad, to domestic destinations could be a viable strategy. Many people still yearn to travel, but fear foreign and exotic places and wish to avoid mass transportation or are simply restricted by local lockdowns.

What if all tourists who headed for foreign destinations in 2018 travel domestically instead in 2020? Across Asia and the Pacific, in more than half of cases, domestic tourism has the potential to fully replace foreign visitors (Figure 8.1). For example, in Armenia, outbound tourists exceed the number of inbound foreign tourists by 30%. This is not the case, however, in countries that depend heavily on tourism, such as Cambodia or Fiji, which would still face large gaps in demand even if they could fully mobilize domestic tourism.

Figure 8.1: Scenario Analysis of Domestic Tourists Replacing Foreign Tourists, based on Number of Tourists
(%)

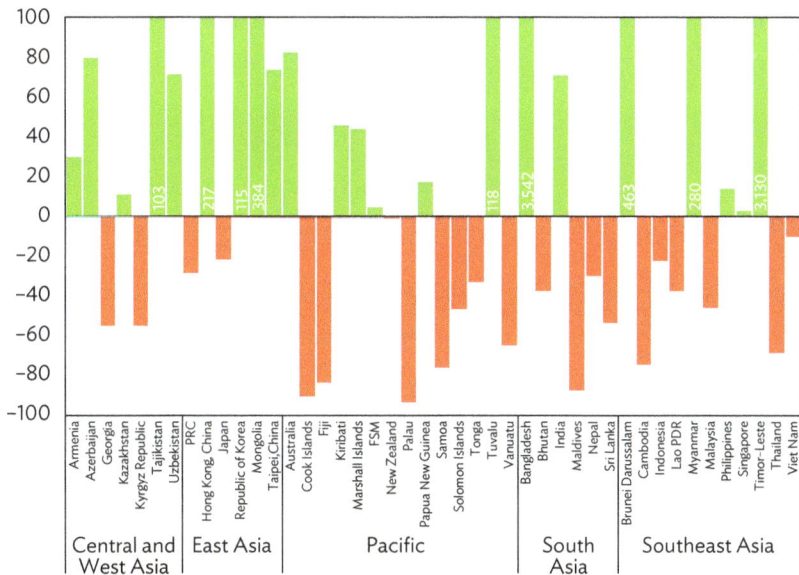

FSM = Federated States of Micronesia, Lao PDR = Lao People's Democratic Republic, PRC = People's Republic of China.
Note: These are the ratios of the difference between outbound and inbound tourists with respect to inbound tourists. Using data from 2018 tourist arrivals, a value of zero suggests an economy's domestic tourists are sufficient to compensate for international tourist arrivals. Economies with green bars indicate the potential of domestic tourism is higher than the gap left by the absence of international tourists. Economies including Bangladesh; Brunei Darussalam; Hong Kong, China; Mongolia; Myanmar; the Republic of Korea; Tajikistan; Timor-Leste; and Tuvalu have values that surpass 100%, suggesting these economies' domestic tourists were more than double their international tourists in 2018. Economies with red bars indicate a gap in arrivals even with mobilization of domestic tourists.
Source: Asian Development Bank calculations based on United Nations World Tourism Organization statistical database (accessed 13 June 2020).

Domestic tourism probably cannot fully replace foreign tourists for other reasons as well. For example, some people might not want to travel at all for fear of the pandemic. Social distancing and other containment measures are required even for domestic tourism, making it difficult to operate at the maximum level. And overall demand for tourism has declined amid job losses and other loss of income in the pandemic. Finally, a gap may exist between the demand of domestic travelers and the supply of available tourism services. Some countries successfully attracted high-income travelers from abroad in the past, but the number of domestic tourists that can afford such high-end services might be limited.

Travel Bubbles

These are agreements to open borders to visitors from a "travel bubble" partner economy. Travel bubbles could be for business travel only or also include leisure travel. They often specify provisions on health protocols that need to be followed when leaving and entering the territory. Access can be reciprocal or only in one direction. They can be formed between two or more partners.

The first travel bubble in Asia and the Pacific was established between the PRC and the Republic of Korea on 1 May 2020. The agreement is limited to business travelers who need to be invited by a company in the receiving country. Visitors need to monitor their health for 2 weeks and get tested for the virus 72 hours before departure from their home country. Upon arrival, they are tested again and quarantined until the results are obtained. The two countries are currently discussing expansion of this program.

Bilateral travel bubbles may help the economies that are highly dependent on tourism from one source (Figure 8.2). For example, the gap for Fiji would drop from 84% to 44% if it entered a bilateral agreement with Australia. Thailand would see an improvement from minus 68% to minus 46% if it established an agreement with the PRC. While these would be significant improvements, they still leave these economies with a large deficit.

Travel bubbles are geared toward redirecting a significant part of the partner economies' international travelers. For example, another travel bubble under negotiation is the Trans-Tasman travel bubble between Australia and New Zealand. Given the strong links between the two countries, the agreement is expected to boost tourism in both, as similar COVID-19 status argues for an agreement. However, a recent outbreak in the Australian state of Victoria has stalled negotiations.

Figure 8.2: Scenario Analysis of Bilateral Travel Bubble with Largest Partner, based on Number of Tourists
(%)

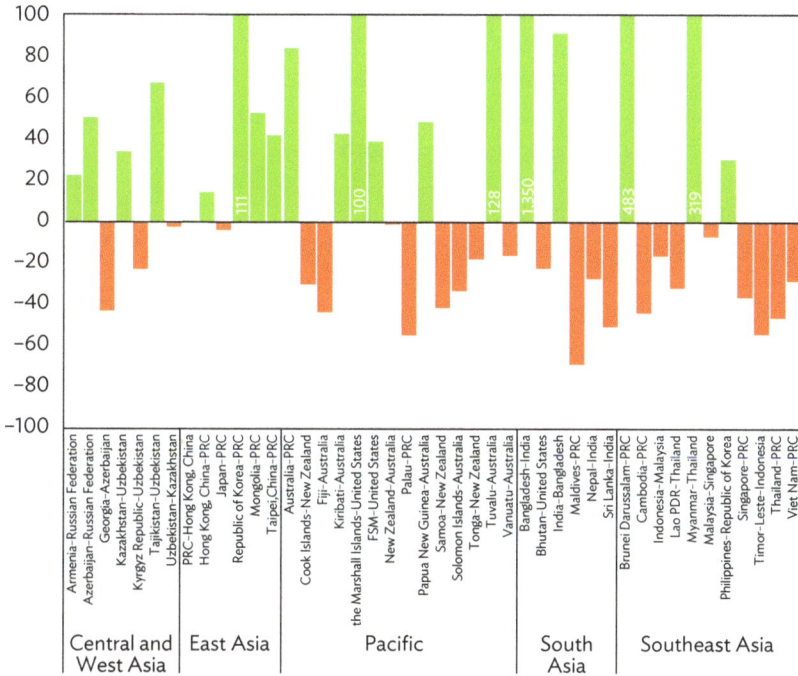

FSM = Federated States of Micronesia, Lao PDR = Lao People's Democratic Republic, PRC = People's Republic of China.

Notes:

1. Using 2018 data, we assumed that domestic tourists which would otherwise leave the economy will stay at home in this scenario. We then get the difference between international tourist arrivals, and the sum of inbound tourists from the economy's preferred partner and its own domestic tourists. We then divide this figure with the total international tourist arrivals to get this ratio.

2. The green bars indicate by how much the combined domestic tourists from an economy and its preferred partner would surpass the number of international tourists. Some economies and their preferred partner including Bangladesh, Brunei Darussalam, the Marshall Islands, the Republic of Korea, Tuvalu, and Myanmar have values that surpass 100% which suggests that their combined tourists are more than double their 2018 international tourist arrivals. Economies with red bars indicate a gap in arrivals even with mobilization of domestic tourists and arrivals from their preferred partner.

3. Arrival data for 2017 was used for the Marshall Islands, Tonga, and Tuvalu, while 2016 and 2014 was used for FSM and Bangladesh, respectively. There was no arrival data available for Afghanistan, Pakistan, Turkmenistan, and Tuvalu for any year.

Source: Asian Development Bank calculations based on United Nations World Tourism Organization statistical database (accessed 13 June 2020).

Other travel bubbles under negotiation aim to allow movement of cross-border commuters (Malaysia and Singapore) and tourists (the "Bula bubble" involving Australia, Fiji, and New Zealand).

Figure 8.3 illustrates large potential benefits of subregional bubbles for the Kyrgyz Republic in Central West Asia, for East Asia, and Palau in case it joined a subregional travel bubble with East Asia, and for most Pacific islands in case of a travel bubble with Australia and New Zealand.

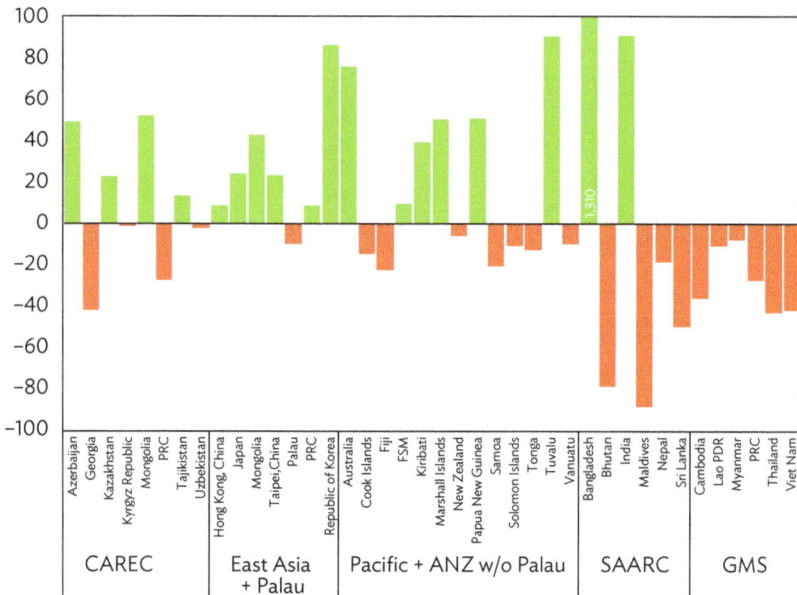

Figure 8.3: Scenario Analysis of Subregional Tourism Bubbles, based on Number of Tourists
(%)

ANZ=Australia New Zealand, CAREC=Central Asia Regional Economic Cooperation, FSM = Federated States of Micronesia, GMS=Greater Mekong Subregion, Lao PDR = Lao People's Democratic Republic, PRC = People's Republic of China, SAARC=South Asian Association for Regional Cooperation.
Note: For this scenario, we used data from 2018 and assumed that the tourists will be able to move freely within their respective bubbles. Tourists who went to a destination outside the bubble were assumed to stay at home. We subtract the number of tourists who stayed at home and those who arrived from the bubble from the total number of international tourists. We then get the proportion of this figure with respect to the number of international tourist arrivals. Arrival data for 2017 was used for the Marshall Islands, Tonga, and Tuvalu, while 2016 and 2014 was used for FSM and Bangladesh, respectively. There was no arrival data available for Afghanistan, Pakistan, Turkmenistan, and Tuvalu for any year.
Source: Asian Development Bank calculations based on United Nations World Tourism Organization statistical database (accessed 13 June 2020).

One challenge when negotiating travel bubbles is that the spread of the COVID-19 has not been brought under control in most economies. Tourists' appetite to travel abroad also depends on the pandemic situation. The opportunity to open for bilateral tourism typically only arises once an economy and its partner are well beyond their peak of new infections. In addition to the pandemic itself, the preparedness of an economy to fight COVID-19 is another important consideration for tourists. Only a few economies in the region seem to be equipped to handle outbreaks swiftly and effectively.

Promoting domestic tourism might be a viable option for some economies, but for most it falls short. The other option, setting up travel bubbles, can also be challenging. As the pandemic remains unpredictable, maintaining the bubbles will not be a simple undertaking. For example, the negotiations on the Trans-Tasman travel bubble were stalled due to a local COVID-19 outbreak in Melbourne. Even with these two strategies, the tourism industry is therefore likely to struggle until a vaccine is widely available. It is also important to note that travel bubbles are only the second-best option and should be a temporary measure that becomes eventually replaced by a fully open, non-discriminatory regime.

Prior to COVID-19, the tourism industry was one of the most dynamic sectors in the Asia and Pacific region. Once the pandemic is over, there are many reasons to believe that the sector will resume its vibrancy.

Managing Public–Private Partnerships for a Post-Pandemic Recovery

Sanjay Grover, Hanif Rahemtulla, and Colin Gin

COVID-19 is directly impacting infrastructure services around the world. Demand for existing infrastructure has fallen sharply. Construction of new infrastructure has slowed, if not stalled, everywhere.

The COVID-19 crisis is also unique in the suddenness and the severity of its impact on the economy and infrastructure usage. While some infrastructure sectors like health and information and communication technology (ICT) are experiencing unprecedented demand, others like airports have seen demand dry up. In a period of 2 months, daily commercial flights have fallen from more than 110,000 to less than 30,000. In April, national highway traffic in Java, Indonesia, plunged by almost 70%. But uniformly, across all sectors the costs of service delivery are going up as governments rush to make service delivery pandemic-proof.

In seeking value for money, public–private partnerships (PPPs) are becoming an important modality for governments to attract private capital and expertise into infrastructure in Asia. PPP projects can be structured so the demand risk, the risk of infrastructure usage, is retained by the investor (usually in transport) or by the government. More than 80% of the PPPs that reached financial closure in Asia in the last 2 decades are in transport sector, and these are usually structured, so demand risk is retained by the project company through user fees.

Pair the impact of declining revenue and increasing costs with the uncertainty of a timeline to complete recovery or an as-yet-unknown new normal, and you can start to see the formidable challenges facing governments and investors in navigating the long-term contractual nature of operational PPPs.

First, a focus on the infrastructure PPP challenges of the immediate.

In Asia, the immediate stress is being felt primarily by the partner carrying the demand risk. Significantly less revenue and significantly higher operating costs will force investors to dig into their reserves to keep critical infrastructure functioning.

Even projects where the investor depends on an availability payment from the government will feel stressed because, at a time when issues of health and economic well-being have stretched governments, little revenue will come in to offset the government's payments.

Even though these infrastructure PPPs are stressed, infrastructure may not form part of the upfront stimulus measures given COVID-related pressing requirements. Yet, where there are payment obligations, governments must continue to honor those obligations.

From a policy/portfolio perspective, in the near term, countries should take lessons from the global financial crisis and the Asian financial crisis. Governments in Asia will need to quickly assess the potential short-term impact of reduced demand and increased costs across their PPP portfolio, differentiating by project type, project status, and assessing government exposure.

While it may be difficult to predict the impact, stress tests should be developed to assess a range of the exposure of the government.

In coming blogs, we will discuss infrastructure PPP challenges and opportunities in the medium term while we wait for clarity on the new normal. With credit and liquidity in short supply, stimulus measures may be needed for the infrastructure sector, as continued payment risks will increasingly impair investors. In light of the pandemic, a significant portion of this stimulus may also be targeted for health care, education, social housing, digital connectivity, and agribusiness sectors.

Even though the number of PPPs has been increasing rapidly in Asia, most Asian countries' PPP programs are still considered developing or emerging by international lenders. Only 13% of the countries in Asia and the Pacific have procedures that align PPPs with public investment priorities, and even fewer may have good contingent liability management processes.

Further, as with the dip in the number of PPPs worldwide in the years following the Asian financial crisis of 1997–1998 and the 2008 global financial crisis, this pandemic will drastically change the risk profile of infrastructure PPPs.

Regardless of the shape of the recovery, V-, U-, or swoosh-shaped, governments should revisit their PPP frameworks and risk sharing to prepare for the longer-term, making government support an integral element for seeking value for money through PPPs.

With declining GDPs and decreasing fiscal headroom, this is not going to be easy, and new sources of revenue—such as bonds, land value capture, and asset recycling—may have to be mobilized. COVID-19 is an opportunity for leadership to strengthen local governments so that cities, many of which are struggling to meet the social and economic challenges of the pandemic, can become frontliners in the recovery process.

Multilateral financial institutions will also have a big role to play in supporting governments in this transitory period, with capacity building, technical, and financial assistance through this period.

In the long run, there is a lot of uncertainty about what the new normal will bring, but a few things can be safely assumed. One, a significant infrastructure gap to attain the UN Sustainable Development Goals will remain, and the private sector will have an even bigger role to play in closing that gap and ensuring we build back better.

Two, the unit cost of infrastructure service provision will increase as we make current projects pandemic-proof, and newer, efficient and disruptive ways of delivering services will have to be found. Think 5G for all.

Finally, in whatever way the new normal shows up, governments in Asia will take a bigger step toward resilient and quality infrastructure, and here PPPs can help by bringing in private sector capital and technical expertise as governments continue to look for value for money in infrastructure provision.

Asia and the Pacific Can Overcome COVID-19 by Working Together

Arjun Goswami

COVID-19 and the response by national governments around the world has prompted many to question the future of globalization and cross-border cooperation. The fear and panic which accompany deadly pandemics such as COVID-19 has led many countries, such as those in the Pacific, to implement national lockdowns, suspend international travel, and close borders. The disruption to global supply chains may well also accelerate existing trends toward onshoring and reshoring of productive capacity.

The preexisting global growth slowdown, the trade war between the US and the PRC, and the impacts of the technological Fourth Industrial Revolution made onshoring and reshoring increasingly attractive. The impact of the pandemic on the PRC, which represents 18% of global parts and components trade, and the loss of confidence in just-in-time logistics, could amplify this. A potential global economic recession will further depress cross-border trade and investment. This has led some thinkers to declare the "end of globalization as we know it,"

Yet, what we need now is not to step back from cross-border cooperation but to redouble such cooperation. It should be deployed to protect human health more effectively from the current pandemic while promoting a recovery of human welfare from the effects of the crisis. COVID-19 reminds us that we are highly interconnected, not just in terms of goods, capital, and information, but also human interaction, and that disease does not respect national boundaries.

It is therefore crucial to cooperate to ensure coordinated responses to effectively mitigate pandemic crises. These could include coordinated travel restrictions. While these may be necessary in the short run, in the longer run this will result in significant economic and financial costs. Consequently, it will be vital over time for countries to cooperate to factor in lessons learned while promoting recovery from the economic effects of this pandemic.

Fortunately, Asia and the Pacific is showing strong signs of understanding the importance of continued regional cooperation. The financial contagion of the 1997 Asian financial crisis led many countries toward deeper regional cooperation and the same appears to be true for this crisis, albeit involving contagion of a quite different nature.

On 13 March, ASEAN senior health officials met online to reaffirm their commitment to regional collective action, share information on the results of disease surveillance and social interventions, and discuss regional access to equipment and testing facilities. The South Asian Association of Regional Cooperation (SAARC) has also acted. On 15 March, SAARC leaders discussed the establishment of an emergency fund to fight COVID-19, a common research platform, and sharing of knowledge and equipment.

ADB has regional cooperation as part of its DNA and is well positioned to help sustain these efforts. It supports regional cooperation platforms such as the South Asia Subregional Economic Cooperation (SASEC), Central Asia Regional Economic Cooperation (CAREC), and the Greater Mekong Subregion (GMS) programs. These platforms have a history of effective mobilization to support regional public goods. The GMS, for example, implemented a Regional Communicable Disease Control Project which helped contain outbreaks of disease, reduced fatalities, and strengthen regional networks.

Moreover, ADB has mobilized $20 billion for developing member countries' response to COVID-19. This includes support to the private sector, including micro, small, and medium-sized enterprises (MSMEs) directly impacted by the crisis, and $2.5 billion in concessional and grant resources.

In the medium term, ADB will need to work with governments and the private sector to reduce the likelihood of future pandemics and respond effectively when they (inevitably) occur. Options for consideration include:

- **Equipment, research, and testing facilities**. Building regional equipment pools which can be deployed where they are needed most; and adopting strategies and action plans for regional research and testing. As part of its COVID-19 regional response in the Pacific, ADB is supporting pooled procurement of personal protective and health equipment through the UN system for two Pacific developing member countries.

- **Regulations and policies**. Helping countries meet regional and international standards on disease surveillance and reporting and enabling cross-border information sharing on emergence of infectious diseases; updating and harmonizing national public health legislation to support safe cross-border travel and tourism; and developing policies to support social protection of mobile, vulnerable groups.

- **Coordination mechanisms and systems**. Using regional cooperation platforms and mechanisms to deepen and extend the use of information technology for trade facilitation to build regional traveler databases and information systems that operate in real time, to support contact tracing and predict community spread. In the Pacific, ADB is using a regional technical assistance to support digital health information systems which improve disease surveillance. The intention is to strengthen country systems and support regional information exchange.

- **Resources and funding**. Establishing regional resources and strengthening the capacity and effectiveness of regional quick-disbursing disaster funds and financing instruments.

To those who say that the pandemic has triggered a "country first" mentality, see how Asia and the Pacific and its regional communities are continuing to stand together in the best tradition of regional cooperation, especially during crisis. They are looking beyond themselves, recognizing that the pandemic represents a transnational threat and involves mutual risks.

Asia Should Lead the Way in Producing a COVID-19 Vaccine

Matthias Helble and Susann Roth

The COVID-19 pandemic is an unfolding global crisis, which goes way beyond public health impacts. It is also an opportunity to take a more holistic approach to health and well-being, invest in health systems, in better collaboration in research, medical technologies, and in resilient supply chains for the long-term benefit of all.

Pandemic experiences in Asia offer valuable lessons to share. These include expansion of COVID-19 testing of the population in order to help authorities track the progress of the disease and determine whether social distancing, hygiene, and health interventions are working. Some Asian countries have strengthened independently managed public health bodies that report directly to the top leadership of the country to ensure quick action and reduce red tape. Emergency procurement mechanisms and market protection to allow the fast purchase of goods and even advanced market commitments for vaccines are other important tools. Transparent communication of risks and frequent updates to the public bolster people's confidence in the government's response. And decentralizing health care back into the communities with stronger community clinics helps to avoid hospital infection hotspots.

These and lessons also give the region a high vantage point. Asia needs to invest in high-quality health services which focus on health promotion and disease prevention, as well as decentralized and cost-effective primary health care. In this context, Asia has also an opportunity to lead the world in collaborating on deploying an efficacious COVID-19 vaccine to population groups at risk. To date, an efficacious vaccine provides the beacon of hope to return to "normal" as soon as possible.

The global vaccine research and development effort in response to the COVID-19 pandemic is unprecedented in terms of scale and speed. Given the imperative for speed, there is an indication that a vaccine could be available under emergency use or similar protocols by early 2021. This is a fundamental change from the traditional lengthy vaccine development pathway, which takes on average over 10 years, even when compared with the accelerated 5-year timescale for development of the first Ebola vaccines.

To achieve the goal of early 2021, we will need parallel and adaptive development phases, innovative regulatory processes and scaled-up manufacturing capacity, and above all particularly good post-market surveillance to monitor adverse side effects.

Asia and the Pacific is playing a critical role in this historic endeavor. Of the confirmed active vaccine candidates, 36 (46%) are in North America, 14 (18%) in the PRC, and 14 (18%) in other parts of Asia and Australia, with 14 (18%) in Europe. This is according to an analysis by the Coalition of Epidemic Preparedness Innovations.

The analysis also states that most efforts come from smaller private sector manufacturers, with 36% coming from Asia. The importance of Asia and the Pacific in the international vaccine market is also reflected in the trade data. Six countries in the region are among the top 20 vaccines exporters worldwide. In order of their export volume, they are: India, the Republic of Korea, Australia, Singapore, Indonesia, and the PRC. Other countries are smaller producers, but still export more than $100 million worth of vaccines yearly—Malaysia, the Philippines, Viet Nam, Fiji, and Thailand.

Being at the forefront of developing new vaccines against COVID-19, Asia can build on its substantial experience in producing vaccines that comply with international standards. The key question is now how to best utilize these existing resources to quickly develop and scale up the production of a COVID-19 vaccine.

The need for expedited and novel approaches requires close coordination between manufacturers, research institutes, governments, and regulatory agencies to ensure quality and safety. Most importantly, we need to find a regional coordination mechanism that ensures the production and distribution of safe vaccines for the entire region within a short amount of time.

The first step would be to map out existing capacities. The governments of vaccine-producing countries should request their vaccine manufacturers to give them detailed overviews of existing production capacity, investment needs to upgrade facilities, technology transfer needed, and the surge potential. Existing production of crucial vaccines should not be unnecessarily interrupted. Starting production from scratch in a country with no previous experience is usually a lengthy process that will take no less than 5 years. Therefore, it would be crucial to expand the existing capacities.

Second, countries need to draw up vaccination schedules and logistics. Vaccines will not become available at once, but in batches. Countries need to decide who will be vaccinated first to understand the amounts needed so that they can make advanced market commitments, which are important to inform manufacturers production. The criteria can be based on the profession, and risk locations and risk profiles. Further, vaccines typically require a consistent cold chain. Existing solutions to distribute traditional vaccines need to be expanded to solve this problem.

The third step would be to coordinate efforts within the region. Governments in the region should meet to exchange information and design a plan for a regional solution. Non-producing countries should be ready to make commitments to provide financial and possibly human resources for the expansion of vaccine production and procurement. In return, the vaccine-producing countries would allot contingencies of newly produced vaccines to those countries. Those negotiations could be thorny, as some vaccine-producing countries might have a strong incentive to first distribute the vaccines domestically or to richer countries.

A regional agreement should include: (i) agreement on vaccination protocols, most importantly who will be vaccinated first among mobile and migrant population groups and health workers; (ii) estimation of vaccines doses needed in the next 10 years; (iii) agreement on funding mechanisms of the vaccine production (including R&D), procurement and delivery; (iv) development of reliance polices for vaccine approval by regulatory agencies; (v) close collaboration of regulatory agencies to ensure post-market surveillance of adverse side effects especially in countries with weak health surveillance capacity; and (vi) agreements on grievance mechanism for adversely affected people.

Upscaling the vaccine production rapidly and reaching as many people as possible within a short amount of time requires a regional response that is based on the principle of regional solidarity. Vaccines should become available to critical staff, like health care frontliners, throughout the region. Having people immunized in only selected countries, while other countries suffer severe consequences is not a scenario Asia would want to envisage.

At the same time, rapid approval of new vaccines needs to be safeguarded by sound regulatory systems and surveillance of severe events to ensure we do not do more harm than good. We need strong regional coordination and cooperation among vaccine developers, regulators, policy makers, funders, public health bodies, and governments to ensure safe and effective vaccines can be manufactured in sufficient quantities and made regionally accessible including to the poorest countries. Regional coordination and cooperation can be a lengthy process, but in the current crisis, delays mean many lives lost.

It is time for the Asia and the Pacific to come together to take a leadership role in not only producing a COVID-19 vaccine, but distributing it to those who need it most.

9. Building Back Better Together

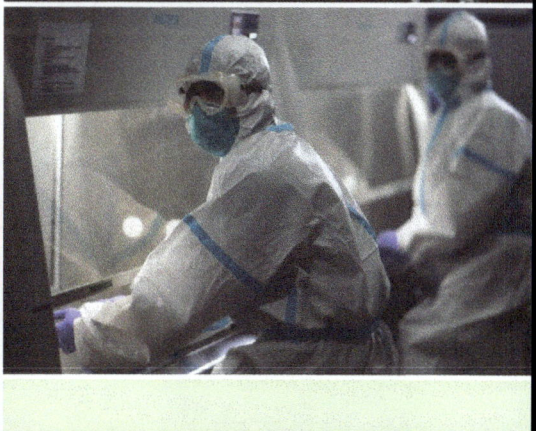

Photos on previous page: [From the top] The climate crisis was already well underway before the COVID-19 pandemic struck; "Greening" Asia's cities will make them more resilient to future pandemics (photo by Vitalijs Barilo); Innovative financing is needed to protect the world's oceans (photo by Dorothea Oldani); Hand washing and other basic hygiene can be challenging on Pacific islands where water is scarce (photo by Nathan Dumlao); With post-pandemic re-opening of economies, Asia's infrastructure projects are getting back on track (photo by Yancy Min); The Pandemic Sub-National Reference Laboratory at the Jose B. Lingad Memorial Regional Hospital in San Fernando City, Pampanga, financed by the $3 million grant from the Asia Pacific Disaster Response Fund, can perform up to 3,000 COVID-19 tests daily, significantly increasing the country's testing capacity (photo by Eric Sales).

Building Back Better, Differently, and Together in Asia and the Pacific

Bambang Susantono

The COVID-19 pandemic is the greatest challenge of this generation thus far. But pandemics are not new. A century ago, the influenza epidemic of 1918–1920 wreaked similar havoc. Strong emphasis was placed on social distancing at that time, but the saving of lives and recovery of livelihoods were constrained by a nascent and limited multilateral architecture and very few technological options.

In contrast to a century ago, there is a much greater arsenal of weapons available to countries in Asia and the Pacific to address the issues arising from the current pandemic. Regional cooperation holds great promise. Pandemics do not respect borders, so the pathway to saving lives and securing livelihoods lies not in national isolation, but in cooperating across borders on information sharing, capacity building, and policy coordination. The digital economy is the best means of working together while minimizing physical contact.

In the short term, Asia and the Pacific governments' emergency assistance packages, many of them supported by ADB, are helping build health system capacity and providing necessities for the poorest households. However, as had happened in the influenza epidemic in 1918–1920, repeated waves are possible. In the medium term, therefore, we need to strengthen countries' resilience and find ways to begin recovery and sustain development progress. For these purposes, ADB has announced a $20 billion pandemic response package to support these efforts.

Developing Asia's Immediate Response Measures

ADB has built a database that contains information about the measures that its members have taken to combat the pandemic. Asian governments and central banks have acted swiftly and decisively. Data collected until early May 2020 indicate that ADB's developing member countries have committed $1.9 trillion (substantially more if we include Asia's advanced economies) in the form of (i) actions to support normal functioning of money markets and short-term lending, (ii) encouraging private credit creation, (iii) long-term lending to the non-financial sector, (iv) equity claims on the private sector, and (v) direct support to income/revenue. This amount represents about 8% of their combined GDP. The packages committed will be decisive for supporting Asia's comeback. Moreover, to maximize the activation of the transformative tools of regional cooperation, digital economy, and financing, ADB and its partners are planning a recovery strategy focused on *"building back better, differently, and together."*

Building Back Better

Past pandemics have shown that social distancing is important but costly. To minimize its economic costs, it is critical to *build better*. This will require making lockdowns "smarter" through testing, tracing, and isolation.

Significant investments need to be made for this. ADB can support countries with weak individual purchasing power and capacity and procure them through regional pooling. ADB has experience of the power of such collective action, for example, in the Pacific region. In the medium term, countries will need to build regional disease surveillance, rapid response teams to investigate disease outbreaks, and coordination mechanisms for harmonizing regional treatment protocols and registration of medicines. ADB is already working through existing regional platforms to build systems and improve the use of digital disease surveillance information and for e-health services. It serves as the secretariat for the Greater Mekong Subregion (GMS) Economic Cooperation Program, the Central Asia Regional Economic Cooperation (CAREC) Program, and the South Asia Subregional Economic Cooperation (SASEC) Program.

Building Back Differently

Over the past 50 years, the region has become more integrated on the back of improved physical connectivity. This has not only driven economic growth but also built resilience. The pandemic threatens this progress.

The need of the hour is for countries to *build differently* the infrastructure required to overcome health risks that come alongside connectivity. For example, using regional traveler databases or mobile health certificates showing travelers COVID-19 status could be rolled out to operate in real time.

Past health crises also highlighted the importance of investing in decongesting cities and making them more livable. This time around, the decongestion of urban development in major cities through trade and transport links to hinterlands in economic corridors will be key.

Building Back Together

Trade and investment had been important drivers of Asian growth and will remain so during the recovery period. Before the pandemic started, we were seeing stress buildup in the multilateral trading system and a move toward increased protectionism.

The crisis, however, has shown that whether it be trade in food or medical equipment, trade increases resilience. The PRC, for example, is the largest producer of personal protective equipment, but 55% of the demand comes from the US and Europe. We need to restart trade, but this time around, we also need to *build together*. South and Central Asia need to become better integrated with the rest of Asia, and Asia with the rest of the world.

Greater attention also needs to be paid to building resilience in sectors such as agriculture and small- and medium-sized enterprises hit hard by the pandemic. This is important not only because the sectors provide a livelihood for a majority of poor, and especially for women-owned businesses, but also because they are storehouses of economic dynamism and critical links in supply chains.

We are faced with a new normal. Public and private resources are stretched worldwide. We need to maximize the impact of every investment we make to save lives and secure livelihoods. However, the COVID-19 crisis can also be used as an opportunity to accelerate change and transform the economy using 21st century tools.

Strengthening Disaster Resilience

Benno Ferrarini

Asia and the Pacific is the most disaster-prone region in the world and therefore more vulnerable to the COVID-19 pandemic.[1] Natural hazards can complicate the efforts to contain and cope with the pandemic. Emergency responses to the effects of disasters triggered by natural hazards will directly impact public health services and health infrastructure already burdened in the time of COVID-19. Social distancing will become extremely challenging among people displaced by disasters. It could also disrupt clean water supplies, provision of adequate sanitation services, and good hygiene practices. Moreover, it will test local governments' capacities and budgets that are already stretched to cope with the pandemic. The COVID-19 pandemic may not be over soon, calling for urgent actions to incorporate disaster resilience in the pandemic responses.

Natural Hazards Are Putting Asia's Prosperity at Risk

Over the past 2 decades, 82% of disasters ensued from extreme weather events such as floods, storms, and droughts. With nearly 38,000 disaster fatalities annually from 2000 to 2018, developing Asia accounted for almost 55% of 60,000 disaster fatalities worldwide, and it accounted for 26% of the $128 billion in global economic damage (Figure 9.1).

The impact of disasters is greater when more vulnerable populations are exposed to hazards. The upshot is harm to people and their physical assets such as property and infrastructure. Hazards can be natural, like hurricanes and earthquakes, or artificial, like industrial accidents and nuclear meltdowns.

---

[1] This section is a summary of the theme chapter of the April 2019 *Asian Development Outlook* report, "Strengthening Disaster Resilience."

Figure 9.1: Deaths from Disasters, 1990-2018

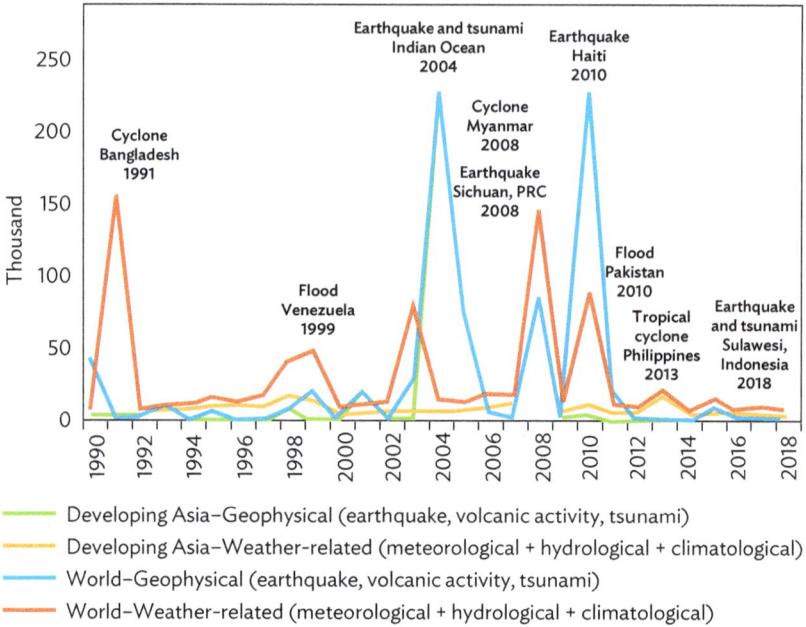

Earthquake and tsunami Indian Ocean 2004

Earthquake Haiti 2010

Cyclone Myanmar 2008

Cyclone Bangladesh 1991

Earthquake Sichuan, PRC 2008

Flood Venezuela 1999

Flood Pakistan 2010

Tropical cyclone Philippines 2013

Earthquake and tsunami Sulawesi, Indonesia 2018

—— Developing Asia–Geophysical (earthquake, volcanic activity, tsunami)
—— Developing Asia–Weather-related (meteorological + hydrological + climatological)
—— World–Geophysical (earthquake, volcanic activity, tsunami)
—— World–Weather-related (meteorological + hydrological + climatological)

PRC = People's Republic of China.
Source: ADB estimates using Centre for research on the Epidemiology of Disasters. The Emergency Events database. https://www.emdat.be/ (accessed 6 February 2019).

This report focuses on disasters that emerge from natural hazards, including severe weather events, geophysical disturbances, and epidemics. They can occur suddenly with little or no warning, or they can build slowly over the span of days, weeks, months, or years.

Development and climate change alter disaster risk. On the one hand, rising incomes enable communities to cope with disasters. On the other, rapidly expanding coastal megacities, for example, create greater exposure to natural hazards. As the frequency and intensity of extreme weather events worsen because of climate change and associated sea level rise, coastal areas and island states across Asia face increasingly dire threats.

More than four in five people affected by natural hazards live in Asia. From 2000 to 2018, developing Asia was home to 84% of the 206 million people affected by disasters globally on average each year.

Those who suffer most are poor, marginalized, and isolated. Surveys after severe flooding in Indian cities found that poor and migrant families were the worst affected, with some losing more than they earned in a year. Many small businesses fell into financial distress, some having to sell their assets and close down. Further, surveys of communities heavily exposed to flooding across five Asian countries found that, among rural households surveyed, 90% had suffered in the past decade either loss of life or significant damage to assets from floods, and their financial recovery took more than three times longer than for urban households. Pacific island economies are especially vulnerable to severe hazards, reflecting their isolation, limited economic diversification, and extreme exposure.

Disaster Impacts and How They Propagate

Immediate impacts on local economic activity can be substantial. New evidence on the economic impacts of tropical storms in the Philippines shows that each of these events reduced local economic activity in that year by 1.7% on average, but by as much as 23% after the most severe storms. More extreme events can have much larger impacts. Cyclone Pam in 2015—the second most intense tropical cyclone ever recorded in the South Pacific—caused damage in Vanuatu equal to 64% of annual GDP. Events that fall short of catastrophic typically affect economic activity for a year or less, allowing households that temporarily migrate away in the aftermath of a disaster to return to their land and livelihoods.

The effects of disaster can persist. Beyond immediate loss of life and wealth, the effects can last for many years. More than a decade after the 1995 Kobe earthquake in Japan, for example, income per capita in Hyogo Prefecture was 12% lower than it otherwise would have been. Case studies of flooding in Indian cities show that, in the absence of social protection, disaster-hit families deplete their savings or borrow at high interest rates from informal sources, pushing them into indebtedness and poverty traps. Recent research reveals that disasters can affect victims for decades as reduced household spending on food, medicine, and education, for example, stunts a child's potential well into adulthood.

Effects can spread and link up with epidemics, conflict, and other risks. Disruption to supply chains, as occurred in 2011 after floods in Thailand and the Tohoku earthquake and tsunami in Japan, can transmit disaster impacts to firms and customers not directly hit by the event. Spatial transmission of impacts happens as well when people are forced to leave a stricken area, creating a displaced population. East, Southeast, and South Asia accounted for over 60% of the estimated 19 million people displaced by disasters in 2017—some briefly, others for much longer. The number of internal climate migrants is projected to increase rapidly. Disaster-induced migration can expose migrants to flooding, landslides, heat stress, and other hazards. It may also facilitate the spread of disease and even spark social disorder in urban areas, as suggested by new evidence on flood-induced migration.

Investing in Development with Disaster Resilience

Asia has achieved substantial mainstreaming of disaster risk management. Many countries in the region are adapting the Sendai Framework for Disaster Risk Reduction, 2015–2030 for national needs and thereby effecting a notable policy shift in disaster response from reactive to proactive. Escalating losses from disasters suggest that these positive trends require reinforcement to translate plans into actions and to address the causes of social vulnerability and the drivers of disaster risk.

Greenfield investment is a natural entry point for disaster resilience. Developing Asia is estimated to need $26 trillion in infrastructure investment from 2016 to 2030, or $1.7 trillion per year. Planning for and investing in climate-friendly and disaster-resilient infrastructure from the start can help avoid locking in further exposure to disaster risk and is a particularly cost-effective way to reduce losses from disasters.

Spending on prevention needs to catch up with spending on response. Globally, governments in developing countries receive seven times more assistance for responding to disasters after they occur than for preparing in advance for rapid recovery and, where possible, taking measures to keep hazards from developing into disasters. In Asia, this spending gap has narrowed slightly over the past few years but remains large. Further closing the gap will yield multiple dividends, especially when investments have development benefits aside from reducing disaster risk. Examples include stable water resource management that integrates flood risk considerations, the construction of cyclone-safe multipurpose evacuation centers that serve daily as classrooms or community centers, the re-establishment of sustainable mangrove forests to absorb storm impacts and prevent coastal erosion, or hydroponic projects that diversify incomes in normal times and safeguard food security when disaster strikes.

Risk shared through commercial credit or insurance is manageable risk. Across Asia including Japan, just over 8% of catastrophe losses since 1980 were covered by insurance. Recent years have seen an increase in programs that offer insurance coverage, especially across developing Asia. New studies show that two-thirds of them offer micro-insurance to cover agriculture losses, and over 80% depend on subsidies or other financial support. The benefits of insurance are clear: pooling risk to preserve human welfare, facilitating investment by containing risk, and making post-disaster support more predictable. While traditional indemnity insurance models are difficult to scale down to the needs of individual households in poor communities, more innovative insurance models such as index-based risk-transfer products (such as drought insurance linked to rainfall) offer potential, and government and international support for reinsurance allows broader pooling of risk.

Hiring victims can help, as can informal support networks and remittances. Labor market interventions can gainfully employ some disaster-affected people in reconstruction after disasters. Informal risk-sharing arrangements such as through private transfers within communities can effectively cope with shocks to individual households, but not with shocks to whole communities from large disasters. Public transfers can help, as can remittances from outside the affected area. In the Philippines, for example, remittances compensated for nearly 65% of income lost in shocks caused by rainfall deviations. The poorest of the poor, however, often lack the social and financial networks necessary to allow family members to migrate and remit.

Community action must complement national efforts. Communities are themselves the first responders to disasters, often with little or no immediate external support, and are key to ensuring sustained recovery and reconstruction. New evidence from flood resilience surveys across 88 communities in Asia shows that community investments can build resilience while delivering broader development benefits, such as better education, transportation, and food supply. Proper waste management, for example, can prevent the spread of disease and keep rivers and drains clear to carry away floodwaters, while benefiting communities more broadly day to day. Recent experience after major earthquakes and tropical cyclones in Asia highlights the role of local communities as custodians of local knowledge and experience that enables the dissemination of early warning messages and timely evacuation, and that can guide the effective delivery of humanitarian response and recovery assistance.

Development agencies support disaster resilience in many ways. Countries have received concessional loans and grants from development agencies to strengthen disaster resilience. Multilateral and regional lenders support the establishment of disaster-contingent financing arrangements designed for quick disbursement. ADB's $6 million contingent financing loan to Tonga, for example, was fully disbursed in just 3 days after that Pacific island country was struck by Tropical Cyclone Gita in February 2018. Other multilateral assistance from ADB has designed and piloted innovative insurance programs, notably a disaster insurance pool for city governments in the Philippines that was the world's first. Meanwhile, international efforts continue to provide to poor countries' access to finance through more traditional emergency assistance loans and grants offered in response to disasters.

Improved financial arrangements enable better disaster management. Delayed or insufficient financing for relief, early recovery, or reconstruction exacerbates the economic and social consequences of direct physical damage, extending the time required to rebuild infrastructure, render it fully functional, and deliver the services that depend on it. Such shortcomings stymie efforts to build back better. Governments increasingly recognize this and work to enhance both sovereign and nonsovereign financing instruments with support from development partners. The Government of the Philippines became the first to position these instruments in a wider framework by establishing in 2015 a national financing strategy for disaster risk to promote a comprehensive approach. The Government of Indonesia launched a similar strategy in 2018, and such strategies are currently under development in Myanmar and Pakistan.

Prepared to Build Back Better after Disaster Strikes

Humanitarian response is a prelude to recovery and reconstruction. Sustainable recovery must overcome operational challenges and bridge the gap between urgent humanitarian response and longer-term recovery and reconstruction. The efficient and equitable allocation of private and public resources in response to disasters is often challenged by deficiencies in governance. Even after finances are secured, reconstruction projects face local implementation challenges such as a lack of skilled personnel, unclear land tenure, transportation bottlenecks, and sudden increases in wage rates and prices for construction materials. Case studies of the 2015 earthquake in Nepal and Cyclone Pam in Vanuatu the same year indicate that successful long-term recovery requires broad collaboration involving central and local governments, civil society, and affected communities. The roles and responsibilities of all stakeholders must be clear, and responsible parties must have the experiential knowledge and capacity necessary to absorb and effectively apply the large influxes of resources that materialize after disasters.

Build back better to equitably realize social and economic potential. Building back better means ensuring that recovery is not only complete but superior to the status quo before the disaster. While building back fast often takes precedence in the immediate aftermath, it must be balanced against other objectives. Strengthening resilience under future hazards should be central to recovery and reconstruction. Crucially, this entails integrating measures that mitigate disaster risk when restoring infrastructure and social capital, as well as ensuring that reconstruction restores and renews economic opportunity and dynamism. Finally, public planning for recovery and building back better must be inclusive and fair to vulnerable segments of society.

Quality Must Prevail in Post-Pandemic Infrastructure Development

Bruno Carrasco and Hanif Rahemtulla

As Asia and the Pacific comes out of the crisis with significantly larger public debts, infrastructure investments will need to be efficient, affordable, and sustainable.

Out of crisis comes opportunity is a common refrain and perhaps there is no better time than now to preview what follows on the COVID-19 relief and recovery support. Infrastructure development has been a cornerstone of Asia and the Pacific's successful growth and development strategy. It has served to strengthen income per capita, improve livelihoods, and lower poverty through investment led growth. In parallel, it has supported the UN Sustainable Development Goals, recognizing the crucial link between infrastructure development and service delivery.

High-quality infrastructure is critical to continue to deliver on these gains. The quality of infrastructure investment was central to the deliberations of the G20 Finance Ministers and Central Bank Governors, who endorsed the new principles for this at their meeting in Fukuoka, Japan in 2019.

The principles mark a broader, robust, and dedicated approach to sound project preparation practices over the project life cycle, including the adoption of innovative technology, environmental and social sustainability, resilience against natural disasters, and governance for procurement transparency and robust institutions. Investments aligned with these principles will support the value for money proposition, help extend the life of the infrastructure asset and thereby increase the returns on investment across both end users and investors, enhancing social welfare.

Gradually, these principles are gaining traction across countries. In the PRC, for example, the Measures for the Administration of Infrastructure and Public Utility Concessions took effect in 2015. They enabled competition for public–private partnerships between private and state-owned bidders, and encouraged bankable projects and risk transfer over the project life cycle.

The preparatory phase of the project cycle is crucial in ensuring that only a well-structured, commercially viable public–private partnership projects—which are more likely to provide value for money—are procured by governments. The preparation phase in the project cycle includes appraisal of fiscal affordability, social and environmental assessment, risk identification, financial viability, comparing public and private options, and sounding out the market.

Asia has some work to do on this score. The *Procuring Infrastructure Public-Private Partnerships Report* by the World Bank found that, based on an index from 0 to 100, of global best practices for project preparation, East Asia and the Pacific scored 40 compared to an average 65 for high-income OECD countries.[2] This demonstrates the need for more work in Asia to bridge the gap between theory and practice when it comes to implementing project preparation practices associated with the quality infrastructure principles.

There is no greater compelling case for quality infrastructure than now. All countries will come out of the crisis with significantly larger public debts. Infrastructure investments will have to meet three key indicators—efficiency, affordability, and sustainability.

On efficiency, considerable progress is needed. In a review of public investment management frameworks of 30 emerging, low-, and middle-income countries, the International Monetary Fund (IMF) concluded that 30% of potential economic benefits of public investments are lost due to inefficiencies in the public investment process.

On affordability and inclusion, COVID-19 has led to the further widening of already yawning inequalities across this region including between those securing and losing their jobs and varied levels of access to health services. Research by the IMF shows that GINI coefficients—a widely

---

[2]   World Bank. Procuring Infrastructure Public-Private Partnerships Report 2018. Washington, DC. http://pubdocs.worldbank.org/en/256451522692645967/PIP3-2018.pdf.

accepted measurement of inequality—have risen by nearly 1.5% five years after pandemics.

From a public policy perspective, greater attention to financing will be required. For example, tariffs should be part of a wider package of financing—and not the driver—including tax revenue and returns from land value capture to ensure wider infrastructure service availability. Infrastructure investment with proper appraisal and aligned to Quality Infrastructure Investment principles can help to turn the tide on inequality by providing inclusive infrastructure that is more affordable and accessible by all.

On sustainability, there is no greater threat than climate change and natural disasters. Addressing these threats requires innovative and inclusive solutions to foster new technologies that enhance resilience, to boost green investment in a decarbonized economy, and to leverage innovative technology throughout the project life cycle.

Economic and financial sustainability and strengthening institutions will be equally important in a world of scarce resources and limited fiscal headroom in the pandemic's immediate aftermath. A recent survey of finance ministries, central banks, and academics in G20 countries showed that green investment has a positive impact on the speed at which the stimulus delivers economic impact for every dollar invested. The question is how to effectively internalize future returns on an infrastructure project against upfront construction costs exacerbated by the pressing fiscal and financing constraints caused by COVID-19.

Emergency financial support should be integrated into a fiscal framework that does not jeopardize debt sustainability. In the medium to long term, however, a sound fiscal framework should be combined with increased investment in high-quality infrastructure that provides direct positive social and economic impacts, climate resilience, and more effective delivery of public goods and services.

Quality infrastructure is not a luxury good that would be nice if affordable. It is a necessary good that delivers a positive return on public investment as well as measurable economic benefits.

Beyond ramping up finance to meet the immediate crisis, multilateral development banks can help their borrowing members by ensuring infrastructure investment is in line with the Quality Infrastructure Investment principles.

Water, Sanitation, and Hygiene Key to Pacific's Ongoing COVID-19 Strategy

Jingmin Huang

Pacific island nations have been among the top performers worldwide in controlling COVID-19. A greater emphasis on water, sanitation, and hygiene practices will help continue that success. COVID-19 has forced Pacific island nations to close borders to prevent the disease's entry. This has been a largely successful strategy, however, more needs to be done. As UNICEF and the WHO have indicated, good water, sanitation, and hygiene practices also play a critical role in blocking transmission, particularly hand hygiene. Most Pacific island nations have a poor track record with regard to water, sanitation, and hygiene policies.

Limited handwashing facilities, high population densities, large household sizes, and weak health services compound the risk that the virus could spread quickly once it has a presence in Pacific communities. To address COVID-19 and other human-to-human transmissible diseases, water, sanitation, and hygiene practices should reach the three major goals: universal access, efficiency, and sustainability.

Universal Access

Water, sanitation, and hygiene campaigns have been conducted in many Pacific countries, but they have never achieved universal access due to a lack of access to reliable water and sanitation infrastructure. Pacific island states have some of the lowest rates internationally of access to basic water supply and sanitation. Handwashing facilities with flowing water and soap are not always available in public areas. Hand sanitizer should be introduced for hand hygiene, with a specific focus on schools, markets, and clinics.

In some countries, the water supply is limited and intermittent. In this case, the provision of small water tank systems to accompany handwashing stations should be considered to provide flowing water for handwashing. Universal access will help women, girls, and other children to maintain their hygiene, at least in schools and public toilets, when they do not have household water connections.

Efficiency

In some areas with continuous water supply, poor hand hygiene behavior is still prevalent. The COVID-19 crisis has greatly undermined the efficiency of water, sanitation, and hygiene, and handwashing, particularly in public areas and health clinics. People should be trained on hand hygiene in the why, when, and how in households and public areas. Following the WHO's "My 5 Moments for Hand Hygiene" approach, proper locations for handwashing facilities should be ensured within 5 meters of toilets, as well as in waiting and dining rooms and other public areas.[3] The efficiency of water, sanitation, and hygiene will also require proper sanitation service and solid waste collection to prevent the virus from spreading with dirty water or infectious waste.

Efficiency here will also require the efficient use of freshwater resources since proper handwashing demands 20–40 seconds of flowing water, which uses 2 to 5 liters of water. In many island countries, the fresh water comes from sea water desalination with high costs. In this case, water conservation taps should be considered.

Sustainability

One of the key challenges is ensuring the sustainability of hygiene interventions where the provision of water supply and sanitation is often inadequate. This can be addressed by supporting water, sanitation, and solid waste management financing. Water and wastewater utilities, government regulators, and decision makers should also actively join water, sanitation, and hygiene activities. After all, it is important to develop a culture that values hand hygiene, especially with the support of senior officials.

---

3   WHO. About SAVE LIVES: Clean Your Hands. https://www.who.int/gpsc/5may/background/5moments/en/

Existing WHO guidance on the safe management of drinking water and sanitation services is adequate to deal with the COVID-19 outbreak. The pandemic makes access to water, sanitation, and hygiene a more urgent priority.

Many co-benefits will be realized through good water, sanitation, and hygiene, including the prevention of other infectious and waterborne diseases which cause many deaths in the Pacific each year. By bringing about a clean, and hygienic environment, good water, sanitation and hygiene practices contribute to safety first in the community. They will also help restore local economies, including tourism, which is critical for many islands.

If Pacific island nations can work toward these three goals, they increase the chances that they will not only survive but thrive in the wake of COVID-19.

Build Green to Help Fend Off the Next Pandemic

Anouj Mehta and Naeeda Crishna Morgado

Governments across the world, including Asia and the Pacific, are struggling to stem a rising tide of infection. For many of us, this will forever remain the memory of 2020. The question now is will 2025 or 2028 look similar, or will we learn from COVID-19 to make real change for an improved version of the "new normal"?

The "old normal" struggled to maintain the balance between the environment, people and economies, and came with a high risk of epidemics and other natural disasters. While growing economies and rising wealth have benefited millions, this region is also associated with entrenched fossil fuel dependence and increasing greenhouse gas emissions, decreasing primary forests and vanishing species, and a never-ending stream of plastic going into the ocean. Storms, drought, tsunamis, and even volcanoes are par for the course for people living in Southeast Asia, where many of us live and work. And in the end, the loss in balance between nature and people also spurred the rise and spread of the coronavirus disease.

Preventing the next pandemic will require a serious rethink of how we develop our economies, especially in Asia and the Pacific. And the starting point for this is infrastructure development, which is key to any post-COVID-19 economic recovery effort, helping to kickstart economies, create jobs, and keep businesses afloat.

Recovery Financing Must go into Green Infrastructure

Infrastructure also lies at the crux of balancing economic, social, and environmental sustainability, as infrastructure projects are still associated with potentially major impacts on climate, oceans and forests, and biodiversity. With an estimated \$210 billion in investment needed per year for infrastructure in Southeast Asia alone, ensuring this investment is targeted toward the cleanest and most sustainable options will be critical in a post-COVID-19 future.

Greening post-COVID-19 infrastructure investment will require concerted action across policy, governance, capacity, and finance domains in the long-term. But most immediately, one practical step decision makers can take is to put in place principles that are practical and quickly implemented to help guide infrastructure choices and ensure they are green.

Such principles are not new. Global, regional, and national "green bond" standards help distinguish bonds that support green objectives from those that do not. In the last two years alone, major efforts by the European Union, the PRC, and others to establish specific lists or "taxonomies" on what is green have taken the discussion a step further.

The Climate Bonds Standard, for example, sets out criteria for different project types to help investors determine their impact. A solar or wind project would almost always automatically classify as "green," whereas a project to support bus systems in a city would only count after considering the type—and associated environmental footprint—of the buses in question.

Green Finance Principles Must Build in Financial Incentives

In addition to calculating the green impact, public incentives need to help green projects become bankable, especially ones that may be associated with more expensive technologies. Green finance principles that link cheaper financing or incentives with climate and environmental criteria are key to moving infrastructure trajectories in Asian countries from "brown" to "green."

Such an approach is being piloted under the ASEAN Catalytic Green Finance Facility, a multi-government-owned (all ASEAN region countries) green finance vehicle in the region, managed by ADB. The facility has published investment principles to screen projects based on green criteria as well as bankability conditions, and links this to cheaper financing.

The timing of the release of the ASEAN Catalytic Green Finance Facility's principles during the COVID-19 pandemic is hopefully also a ringing bell for decision makers who are struggling to weigh their options in designing their post-COVID-19 economic recovery packages.

Investments in climate-resilient infrastructure that help to maintain natural capital and protect oceans should be the centerpiece for the billions of dollars in economic stimulus being considered. Greening post-COVID-19 recovery can spur industry and maintain jobs, but can also help us stave off and build resilience for the next major shock or crisis that hits.

In the long term, hopefully, a greener, more balanced growth pathway in Asia and the Pacific will become our "new normal."

The Response to COVID-19 Should Also Be a Response to the Climate Crisis

Preety Bhandari and Arghya Sinha Roy

Now is the time to ramp up actions on resilience so that society can beat the COVID-19 crisis while reducing the impact of climate threats. The last few weeks have taken all of us by surprise. We are confined to our homes. Weaknesses in health care systems have been exposed. Jobs are uncertain. Women are bearing the burden of providing informal care within families. Millions are being pushed back into poverty. Stock markets are reeling.

We long for normality. But when life was normal, we were already in crisis—a climate crisis. Returning to that status quo is not an option. Instead, we should ensure our decisions to tackle this pandemic do not compound the climate crisis. Rather, they should help shape an inclusive and sustainable future for all. Now is the time to ramp up our actions on resilience so that our society can beat the COVID-19 crisis and reduce the impact of climate threats.

The following five approaches can drive this shift.

First, use the opportunity to tackle the climate crisis head-on, as well as the pandemic. Though national borders are closed, global solidarity is high. Time and resources are in short supply. We do not have the luxury nor the financing to deal with each crisis separately. More importantly, dealing with the impact of both requires us to urgently address underlying vulnerabilities— poverty, limited social safety nets, weak health systems, and structural gender inequalities.

Tackling issues together can redouble resilience. For example, more resilient health care systems would cope better during pandemics. They could also deal more effectively with diseases caused by climate change, such as respiratory ailments due to higher temperatures and waterborne illnesses from changes in precipitation.

Second, reforms, tax cuts, subsidies, and incentives designed to help economies recover should also examine the implications for longer-term climate-resilient development. Sustainable recovery will require a long-term systemic shift so that short-term fixes do not have adverse consequences for the environment and equity.

Actions for climate resilience have always prioritized long-term thinking. Still, climate risk information has only very rarely found its way into fiscal policy and management processes. Now is the time to make this happen. Proposed reforms to meet immediate needs should also promote green infrastructure, create jobs in sectors that reduce carbon emissions, and incentivize actions such as business continuity planning across supply chains that promote longer-term sustainability and equity by addressing climate risks.

Third, measures should have an explicit focus on the poor and marginalized. The pandemic is having a disproportionate impact on poor and marginalized populations. These people are already burdened with the ill-effects of climate-related shocks and stresses such as salinity intrusion at coastal areas and urban "heat islands" endured by outdoor workers.

To prevent millions slipping back into poverty, a sharp focus on strengthening the resilience of the poor will be needed. This calls for tailored solutions to support the chronic and near-poor in both urban and rural areas. Large-scale pro-poor development programs should proactively introduce explicit resilience-building measures. Technical and vocational education and training programs can build skills for climate-friendly livelihoods, such as producing drought-resistant high-value crops. Cash-for-work programs can help protect wetlands and mangroves.

Equally important is to invest in social protection systems with adaptive features. For example, using climate risk information to target vulnerable populations and flexibly allowing cash transfer programs to add temporary new beneficiaries can cushion the impacts of a crisis. It will be important to strengthen linkages between various programs—public health, community infrastructure, sustainable livelihoods, microfinance—to deliver resilience solutions.

Fourth, let's take a transformational approach to resilience. The effects of climate change are not linear. Therefore, additive incremental actions taken to combat a pandemic will not necessarily protect assets, livelihoods, and well-being over the long term.

Instead, we need to address the systemic, structural, and gendered dimensions of vulnerability. The focus should be on underlying inequalities, balancing bottom-up and top-down planning approaches, and requiring behavioral and lifestyle changes. For example, investments to support populations in urban informal settlements should involve communities, especially women, in decision making about selection, construction, and maintenance of water supply and sanitation infrastructure.

We can promote behavioral change through improved hygiene and by forming self-help groups to kickstart sustainable livelihoods in climate-friendly roles such as management of wetlands and mangroves.

Finally, invest in communities. Managing any crisis boils down to individual communities—their capacity, resources, and level of preparedness. Communities that are well informed about risks and involved in local decision making can play critical roles in helping local governments to identify and serve vulnerable populations.

This can improve the targeting of resources and distribution of food. Self-help groups have spread awareness about climate and disaster risks, performed caregiving roles, and implemented farm-to-home models to deliver agricultural produce. Grassroots women's groups are better aware of local vulnerabilities and can ensure that government support reaches the last mile.

Building the adaptive capacity of communities requires sustained investments in organizing communities and empowering them economically and socially. The Global Commission on Adaptation has estimated that investing $1.8 trillion globally from 2020 to 2030 in resilience-building measures could generate $7.1 trillion in total new benefits.

It pays to invest in resilience. Let's make those investments now so our communities can thrive—before, during, and after crises.

Back to Blue: Let's Value Our Oceans Again

Ingrid van Wees

In the midst of perhaps the worst crisis of our lifetime with loss of life, livelihoods, and a spreading fear across the world as a result of the COVID-19 pandemic, there have also been glimpses of the possibility to reverse decades of environmental damage. This opportunity must be grasped to avoid the catastrophes likely to be unleashed if the damage continues unabated. As the world works to recover from the ongoing crisis, governments need to include in their recovery strategies, actions that can especially focus on sustaining and improving one of the most critical, visible, and universally needed environmental resources, our oceans—including all water bodies, seas, lakes, and rivers.

The case for the oceans. The case, if ever needed, for protecting oceans is the sheer importance of this resource to every sphere of life, including climate change. Oceans have been acting as a giant carbon sink, absorbing about a third of the carbon dioxide generated by human activities since the Industrial Revolution. However, while helping mitigate climate change, with greater carbon absorption, the oceans are also facing a 30% rise in seawater acidity since the Industrial Revolution—an acidification rate estimated to be 10 times faster than at any other period during the preceding 55 million years. This is already impacting marine biodiversity, and with an estimated 1 billion people dependent on seafood, and a global fishing market worth an annual $100 billion, it will eventually affect the global economy.

An 8 million-ton problem. The specter of polluted rivers across the region, several having already lost their battle against a tide of municipal and industrial waste and deemed "dead," is worsened by 8 million tons of plastic ending up in the oceans each year. And this is also coming back full circle with cities such as Bengaluru, Chennai, Cape Town, Jakarta, and Karachi, included in the lists of global cities facing water stress and water crises.

Projects are clear, funds are not. The projects that need to be done to address these challenges have always been well known: municipal and industrial effluent treatment, agribusiness runoffs, plastic waste management, coastal protection, marine protected areas, and river basin pollution control. The challenge has always been that of a shortage of funds, conducive institutional and regulatory environments, and financial incentives. This shortage of funds, an estimated annual gap of $459 billion, according to ADB, can only be met by a significant ramp-up in flows from commercial and institutional finance, capital markets, and public-private partnerships.

However, such 'blue' projects suffer from a lack of bankability, with many having either low tariff and revenue levels due to affordability considerations or no revenue streams at all. Other risk factors include high-cost technology, environment clearances, and land acquisition risks, further deterring the flow of private capital and resulting in a growing demand supply gap for capital. This is only likely to be exacerbated in the post-COVID-19 scenario, causing further budgetary pressures on governments to fund such projects.

A time for 'blue credits.' How then can one persuade private capital into such projects? Several models exist within blended or leveraged finance approaches, which aim to better apportion risk to the party—public or private—best suited to manage that risk and hence create a more bankable project structure.

One mechanism that could be included to address the lack of revenues in many of these projects is that of blue credits, being developed by the ADB's Southeast Asia Department's innovative finance hub. Based on the concept of the 'hybrid annuity' model that India tried successfully for its public–private partnership road projects, this would essentially entail a local or national government providing a predetermined annual payment or blue credits to a project-implementing entity (whether a government-owned company, a public–private partnership, or private sector entity), linked to performance or impact indicators that a project needs to achieve, such as chemical oxygen demand and biochemical oxygen demand levels.

The main aim would be for private capital to finance most of the capital expenditure, take the construction risk and subsequently focus on operational efficiencies, while insulated from revenue risks as long as project benefits are delivered. The mechanism of blue credits should be seen as aligned with the principle of 'avoided costs' from alleviating future economic or health disasters, such as diseases arising from lack of access to clean water, polluted river bodies, or decline in fishing stocks. An estimate of such avoided costs could provide a benchmark to limit the level of blue credits provided to a project.

Similar to initially higher feed-in tariffs for wind and solar energy plants, the need for this financial support will likely fade over time once scale and technologies improve, costs are reduced and 'grid parity' is achieved. The circular economy for waste and water treatment plants will improve when the sector develops, governments create conducive regulatory environments and financial (tax) incentives, and counterproductive (fuel) subsidies are eliminated.

The payment mechanism for such blue credits could be ring-fenced into dedicated special purpose vehicles funded by governments, multilateral development banks, and donors. ADB could work with interested governments in developing the mechanisms and structures for such vehicles or 'blue credit funds' as well as in implementation of some early pilots.

A visible commitment. The elements of the idea above are not new, however, creating a visible mechanism such as this would clearly and strongly signal a government's intent and commitment to both project sponsors and private capital sources creating a clear momentum for leveraging in private capital of three or four times the government funds committed. Including such mechanisms along with credible sovereign funds into post-COVID-19 recovery packages would be a critical step forward to renewing the attention on this hugely critical theme and lead to safer, healthier, and sustainable economic growth in the region.